Cooking Smart for a Healthy Heart

Cooking Smart for a Healthy Heart

Over **150** flavorful eat-right recipes to lose weight and live longer

Reader's Digest

The Reader's Digest Association, Inc.
Pleasantville, New York/Montreal

A READER'S DIGEST BOOK

First printing in paperback 2009

This edition published by The Reader's Digest Association, Inc., by arrangement with NOVA Graphic Services, Inc.

FOR NOVA GRAPHIC SERVICES
NOVA Graphic Services, Inc.
2370 York Road, Suite A9A
Jamison, PA 18929

President: David Davenport
Composition Manager: Steve Magnin
Manager, Editorial Services: Sandra Kear
Associate Editor: Kimberly L. Gana
Indexer: Kathleen Rocheleau

CONTRIBUTORS
Project Editors: Susan McQuillan,
Martha Schueneman, Nancy Shuker
Photographers: Beatrice da Costa, Elizabeth Watt
Produced by: Beth Allen Associates; Rebus, Inc.

READER'S DIGEST TRADE PUBLISHING
Project Editor: Kimberly Casey
Copy Editor: Marcy Gray
Contributing Writer: Eric Oatman
Project Designer: Martha Grossman
Senior Designer: George McKeon
Executive Editor, Trade Publishing: Dolores York
Director of Production: Michael Braunschweiger
Production Technology Manager: Douglas A. Croll
Associate Publisher, Trade Publishing: Christopher T. Reggio
President & Publisher, Trade Publishing: Harold Clarke

READER'S DIGEST ILLUSTRATED REFERENCE BOOKS
Vice President, Editor-in-Chief: Christopher Cavanaugh
Art Director: Joan Mazzeo
Senior Design Director: Elizabeth Tunnicliffe

Library of Congress Cataloging-in-Publication Data:

Cooking smart for a healthy heart : Over 150 flavorful eat-right recipes to lose weight and live longer / Reader's Digest.
p. cm.
Includes index.
ISBN 0-7621-0615-8 (hardcover)
ISBN 978-0-7621-0996-8 (paperback)
1. Heart–Diseases–Diet therapy–Recipes. 2. Reducing diets–Recipes. 3. Nutrition. I. Reader's Digest Association.

RC684.D5C658 2005
641.5'6311–dc22

2004059863

Address any comments about *Cooking Smart for a Healthy Heart* to:
The Reader's Digest Association, Inc.
Adult Trade Publishing
Reader's Digest Road
Pleasantville, NY 10570-7000

For more Reader's Digest products and information, visit our website:
www.rd.com (in the United States)

NOTE TO OUR READERS
The information in this book should not be substituted for, or used to alter, medical therapy without your doctor's advice. For a specific health problem, consult your physician for guidance.

Printed in China

1 3 5 7 9 10 8 6 4 2 (hardcover)
1 3 5 7 9 10 8 6 4 2 (paperback)

The wise man should consider that health is the greatest of human blessings. Let food be your medicine.

—Hippocrates

Contents

Cooking with Heart

Heart attacks happen swiftly, usually without warning. The cause of most of them is atherosclerosis, the build-up of fats like LDLs (the "bad" cholesterol), on and inside artery walls. As these fatty deposits accumulate, substances like fibrous tissue, blood cells, and calcium stick to them. This gluey mixture hardens into plaques that narrow the blood vessels. An area of plaque or a blood clot can break loose and plug up an already narrowed artery. Most often this happens in the coronary arteries, which feed oxygen-rich blood to the heart.

Preventing Heart Disease

What's remarkable about atherosclerosis is that it is almost entirely preventable. Smoking and heavy drinking are two causes of the problem. Heredity is another. But at the root of heart disease is poor nutrition that results in obesity, high blood pressure, and high cholesterol. *Cooking Smart for a Healthy Heart* is designed to help you and your family meet these challenges to your well-being.

The most common form of atherosclerosis is coronary artery disease (CAD). This year, CAD is expected to trigger 950,000 heart attacks in the United States. Two of every five of its victims will die. CAD is an equal-opportunity killer. Men tend to develop heart disease earlier than women, but heart disease is the number-one killer of women older than 55.

The focus on adults obscures one of the saddest facts about heart disease: In most cases, it begins in childhood. Autopsies performed on children and young adults provide the most revealing evidence—fatty streaks on the blood vessel walls. According to some studies, nearly 15 percent of all children in the United States have elevated levels of cholesterol. Many suffer from familial hypercholesterolemia, an inherited condition that causes the liver to overproduce cholesterol. But most have high cholesterol simply because they consume too much saturated fat either at home or when dining out.

Findings like these are a reminder that it's never too early to start down the path to a healthy heart, nor is it ever too late. University of California heart expert Dean Ornish, M.D., has shown that people with advanced heart disease can improve the

Warning signs for your heart: Chest pain, breathlessness, and palpitations (a fluttering sensation in the chest) are possible signs of heart problems. If you experience them, you should visit your doctor.

health of their arteries through following a combination of exercise, stress-reduction techniques, and a rigorous heart-smart diet.

The 158 recipes in this cookbook follow the recommendations of the American Heart Association (AHA). Fixing these easy-to-prepare meals will help teach your family just how high-in-taste low-calorie, low-fat (especially saturated fat), low-cholesterol, and low-sodium meals can be.

FATS: THE GOOD, THE BAD, AND THE UGLY

Monounsaturated Fats: Vegetable oils such as peanut, olive, and canola; peanuts, pecans, almonds, and avocados.

Polyunsaturated Fats: Vegetable oils such as corn, soybean, sunflower, flaxseed, and safflower; fatty fish including salmon, tuna, mackerel, trout, and sardines; most nuts.

Saturated Fats: Animal products, especially beef, full-fat dairy products, any type of fried meat, and any type of ground meat that may have the skin mixed in to add moistness; tropical oils including palm, palm kernel, and coconut.

Trans Fatty Acids (TFAs): Some margarines; virtually all prepackaged, prepared foods including frozen dinners, breakfast foods, vegetable dishes, and desserts; dry mixes for dressing, rice, macaroni, and hamburger dishes; chips; baked goods including breads, cookies, cakes, and crackers; fried fast foods.

Putting Our Recipes to the Test

In 2000, the AHA published the *Dietary Guidelines for Healthy American Adults*. The title is a bit off base: The AHA created the recommendations for all healthy Americans older than two years old.* But how well does *Cooking Smart for a Healthy Heart* measure up to the AHA guidelines? Let's take the guidelines one by one:

AHA Guideline: Eat a variety of fruits and vegetables, especially dark green, orange, or yellow—the high-oxidant foods. *Cooking Smart*: More than 25 recipes in this book celebrate fruit. More than a third put vegetables of every hue on center stage.

AHA Guideline: Eat a variety of grain products, especially whole grains. *Cooking Smart*: The Pasta and Grains section features 17 recipes ranging from rice and pilaf to fusilli and sesame noodles. The Breads and Pizza section contains even more. Multigrain Soft Pretzels, anyone?

AHA Guideline: Eat low-fat or fat-free dairy products. *Cooking Smart*: To fix these meals, you'll use low-fat cheese and yogurt, fat-free sour cream, fat-free cottage cheese, and reduced- or low-fat milk. You won't be scrimping on taste. Trust us.

AHA Guideline: Make seafood a key part of your diet. *Cooking Smart*: The 16 recipes in the Fish and Shellfish section will give you a selection to help you stay on top of this guideline.

AHA Guideline: Include legumes—beans of any sort, from navy and fava to black and green. *Cooking Smart*: More than a dozen recipes call for beans, which are rich in protein and soluble fiber—the kind that sweeps away cholesterol before it can clog your arteries.

AHA Guideline: Add poultry (skin removed) and lean meats. *Cooking Smart*: The collection includes 20 low-fat poultry recipes and 20 more that call for lean beef, pork, lamb, and veal.

AHA Guideline: Limit cholesterol-boosters such as saturated fats and trans fatty acids. *Cooking Smart*: Except for recipes that call for lean meat and low-fat cheese, saturated fat is all but banned from this book. Trans fats? Our recipes don't call for any. Trans fatty acids are found in vegetable oil that has been mixed with hydrogen, or hydrogenated. The process transforms the unsaturated vegetable oil to a more saturated form, such as solid margarine. Our recipes call for foods rich in monounsaturated fats and polyunsaturated fats. Monounsaturated fats (for example, olive, canola, and peanut oils) are those that begin to harden when refrigerated. Polyunsaturated fats (for example, safflower, corn, and other oils) always remain completely liquid.

AHA Guideline: Limit intake of foods that are high in calories and low in nutrition, including foods with

*The AHA's *Dietary Guidelines* is an eating plan for healthy Americans. For higher-risk individuals—those with diabetes, cardiovascular disease, or lipid disorders, for example—the AHA advises following the National Cholesterol Education Program's *Therapeutic Lifestyle Changes* (TLC) diet, a form of medical nutrition therapy developed by the National Institutes of Health (www.nhlbi.nih.gov/chd/lifestyles.htm). Women who are pregnant or breast-feeding should talk to their healthcare provider, a registered dietitian, or a licensed dietitian or nutritionist about their special dietary needs.

high sugar content such as soft drinks or candy. *Cooking Smart*: Empty calories have little place in these recipes. Only the bare minimum of sugar is called for, even in the 22-recipe Cakes, Pies and Sweets section.

AHA Guideline: Consume less than a level teaspoon (2,400 milligrams) of salt per day. *Cooking Smart*: To us, "Salt to taste" means lots of taste, not much salt. Even our chicken broth is low in sodium. People with high blood pressure should consider adhering to the more stringent Dietary Approaches to Stop Hypertension (DASH), an eating program created by the National Heart, Lung, and Blood Institute.

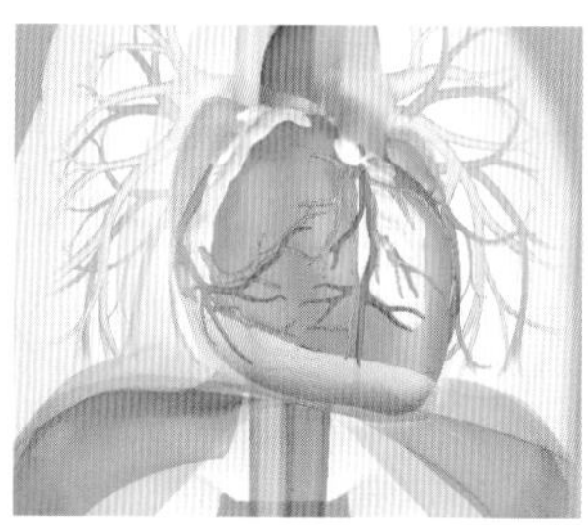

AHA Guideline: Women should consume no more than one alcoholic drink per day; men no more than two. (One drink amounts to 12 ounces of beer, 4 ounces of wine, or 1.5 ounces of 80-proof liquor.) *Cooking Smart*: This is not a bartender's manual. But we've kicked up the taste of a few classic recipes by adding a touch of beer, wine, and even bourbon. After all, a little bit of alcohol may be good for you. Not long ago, doctors at Beth Israel Deaconess Medical Center in Boston completed the largest study on alcohol and heart health to date. Their findings: Men who consumed one alcoholic drink three to seven days a week had a much lower risk of heart disease than those who drank less often.

A Tour of the Healthy Heart

What is the healthy heart that the recipes in this book were created to strengthen? It's the heart that most people are born with—a powerful, four-chambered miracle of efficiency about the size of a clenched fist. A healthy adult heart pumps five quarts of blood through 60,000 miles of flexible, smooth tubing every minute. Arteries carry blood away from the heart, bringing oxygen and nutrients to every part of the body, including the heart muscle. On the return trip through the veins, the blood carries very little oxygen.

For the healthy heart, "tired blood" flowing into the right side of the heart is an easy problem to solve. The heart pumps the blood into the lungs, where waste such as carbon dioxide is discharged. After loading up with oxygen, the blood flows back to the left side of the heart, which—once again—pumps it to every tissue in the body.

Smokers' risk for heart disease is four times greater than the risk for non-smokers.

One of the heart's marvels is its electrical system, a group of cells that generate the electrical impulses that make the heart contract. Between contractions, the heart relaxes, enabling it to refill with blood. Though you hear only one beat, a contracting heart beats twice, once in the atria, or upper chambers, and once in the ventricles, or lower chambers. This squeeze-relax process occurs an average of 70 times a minute, 100,800 times a day, and nearly 37 million times a year.

Healthy hearts can also be defined by what they aren't. They aren't pooped. A weakened heart may not contract and relax easily. Fluids will back up in the veins and congest the legs, lungs, and other parts of the body.

Nor are healthy hearts dependent on off-again, on-again electrical systems, a challenge for aging heart muscles. Healthy hearts don't need battery-driven pacemakers to keep them beating regularly.

Healthy hearts aren't fed by arteries that are narrowed by plaque. Their owners take good care of them: They don't sit too much, drink too much alcohol, smoke, weigh too much or consume foods that have too much saturated fat.

Cutting the Risk

In ancient times, people thought the heart was the seat of memory. We know it isn't. Something else we know: We can't forget to give the heart a lot of TLC. Fortunately, it's not really hard to provide that extra care. Among other things, we can:

Stop smoking Each year, smoking—the single most preventable cause of death—kills about 400,000 Americans. Smokers' risk for heart disease is four times greater than the risk for nonsmokers.

GETTING A GRIP ON GENES

Apart from the risk factors for heart disease that we can change, there are at least an equal number that we cannot. But we can manage them with exercise and healthy food, and, when necessary, with medicine. Here's how you might deal with five risk factors:

Gender: Men are more at risk for heart attacks than women. After reaching menopause, women's risk rises, but it never equals men's. Staying fit and cooking smart makes sense for both men and women. But men, especially those over 50, must remain especially vigilant.

Age: The older you are, the greater your chance of getting heart disease. We can't reverse aging, but we can make sure that as we get older, we don't stop exercising and eating heart-healthy food.

Family history: The children of parents who have coronary artery disease (CAD) are more likely than others to contract CAD. Children can also inherit a predisposition to high cholesterol, hypertension, diabetes, and obesity. While drugs and a change in eating habits may not eradicate this risk factor, they can go a long way toward minimizing it.

A history of heart disease: If you have suffered a heart attack in the past, you are more likely than others to experience one in the future. In this case, listen to the experts: reduce stress, exercise, don't drink too much, don't smoke, and eat healthy foods.

Race: Physicians have found a higher risk for heart disease among African Americans, Native Americans, Mexican Americans, Native Hawaiians, and some Asian Americans. The reason: Members of these ethnic groups are more likely than whites to suffer from diabetes, hypertension, and obesity. In most people, hypertension and obesity can be controlled or reversed. Diabetes is often an inherited disease. Because it is also a consequence of obesity, in most cases, it can be avoided.

Eat to beat high blood pressure Blood pressure is the force of blood coursing through your arteries when your heart beats. Over time, high blood pressure, also called hypertension, tires the heart muscle by making it work harder. Heart attacks and heart failure can follow, and so can strokes.

Hypertension rates are much higher in modern, fast-moving cultures like ours than in less industrialized parts of the world. The main difference is the quality of the diet. In the United States, we eat huge portions of highly processed foods and minimal amounts of fruits, vegetables, and unprocessed grains. People in less industrialized cultures have simpler, healthier diets.

Cook smart to knock out cholesterol Cholesterol, a fatlike substance, circulates in the blood primarily in two forms. LDL cholesterol can clog arteries and contribute to cardiovascular disease. HDL, the "good" cholesterol, sweeps harmful cholesterol out of the arteries. Medical experts believe HDL cholesterol levels should be no lower than 40mg/dL. They recommend that LDL levels be no higher than 70-100mg/dL and that total cholesterol levels be no higher than 200mg/dL.

Our livers produce as much cholesterol as our bodies need. Genetic factors, smoking, inactivity, and obesity raise total cholesterol to dangerous levels. The major culprit here is the meat-and-potatoes American diet. Its saturated fat and trans fatty acid content is simply out of control. Substituting monounsaturated fat for saturated fat, as the recipes in this book do, will go a long way toward bringing cholesterol down to a safe level and keeping it there.

What foods are best for controlling high cholesterol? The top-of-the-line foods are plant-based. Most vegetables and fruits are free of saturated fats. But this isn't their only advantage. Just as important is the power of plant foods to lower cholesterol levels. In a recent study, women who ate 8 to 11 walnuts every day in place of other fats cut their LDL cholesterol levels significantly. In another research project, men and women who ate a cup of carrots a day for three weeks experienced an 11 percent decrease in their blood cholesterol.

One reason for the drop is that carrots are high in soluble fiber. The soluble fiber in oats, carrots, and psyllium (available in health food stores) is particularly helpful, researchers say. Soy protein and other plant proteins seem to have a similar effect. The recipes in this book will show you how to use soluble fiber to enhance the taste—and the healthfulness—of the meals you prepare.

Eat more and weigh less Fiber comes in two basic forms. The insoluble form passes through your digestive tract mostly unchanged. Bran, whole grains, and fruit skins are insoluble fibers. The other form of fiber is soluble.

Love: The Great Healer

British researchers made an interesting discovery in 2004: Love can protect the heart. They enlisted 1,034 patients in the study. All of them had just suffered heart attacks. The patients who had close relationships with friends or family members were the lucky ones. Those without a support group were twice as likely as the others to have a second heart attack within a year's time.

"The fact of having at least one close, intimate relationship seems to be the important factor," said Dr. Francis Creed, the professor of psychological medicine who headed the study. The researchers found no relationship between depression and recurring heart disease, he said. "We did find that lack of social support—not having a person with whom one can share all—was related to an increased chance of a further heart attack or severe angina." Angina is chest pain caused by constricted coronary arteries.

What is the link between heart health and social support? People close to the patients might encourage them to take better care of themselves. But hormones might come into play, too. "We also know that those with a close confidant react to stress with less of an upsurge of hormones," Creed said. "This may be particularly important after a heart attack when the heart is particularly susceptible to an increase in stress hormones."

SOURCE: *HealthDayNews*, April 15, 2004, found at http://www.madhoo.com/archives/003056.php

Soluble fiber dissolves, forming a gummy substance in the intestines. Oat bran, beans, citrus fruits and strawberries are a few of the foods that are rich in soluble fiber.

Both kinds of fiber are good for your heart. Soluble fiber traps cholesterol and removes it from your body. Insoluble fiber slows down the movement of food in your digestive tract. It makes you feel full more quickly and for a longer period of time than foods that contain little fiber. A half-cup of bran will fill you up faster than two sugar doughnuts. A bean salad vs. pasta? No contest. Fiber-rich foods are a blessing to dieters and nondieters alike. They're heart healthy, filling, and when prepared correctly, as tasty as any food on the planet.

Exercise more People who get too little exercise are twice as likely to develop heart disease as people who are active. Medical experts recommend that you get at least 30 minutes of moderate activity, such as brisk walking, five days a week. Do that, and you are likely to lower your blood pressure, resting heart rate, and total cholesterol. And like the heart-smart recipes in this book, exercise will also help you maintain your weight.

Stay cool and in control Less important than the main risk factors discussed are what doctors call "secondary risk factors." Among these are stress and alcohol. People under stress often eat, smoke, and drink too much. Overdoing alcohol can raise blood pressure and triglycerides (fat particles in the blood), tighten coronary arteries, and lead to obesity. Learn how to relax without alcohol. Slow down. Ease up on yourself. Let go of whatever is nagging at you. Distract yourself with a positive activity—a bath, a book, a movie, a phone call to a relative. Exercise. Laugh.

Fix a heart-healthy recipe, and share it with a friend.

How to Use This Book

To help you find just the right recipe for your particular needs, we've placed At-a-Glance icons above each full-page photo. Want to lower your cholesterol? Find a recipe with a red heart. Or perhaps you're in a hurry but still want a heart-healthy meal. Look for the blue stopwatch. From high-fiber snacks to crowd-pleasing entrees, we've provided the following icons to lead the way.

At-a-Glance Icons

Look for these symbols to find just the right recipe.

LOW-CHOLESTEROL

Recipes that provide 20 milligrams or less of cholesterol and 2 grams or less of saturated fat per serving.

CALORIE-COUNTER

Recipes with the following calorie limits: complete meal, 500; main dish, 350; main dish soup, 300; side dish, 150; appetizer, snack, bread, 125; dessert, 250.

HIGH-FIBER

Recipes that provide at least 5 grams of dietary fiber per serving.

30 MINUTES OR LESS

When you're in a hurry to get dinner on the table.

CROWD-PLEASER

Perfect dishes to prepare when family and friends are coming over.

SHOWSTOPPER

Dishes that only look as if you pulled out all the stops.

TIME-SAVER

Make it now and serve it later.

GIFT BASKET

Recipes that make special presents for any occasion.

If you suspect you have some form of heart disease, please consult your doctor. *Cooking Smart for a Healthy Heart* is not a medical program, but it can become an integral part of your efforts toward better health.

Eggs and Breakfast Foods

Zesty Cheddar–Asparagus Quiche

How do you get the rich taste of a classic quiche with a fraction of the fat? One technique: Make the crust with thinly sliced potatoes and bake to crisp perfection. It's a heart-smart substitute for traditional piecrust!

PER SERVING

165 calories / 22% from fat
1 g saturated fat, 4 g total fat
41 mg cholesterol
415 mg sodium
18 g total carbohydrate
2 g dietary fiber
14 g protein

PREP TIME 30 min. | **COOK TIME 45 min.** | **SERVES 6**

- 1 tablespoon plain dry bread crumbs
- 8 ounces small all-purpose potatoes, peeled and sliced thin
- 1 pound asparagus, trimmed
- ½ teaspoon salt
- ¾ cup shredded reduced-fat sharp cheddar cheese
- 3 scallions, sliced
- 1 can (12 ounces) evaporated fat-free milk
- ½ cup fat-free egg substitute
- 1 large egg
- 2 teaspoons margarine, melted
- 1 teaspoon dry mustard
- ¼ teaspoon freshly ground black pepper

1 Preheat oven to 400°F. Coat 9-inch pie plate with nonstick cooking spray and sprinkle with bread crumbs. Beginning in center, arrange potato slices in slightly overlapping circles up to rim. Lightly coat with nonstick cooking spray and press down gently. Bake 10 minutes.

2 Set 8 to 12 asparagus spears aside. Cut remaining spears into 1-inch pieces.

3 Sprinkle crust with ¼ teaspoon salt and ¼ cup cheddar. Cover with asparagus pieces, then sprinkle with scallions and another ¼ cup cheese.

4 Beat evaporated milk, egg substitute, egg, margarine, mustard, black pepper, and remaining salt in medium bowl. Pour into pie plate and sprinkle with remaining cheddar. Arrange whole asparagus spears on top. Bake until knife inserted in center comes out clean, about 35 minutes.

STEP 1 *Slightly overlap potato slices to cover bottom and go up sides of pie plate.*

STEP 4 *Arrange asparagus spears in a decorative design over cheese.*

Round Out the Meal

Serve with a salad of marinated cucumbers. Stuff cored apples with a bit of brown sugar and golden raisins and bake along with the quiche.

Cook's Clue

Before you place asparagus spears on top of quiche, blanch them. Place asparagus in boiling water for 1 minute, then place in an ice bath (a glass bowl filled with ice and cold water) for 30 seconds to set its vibrant green color.

HEALTH HINT

Although eggs are high in cholesterol (a large egg contains 213 milligrams, about two-thirds of the recommended daily amount), they are loaded with nutrition. One large egg has 6 grams of protein, as well as riboflavin, vitamin E, folate, B vitamins, and iron.

living smart
FOR A HEALTHY HEART

You probably keep an eye on how many eggs you eat, and the American Heart Association recommends a limit of four egg yolks a week to keep blood cholesterol in check.

Current research says strict limits might not be necessary. A Harvard University study found that eating an egg a day did not increase the risk of a heart attack, stroke, or death from heart disease. Other research says that eating eggs does not often affect cholesterol levels.

Eggs Florentine

The word Florentine *refers to food that's served on a bed of spinach and means in the style of Florence, a city famous for its artistic treasures and fine food. Let your eyes and taste buds feast on this dish—it's been made over to meet your heart-healthy eating goals. It's a nutritional powerhouse, thanks to spinach that's rich in iron, potassium, riboflavin, and vitamins A and C.*

PER SERVING

367 calories / 29% from fat
4 g saturated fat, 12 g total fat
237 mg cholesterol
1,279 mg sodium
41 g total carbohydrate
8 g dietary fiber
28 g protein

PREP TIME 15 min. | **COOK TIME 15 min.** | **SERVES 2**

- 1 package (10 ounces) frozen chopped spinach
- ¼ teaspoon freshly ground black pepper
- 2 large eggs
- 2 thin slices Canadian bacon (2 ounces)
- ⅔ cup reduced-fat milk (2%)
- 1 tablespoon all-purpose flour
- 2 tablespoons shredded nonfat cheddar cheese
- 1½ tablespoons freshly grated Parmesan cheese
- 2 whole-wheat English muffins, split and toasted
- 1 teaspoon snipped fresh chives

1 Preheat oven to 350°F. Coat a small nonstick skillet and 2 shallow au gratin dishes (about 4 inches in diameter) with nonstick cooking spray. Rinse the spinach under warm water in a colander to thaw and squeeze dry. Sprinkle with a pinch of black pepper. Divide the spinach mixture between au gratin dishes and shape into a "nest" in each dish, forming indentations with your fingers.

2 Crack 1 egg into a separate small dish, then slide into a spinach nest and season with pinch of pepper. Repeat. Bake until eggs are just set, about 15 minutes. Meanwhile, cook the Canadian bacon in a small skillet until lightly browned, 2 minutes on each side. Remove from heat; keep warm.

3 Shake ⅓ cup milk and flour in a small jar with a tight-fitting lid until well blended. Pour into a small saucepan; add remaining milk. Whisk constantly over medium-high heat just until bubbles form around the edge, about 3 minutes. Add cheddar and Parmesan and whisk until cheese melts and the sauce is smooth, about 4 minutes more.

4 For each serving, place 1 slice of bacon on the bottom half of an English muffin and slide the spinach nest on top. Spoon over half of cheese sauce and sprinkle with chives. Arrange the top half of muffin on the plate.

STEP 2 *Slide raw egg from small dish onto spinach nest.*

STEP 3 *Whisk cheese sauce until smooth and thickened.*

STEP 4 *Push spinach nest onto bottom of muffin with spatula.*

secret to success

This skinny cheese sauce has the same delicious taste and texture of the typical hollandaise, but with much less fat.

HEALTH HINT

Although eggs are high in cholesterol, they're low in saturated fat and sodium. They provide high-quality protein, vitamin B_{12}, and many other nutrients, with only 75 calories per egg.

Cook's Clue

Be careful not to overcook the eggs, or they'll turn tough and rubbery. The whites should be completely set and opaque, and the yolks should begin to thicken but not turn hard.

Vegetable Frittata

Looking for a quick, meatless meal that's perfect for brunch, lunch, or a light supper? Your search has ended! This flat, Italian-style omelet has its "filling" piled on top of the eggs, so you don't have to fuss with folding it inside. And the combo of mushrooms, tomatoes, and cheese turns this simple skillet meal into a great-tasting treat.

PER SERVING

105 calories / 26% from fat
1 g saturated fat, 3 g total fat
57 mg cholesterol
358 mg sodium
6 g total carbohydrate
1 g dietary fiber
14 g protein

PREP TIME 10 min.	COOK TIME 14 min.	SERVES 4

- 4 ounces white or cremini mushrooms, thinly sliced
- ⅓ cup thinly sliced red onion
- 2 cups fat-free egg substitute
- 1 large egg
- ½ teaspoon chopped fresh oregano
- ½ teaspoon fresh thyme leaves
- ¼ teaspoon salt
- ¼ teaspoon black pepper
- 4 small plum tomatoes, thinly sliced
- 2 tablespoons shredded part-skim mozzarella cheese

1 Preheat broiler. Coat 9- or 10-inch ovenproof nonstick skillet with nonstick cooking spray and set over medium-high heat. Sauté mushrooms and onion until tender, about 5 minutes. Transfer to plate. Wipe out skillet, coat again with cooking spray, and place over medium heat.

2 Whisk egg substitute, egg, oregano, thyme, salt, and black pepper in medium bowl; pour into hot skillet. Cook, *without stirring,* until eggs begin to set, about 2 minutes, lifting up edge with heat-proof rubber spatula while tilting skillet and letting uncooked portion flow underneath.

3 Arrange tomato slices and sautéed vegetables in concentric circles on top. Continue cooking frittata until eggs are golden brown on bottom and almost set on top, 2 to 3 minutes longer.

4 Sprinkle mozzarella around edge of frittata. Transfer skillet to broiler and broil until cheese melts and begins to brown, about 2 minutes. Cut frittata into quarters.

STEP 2 *Add eggs to hot skillet.*

STEP 3 *Top with tomatoes and sautéed vegetable mixture.*

STEP 4 *Broil to melt cheese.*

HEALTH HINT

Egg whites, which are used as the base of most egg substitutes, are considered the perfect protein because they supply all the essential amino acids our bodies need to maintain good health.

secret to success

Buy mushrooms that are firm, plump, and appear clean. Avoid wrinkled mushrooms or those with slimy spots. Wrap them in a towel to store in the refrigerator so they retain their moisture. The trick to cleaning mushrooms is to wipe thoroughly with a damp paper towel, which preserves their taste and texture. The mushrooms will turn mushy if exposed to too much water.

Cook's Clue

If your skillet has a plastic handle, wrap the handle well in aluminum foil before putting it under the broiler.

Chive and Swiss Cheese Stratas

Not quite soufflés, not quite puddings, not just baked cheese toast. They're stratas, similar to those made in the early 20th century—but much quicker to make because they're not layered. They're so creamy and cheesy that your guests will never guess they're heart healthy!

PER SERVING

240 calories / 17% from fat
2 g saturated fat, 4.5 g total fat
81 mg cholesterol
410 mg sodium
28 g total carbohydrate
1 g dietary fiber
17 g protein

PREP TIME 25 min. + standing | **COOK TIME 25 min.** | **SERVES 6**

- 9 slices white bread (preferably day-old)
- 2 large eggs
- 4 egg whites
- 2 cups nonfat half-and-half
- ½ teaspoon black pepper
- 1½ cups shredded low-fat Swiss cheese
- ¼ cup snipped fresh chives

1 Preheat oven to 350°F. Lightly coat one 11 x 7-inch baking dish or six 1½-cup individual au gratin dishes with nonstick cooking spray. Stack up 4 or 5 slices bread and cut into ½-inch cubes; repeat with the remaining slices.

2 Whisk eggs, egg whites, half-and-half, and black pepper in a large bowl. Mix in ¾ cup cheese, then sprinkle in chives. Add the bread cubes and stir until well coated with the egg mixture. Cover and refrigerate at least 30 minutes or overnight. Spread the mixture evenly into the large baking dish or divide among the six au gratin dishes. Sprinkle with remaining cheese.

3 Bake on middle rack until the knife inserted in the center comes out clean, about 35 minutes for a large strata; 25 minutes for smaller ones. Place a foil tent, shiny-side up, over the strata during the last 10 minutes of baking to prevent overbrowning.

STEP 1 *Cut a stack of bread into ½-inch cubes.*

STEP 2 *Add bread cubes to egg-cheese mixture.*

STEP 3 *Cover with foil tent to prevent overbrowning.*

living smart
FOR A HEALTHY HEART

Lower-fat cheeses taste and act different from full-fat cheeses, so you have to use them in different ways.

♥ **Reduced-fat cheese** contains 25% less fat. Because there's only a slight reduction, reduced-fat cheeses can be substituted for full-fat varieties in most recipes.

♥ **Light and low-fat cheeses,** with 3 or 4 grams of fat per ounce, can be used in soups, stews, stratas, and other moist dishes that are served hot. These cheeses melt well into liquids but tend to get rubbery as they cool.

way back when... Some of the first stratas were found in cookbooks and on dinner tables at the beginning of the 20th century. The names varied from Cheese Pudding to Escalloped Cheese, but the ingredients were the same: slices of buttered bread, eggs, cheddar, and milk. Stratas were a particular favorite during the Depression and both World Wars because they were low in cost, high in flavor, and a great source of protein when meat was scarce.

(Source: American Century Cookbook, by Jean Anderson, Clarkson N. Potter/Publishers, NY, 1997)

HEALTH HINT

To enhance the nutritional value of this meal, substitute white bread with whole grain.

Cook's Clue

Create your own stratas by substituting different breads and cheeses. Just be sure to choose bread with a firm, not spongy, texture. Try rye bread with reduced-fat cheddar, whole grain with reduced-fat peppered Jack cheese, or Italian bread with part-skim mozzarella.

Breakfast Sausage Patties

If you've changed your eating habits for the better, you've probably said "so long" to sausage. But picture this: juicy, crisp-crusted sausage patties, redolent of rosemary and sage and spiced with Dijon mustard. Now imagine that they have less than 1 gram of fat apiece. That's just what you get with this recipe, thanks to lean turkey breast and a few secret ingredients.

PER PATTY

69 calories / 7% from fat
0 g saturated fat, 0.5 g total fat
23 mg cholesterol
196 mg sodium
6 g total carbohydrate
0.5 g dietary fiber
10 g protein

PREP TIME 10 min. | **COOK TIME 6 min.** | **12 PATTIES**

- 1 pound skinless, boneless turkey breast
- ¾ cup cooked brown or basmati rice
- ¼ cup prune butter
- 1 tablespoon Dijon mustard
- ¾ teaspoon salt
- ½ teaspoon rubbed sage
- ½ teaspoon dried rosemary, minced

1 Cut the turkey breast into large chunks. Place in a food processor and pulse until coarsely ground.

2 Transfer ground turkey to a medium bowl. Add rice, prune butter, mustard, salt, sage, and rosemary and stir to combine.

3 Shape the mixture into twelve 2-inch patties. Spray a broiler pan with nonstick cooking spray. Preheat broiler.

4 Place patties on the pan and broil 4 inches from heat, turning once, until cooked through, about 3 minutes per side.

STEP 1 *Cut turkey breast into large chunks for grinding.*

STEP 2 *Add prune butter to ground turkey and cooked rice.*

STEP 3 *Divide ground turkey mixture into 12 equal portions, and shape each portion into a patty, 2 inches in diameter.*

living smart
FOR A HEALTHY HEART

How to lower the fat content in your meat and poultry dishes:

♥ **Purchase meat with little fat,** or trim off all visible fat before cooking. This will save up to 5 g of fat per 3-ounce serving.

♥ **Buy leaner cuts of meat,** especially ground meat.

♥ **Grill or broil poultry,** so the fat drips off. You can leave the skin on during cooking to keep meat moist, and then discard.

Round Out the Meal

Serve with a one-yolk omelet, sautéed apples, and whole-grain toast.

secret to success

You might have used prune butter (pureed prunes) as a fat substitute in baking, but you may be surprised to discover that it can also replace some of the fat in savory recipes like this one. The rice adds sturdy texture, and both ingredients contribute fiber to the patties.

Cook's Clue

Even for a leisurely weekend breakfast, you may want to make the sausage patties the night before. Shape the mixture into patties, place them on a platter, and cover closely with plastic wrap. When you broil the patties, add an extra 30 seconds or so per side to the cooking time to compensate for the fact that the meat is chilled.

Denver Omelet

Whip up an omelet the Denver way but in a more healthful fashion. This omelet is made with the same peppers and onions used in the original, but egg whites replace some of the whole eggs, and red-skinned potatoes replace the ham—making a good-for-you breakfast that's ready in under 30 minutes.

PER SERVING

307 calories / 18% from fat

2 g saturated fat, 6 g total fat

212 mg cholesterol

589 mg sodium

46 g total carbohydrate

6 g dietary fiber

18 g protein

PREP TIME 10 min. | **COOK TIME 18 min.** | **SERVES 2**

- 1 medium red-skinned potato, chopped (about ¾ cup)
- 1 medium onion, chopped
- ½ cup green bell pepper, chopped and seeded
- ½ cup red bell pepper, chopped and seeded
- 2 large eggs
- 3 large egg whites
- ½ teaspoon hot red pepper sauce
- ¼ teaspoon salt
- 2 slices whole-wheat bread, toasted

1 Preheat oven to 400°F. Coat an 8-inch oven-proof nonstick skillet with nonstick cooking spray and set over medium heat. Sauté the potato until soft, about 5 minutes.

2 Stir in the onion and green and red peppers. Sauté until soft, about 5 minutes. Remove the skillet from heat. Transfer vegetables to a plate. Coat the skillet again with cooking spray and return to heat.

3 Meanwhile, whisk the eggs, egg whites, red pepper sauce, and salt in a medium bowl. Pour into the hot skillet. Cook until set on the bottom, lifting up the edge with a heatproof rubber spatula to let the uncooked portion flow underneath.

4 Spoon the vegetables over half of the omelet and fold omelet over the filling.

5 Transfer the skillet to the oven and bake until the eggs are completely set, about 3 minutes. Cut the omelet in half and serve with toast.

STEP 3 *Lift edge of omelet, letting uncooked eggs flow to hot skillet underneath.*

STEP 4 *Gently fold half of omelet over filling with wide, long spatula.*

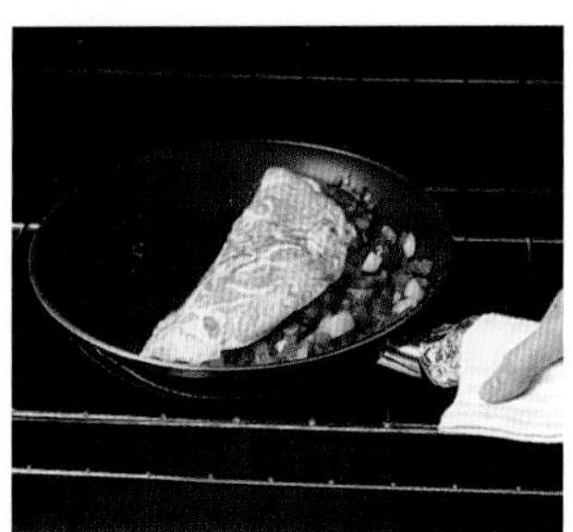

STEP 5 *Cook in oven until eggs are set.*

secret to success

You can eat healthfully and still enjoy an omelet! All the fat and cholesterol in eggs is in the yolks. This omelet, which is made from three egg whites and just two whole eggs, serves two and has half the fat and cholesterol per serving of a regular two-egg omelet.

HEALTH HINT

Leaving the skin on red-skinned potatoes significantly raises the fiber and vitamin content in this meal.

way back when... In the 1920s, customers ordering a Denver omelet were often brought a sandwich—an omelet filled with ham, onion, and green pepper on white bread or toast. Over the years, it has taken on a life of its own. Across the country, the fillings change from place to place. Even the name changes, as it is frequently found on menus as a "Western" or a "Western Omelet."

(Source: The Encyclopedia of American Food and Drink, *by John F. Mariani, Lebhar-Friedman Books, NY, 1999)*

Cook's Clue

The secret to a tender omelet is to cook the eggs slowly and evenly. Gently cook the omelet first on the range top over medium heat, then finish for a few minutes in the oven. This ensures an omelet that is perfectly cooked throughout.

Sour Cream Waffles with Glazed Nectarines

PER SERVING
310 calories / 29% from fat
3.5 g saturated fat, 10 g total fat
83 mg cholesterol
597 mg sodium
48 g total carbohydrate
2 g dietary fiber
8 g protein

Waffles aren't just for weekends anymore! You'll have time to dig into this hot breakfast any weekday morning if you make the batter the night before. Reduced-fat ingredients and plenty of juicy nectarines make these wonderful waffles a heart-healthy way to start the day.

PREP TIME 20 min. | **COOK TIME 25 min.** | **SERVES 6**

- 1½ cups self-rising flour
- ½ teaspoon baking soda
- 2 large eggs
- ⅔ cup reduced-fat sour cream
- ⅔ cup reduced-fat milk (2%)
- 2 tablespoons margarine, melted
- 1 teaspoon vanilla
- 3 medium nectarines (about 1 pound), thinly sliced
- ¼ cup packed light brown sugar
- ½ cup orange juice
- 1½ tablespoons cornstarch

1 Preheat the waffle iron. Whisk the flour and baking soda in a small bowl.

2 Whisk eggs in a medium bowl until pale, about 1 minute. Blend in the sour cream, milk, margarine, and vanilla with a rubber spatula. Fold in the flour mixture until combined. Let it stand while you prepare the nectarines.

3 Lightly coat a large nonstick skillet with nonstick cooking spray and set over medium heat. Sauté the nectarines until lightly browned, about 5 minutes. Stir in the brown sugar and cook until the sugar dissolves and becomes syrupy, about 2 minutes. Transfer the nectarines to a bowl with a slotted spoon.

4 Whisk the orange juice and cornstarch in a small bowl until smooth, then add 1 cup cold water. Whisk this mixture into a skillet. Bring to a boil over medium-high heat and cook, whisking until the sauce boils and thickens, about 2 minutes. Return the nectarines to the skillet and heat through.

5 Spoon the batter (about 1 cup for 9-inch-square waffle iron) onto the hot waffle iron. Bake the waffles according to the manufacturer's directions.

6 When done, remove from the iron and keep them warm. Repeat with the remaining batter to make three 9-inch-square waffles. Separate each waffle into four squares and serve two 4½-inch squares topped with about 6 slices of nectarines per person.

Round Out the Meal

Serve with assorted low-fat yogurts with crunchy grains and nuts for required protein and even more fiber.

STEP 5 *Spread batter evenly with heatproof rubber spatula.*

STEP 6 *Use a fork to loosen and remove waffles.*

If you don't have self-rising flour for this recipe, use 1½ cups sifted all-purpose flour mixed with 2¼ teaspoons baking powder and ¼ teaspoon salt.

HEALTH HINT

The skins of nectarines are high in pectin, a soluble fiber that aids in controlling your blood cholesterol level and keeping you heart healthy.

secret to success

Incorporate all ingredients into the waffle batter, but be careful not to overbeat the mixture, otherwise the gluten in the flour will be overworked, giving a less than feather-light waffle.

Dutch Mama

In spite of its name, this pancake is more German than Dutch. It resembles the egg-rich German pancake, which is poured into a hot skillet and baked in the oven with sautéed apples underneath. This recipe is made with fewer whole eggs and more egg whites; cinnamon-spiced apples and strawberries end up on top. It's just as good as the original and a whole lot better for you!

PER SERVING

335 calories / 30% from fat
3 g saturated fat, 11 g total fat
162 mg cholesterol
476 mg sodium
50 g total carbohydrate
4 g dietary fiber
12 g protein

PREP TIME 15 min. | **COOK TIME 25 min.** | **SERVES 4**

- 2 tablespoons margarine
- 3 crisp, sweet apples, peeled and sliced ½ inch thick
- ¼ cup sugar
- ¼ teaspoon ground cinnamon
- ⅓ cup fresh orange juice
- 1 pint strawberries, hulled and quartered
- 3 large eggs
- 4 egg whites
- ½ cup reduced-fat milk (2%)
- ½ teaspoon grated orange zest
- ½ teaspoon salt
- ½ cup all-purpose flour

1 Preheat oven to 425°F. Generously coat a large nonstick ovenproof skillet with nonstick cooking spray and set over medium-low heat. Melt the margarine; remove 1 tablespoon and set aside. Add apples to the skillet and sprinkle with 1 tablespoon sugar. Sauté until the apples are browned and tender but still hold their shape, about 10 minutes.

2 Combine 2 tablespoons of sugar and ground cinnamon; sprinkle evenly over the apples and stir in the orange juice. Bring to a boil, then reduce heat and simmer until the sauce is syrupy, about 2 minutes. Transfer apples to a bowl and stir in the strawberries.

3 Wipe out the skillet and put in the oven to keep hot. Whisk eggs, egg whites, milk, remaining sugar, orange zest, and salt in a medium bowl until combined. Sift in flour and whisk the batter until smooth, then whisk in the reserved margarine.

4 Remove the skillet from the oven and coat with cooking spray. Pour in the batter. Return it to the oven and bake until the pancake is high and puffy, about 10 minutes. Remove from the oven and top with fruit; serve quickly.

STEP 1 *Sauté apples and sugar until apples are tender, yet still hold their shape.*

STEP 4 *Bake pancake until puffed, light golden, and set.*

HEALTH HINT

Strawberries are a good source of the important antioxidant vitamin C, which may help prevent some cancers. Recent research also indicates that vitamin C may raise the level of HDLs (the "good" cholesterol), which helps in removing artery-clogging deposits. The water-soluble fiber from the apples helps lower cholesterol in the body, thus also reducing the risk of heart disease.

way back when... In Latin, the word for pancake was *crispus*, which means curly or wavy. In France, the pancake used to be called a *galette crêpe*. Traditionally, pancakes were served during Candlemas and Shrove Tuesday to celebrate renewal, family life, hopes for good fortune, and future happiness. It is a French custom to touch the frying pan's handle, and make a wish while flipping the pancake, while holding a coin in your hand.

(Source: Larousse Gastronomique, edited by Jenifer Harvey Lang, Crown Publishers, Inc., Reprinted 1988

Cook's Clue

A hot skillet is the secret of a high-puffed pancake. While mixing the batter, heat the skillet in the hot oven. Bake and eat quickly. If you like, you can make the fruit ahead, and let it stand at room temperature for up to 2 hours.

Light 'n' Luscious Blueberry Pancakes

PER SERVING
348 calories / 26% from fat
2 g saturated fat, 10 g total fat
56 mg cholesterol
674 mg sodium
58 g total carbohydrate
4 g dietary fiber
8 g protein

Wake up your family with pancakes sizzling on the griddle. These are overflowing with juicy berries and are so light they melt away with every bite. Call them griddle cakes, batter cakes, hoecakes, or flapjacks—or just plain pancakes. But make them often, for they're a healthful way to start the day.

PREP TIME 15 min. | **COOK TIME 12 min.** | **SERVES 4**

- 1 cup self-rising flour
- 1 tablespoon sugar
- ½ teaspoon baking soda
- 1½ cups low-fat buttermilk
- 2 tablespoons vegetable oil
- 1 large egg
- 1 teaspoon vanilla
- 1 pint fresh blueberries
- ¼ cup blueberry or maple syrup

BLUEBERRIES CONTAIN ANTIOXIDANTS

Antioxidants are compounds found in a wide variety of plant foods, particularly fruits and vegetables. Antioxidants help neutralize destructive forms of oxygen in our bodies called free radicals that can harm cells and are thought to contribute to chronic disease. Free radicals are a result of normal metabolism and are also caused by environmental factors, such as ultraviolet radiation from sunlight, cigarette smoke, and other forms of pollution. While there are hundreds of different antioxidants, those most recognized for their ability to fight disease and enhance immunity include vitamins E, C, and beta-carotene, and the mineral selenium.

1 Whisk the flour, sugar, and baking soda in a medium bowl. Make a well in the center of the mixture. Measure the buttermilk in a large measuring cup; whisk in the oil, egg, and vanilla until blended. Pour into the well and whisk until moistened. Let stand 5 minutes.

2 Meanwhile, coat a large nonstick griddle or skillet with nonstick cooking spray and set over medium heat until it's hot but not smoking. For each pancake, pour about 2 tablespoons of batter onto the griddle.

3 Scatter a few blueberries onto each pancake.

4 Cook until bubbles appear all over the cakes and those around the edge start to burst, about 3 minutes. Turn and cook until the undersides are golden, 1 to 2 minutes longer. Serve the pancakes topped with the remaining berries and syrup.

Round Out the Meal

Serve pancakes with a wedge of honeydew, a couple of strips of crisp turkey bacon, and a cup of fragrant orange-spiced tea.

Cook's Clue

Cook pancakes just the way you like them. For light-golden cakes with no crispy edges, turn them just when the tops are covered with bubbles but none have burst, about 2 minutes. For crispier edges, as in this recipe, wait until the bubbles around the edges have just started to burst before turning, about 1 minute longer. Then cook the underside about 2 more minutes until lightly browned.

STEP 2 *For each pancake, pour about 2 tablespoons batter onto griddle.*

STEP 3 *Scatter a few blueberries onto each cake.*

STEP 4 *Flip cakes over when filled with bubbles and when a few bubbles around the edge start to burst.*

HEALTH HINT

If possible, use fresh fruit with your pancakes; avoid frozen. When fruit is frozen, it often loses its color and taste.

Cinnamon French Toast with Sautéed Apples and Raisins

PER SERVING
469 calories / 19% from fat
3 g saturated fat, 10 g total fat
59 mg cholesterol
489 mg sodium
85 g total carbohydrate
4 g dietary fiber
11 g protein

Begin the day the Parisian way, with pain perdu—that's French for "lost bread." (Soaking day-old bread is a way to revive it.) Top off this heart-smart breakfast with cinnamon-spiced apples and raisins. Help yourself to two slices: This nutritious dish has been trimmed down in fat and calories.

PREP TIME 15 min. + soaking | **COOK TIME** 30 min. | **SERVES** 4

- ½ cup sugar
- 1½ teaspoons ground cinnamon
- ¼ cup fat-free egg substitute
- 1 large egg
- 1¼ cups reduced-fat milk (2%)
- 1 teaspoon vanilla
- 8 slices (about 1 ounce each) French or white bread
- ½ cup golden raisins
- 2 tablespoons margarine
- 2 firm, tart apples, peeled and thinly sliced
- 3 tablespoons apple cider
- 1 tablespoon fresh lemon juice

1 Mix the sugar and cinnamon in a small bowl; set aside. Whisk the egg substitute, egg, milk, vanilla, and 2 tablespoons of cinnamon sugar in a pie plate. One slice at a time, dip bread into the egg mixture, coating both sides, and arrange in a 13 x 9-inch baking dish, slightly overlapping the slices. Cover and refrigerate at least 30 minutes or up to 2 hours.

2 Preheat oven to 375°F. Sprinkle the bread slices with 2 tablespoons of cinnamon sugar. Bake until browned and puffed, about 30 minutes.

3 Meanwhile, cook the raisins in enough boiling water to cover until they're soft and plump, about 5 minutes; drain well.

4 Melt the margarine in a large skillet over medium heat. Sauté the apples until golden brown and almost tender, about 4 minutes. Stir in the raisins, apple cider, and lemon juice, then sprinkle with the remaining cinnamon sugar. Cook until apples are tender but still hold their shape, about 3 minutes longer. Serve with French toast.

Round Out the Meal

Serve French toast with homemade sausage and a glass of hot apple cider with a cinnamon stick.

HEALTH HINT

Bread is a good source of carbohydrates. And thanks to enriched flour, bread also contains useful amounts of iron, niacin, riboflavin, thiamin, and folate. Apples are good sources of pectin, which helps control cholesterol.

STEP 1 *Slightly overlap slices of soaked bread in baking dish.*

STEP 3 *Boil raisins until they are plump and doubled in size.*

STEP 4 *Cook apples and raisins in cider sauce until they are tender but still have their shape.*

living smart
FOR A HEALTHY HEART

ARE YOU AN APPLE OR A PEAR?

Obesity can increase your risk of heart disease, but where you carry extra weight might be as important as how much you carry. If your body is a "pear," excess weight gravitates to hips and thighs—not pleasant in swimsuit season, but a boon as far as your heart's concerned. "Apples" gain weight in their midsections, increasing the potential for heart disease, hypertension, and other ailments. Women whose waists measure 35 inches or more and men with 40-plus waists are at the highest risk.

secret to success

Many ovens have "hot spots," or areas that may brown food quicker than other areas. Be sure to watch over the toast and rotate when necessary.

Breakfast Bread Pudding with Mixed Berries

Pudding for breakfast sounds like a child's dream come true, but it can also be a healthy way to start the day. An exemplary breakfast, this bread pudding brings together fiber from the whole-grain bread and berries, vitamin C from the fruit, and protein from the egg whites.

PER SERVING

224 calories / 10% from fat

0.5 g saturated fat, 2.5 g total fat

71 mg cholesterol

378 mg sodium

41 g total carbohydrate

7 g dietary fiber

9 g protein

PREP TIME 10 min. + soaking | **COOK TIME** 40 min. | **SERVES** 6

- ¼ cup sugar
- 2 large eggs
- 3 large egg whites
- 2 cups fat-free half-and-half
- 1 teaspoon vanilla
- ¼ teaspoon salt
- 8 slices light oatmeal bread, toasted
- 2 cups blueberries
- 2 cups raspberries

1 Spray an 8-inch-square baking pan with non-stick cooking spray.

2 Combine 3 tablespoons of sugar, whole eggs, egg whites, half-and-half, vanilla, and salt in a large spouted measuring cup (or medium bowl) and whisk to combine.

3 Place 4 slices of toast in the bottom of the baking pan. Pour half of the egg mixture over. Top with remaining toast and egg mixture. Let it stand for 20 minutes. (The recipe can be made ahead to this point. Cover and refrigerate overnight.)

4 Preheat oven to 350°F. Place the baking pan in a slightly larger pan. Set the pan on the oven rack and pour in enough hot water to come halfway up the outside of the baking pan. Bake until the pudding is set and the top is golden and puffed, about 40 minutes. Let cool slightly.

5 Meanwhile, toss together the blueberries, raspberries, and remaining 1 tablespoon sugar in a medium bowl. Serve the warm pudding topped with berries.

STEP 3 *Pour the egg mixture over toasted bread in the baking pan.*

STEP 4 *Place the baking pan in a larger pan and pour in enough water to come halfway up the outside of the smaller pan.*

STEP 5 *Sprinkle sugar over the berries and toss to coat.*

HEALTH HINT

Blueberries and raspberries are nutritional storehouses, brimming with vitamin C, fiber, and a number of disease-fighting phytochemicals that sweep harmful free radicals out of your body. You can use frozen berries because freezing doesn't destroy their nutritional value or their flavor—though their texture and color do suffer slightly.

Cook's Clue

You can use toasted whole-wheat bread instead of oatmeal bread. When berries are not in season, try apple slices sautéed with cinnamon as a topping.

way back when... The word pudding, in the past, applied to all boiled dishes. The French word 'boudin' (blood sausage, black pudding) had the same origin. This sweet pudding did not form until the 17th century. The name 'pudding' in France also refers to cake made with dry bread or stale brioche. It is sweetened, then mixed with raisins, rum, milk, eggs, and candied orange peel. It is cooked in a small brioche mould and covered lightly with frosting. The English bread pudding is similar, but the French pudding is much more elaborate.

(Source: Larousse Gastronomique, edited by Jenifer Harvey Lang, Crown Publishers, Inc., Reprinted 1988)

secret to success

To test if batter is done, insert a toothpick or skewer into the center of pudding; if it comes out clean, the pudding is set.

Sweet Carrot–Raisin Muffins

This yummy golden breakfast bread makes a satisfying start to any day. Whole-wheat flour and sunflower seeds sneak some heart-protective fiber and vitamin E into your diet, while applesauce replaces some of the fat usually found in muffins. Carrots, raisins, and a trio of spices please the nose and tongue.

PER MUFFIN

177 calories / 7% from fat
1 g saturated fat, 6 g total fat
35 mg cholesterol
126 mg sodium
28 g total carbohydrate
2 g dietary fiber
3 g protein

PREP TIME 10 min. | **COOK TIME 5 min.** | **MAKES 12**

- 1 cup all-purpose flour
- ½ cup whole-wheat flour
- ½ cup sugar
- 2 teaspoons baking powder
- ¼ teaspoon salt
- ½ teaspoon ground cinnamon
- ¼ teaspoon ground allspice
- ¼ teaspoon ground nutmeg
- ½ cup unsweetened applesauce
- ¼ cup vegetable oil
- 2 large eggs, lightly beaten
- 1 large carrot, peeled and finely shredded
- ½ cup raisins
- 2 tablespoons unsalted, shelled sunflower seeds

1 Preheat oven to 400°F. Coat 12 standard muffin-pan cups with nonstick cooking spray or line with paper liners.

2 Combine the all-purpose flour, whole-wheat flour, sugar, baking powder, salt, ground cinnamon, allspice, and nutmeg in a large bowl.

3 Combine the applesauce, oil, and eggs in a medium bowl. Fold in the carrot, raisins, and sunflower seeds. Stir in the flour mixture until evenly moistened. Spoon into the muffin cups, filling each two-thirds full.

4 Bake until a toothpick inserted in the centers comes out clean, about 15 minutes. Cool muffins on a wire rack. Serve warm.

Round Out the Meal

Serve muffins with pineapple and strawberries, and top off with a glass of prune juice or a cup of herbal tea.

STEP 3 *Spoon the batter into the prepared muffin cups.*

STEP 4 *Remove the muffins to a rack as soon as they finish baking to prevent soggy bottoms. Use a spatula, if necessary.*

secret to success

Don't overmix the batter. Only a few strokes are necessary to obtain light, textured muffins.

way back when... In Great Britain, a muffin is a flat, round, light textured roll, made with yeast dough. Muffins usually are split, toasted, buttered, and sometimes jammed. In Victorian times, muffins were sold in the streets. Street sellers carried trays of muffins on their heads, while ringing a hand bell to attract customers. North American muffins are different: Instead of using yeast, they use baking powder, and deep muffin tins are used. Sometimes instead of flour, cornmeal and bran are used.

(Source: Larousse Gastronomique, *edited by Jenifer Harvey Lang, Crown Publishers, Inc., Reprinted 1988*)

Cook's Clue

To reheat a muffin the second day, put it in a brown paper bag and fold the end over. Splash a little water on the bag, and place it in a 350°F oven for 7-8 minutes. It will emerge warm and moist.

Granola with Toasted Walnuts and Cranberries

Many commercial cereals and cereal bars seem to be vying for junk-food status, not to mention for highest-price honors. It's good to know that you can easily toast up a wholesome, delicious batch of whole-grain cereal at home. Serve it with skim milk or soy milk.

PER ⅓ CUP
154 calories / 29% from fat
0.5 g saturated fat, 5 g total fat
0 mg cholesterol
41 mg sodium
25 g total carbohydrate
3 g dietary fiber
4 g protein

PREP TIME 25 min. | **COOK TIME 5 min.** | **5 CUPS**

- 3 cups old-fashioned or quick-cooking oats
- ½ cup coarsely chopped walnuts
- 2 tablespoons wheat germ
- 2 tablespoons sesame seeds
- ¼ teaspoon salt
- ⅓ cup honey
- 1 tablespoon light brown sugar
- 1 tablespoon extra-light olive oil
- 1 teaspoon vanilla
- 1 cup dried cranberries

1 Preheat oven to 300°F. Combine the oats, walnuts, wheat germ, sesame seeds, and salt in a 13 x 9-inch baking pan. Bake until the oats and nuts are toasted and fragrant, about 30 minutes. Remove the pan from the oven. Increase the oven temperature to 350°F.

2 Meanwhile, combine the honey, brown sugar, and oil in a small skillet over medium heat. Cook until the sugar has melted, about 1 minute. Remove from the heat and stir in vanilla.

3 Drizzle the honey mixture over the oat mixture and stir to coat. Return to the oven and bake, stirring occasionally, until the oats are crispy, about 10 minutes.

4 With a spoon, break up any clumps. Stir in the cranberries. Store in an airtight container.

STEP 1 *Toast the oats, walnuts, wheat germ, sesame seeds, and salt together in a baking pan.*

STEP 3 *Drizzle the honey-sugar mixture over the granola mixture.*

STEP 4 *After the granola is toasted, stir in the dried cranberries.*

living smart
FOR A HEALTHY HEART

SHOPPING FOR GOOD HEALTH

Most large supermarkets carry heart-healthy foods such as tofu, edamame (tender young soy beans), low-fat dairy products, and whole-grain cereals. But it pays to check your local health-food store for a wider selection. In a good health-food store, you'll find more unusual whole grains, more alternatives to meat and dairy products, a wider variety of low-sodium foods, heart-healthy seeds and nuts, and more healthful snacks and convenience foods.

HEALTH HINT

A host of hard-to-find restorative oils abounds in this flavorful granola. Walnuts contain alpha-linolenic acid, which is similar to the heart-healthy omega-3 fatty acids found in fish oils. Wheat germ, in addition to its protective oils, provides cholesterol-reducing, fat-soluble vitamin E.

Cook's Clue

Granola is more than just a breakfast cereal. You can sprinkle it over vanilla yogurt, or cottage cheese and sliced bananas, for a quick lunch. You can also use it as a topping for puddings and frozen desserts.

Orange Marmalade

PER TABLESPOON
52 calories / 0% from fat
0 g saturated fat, 0 g total fat
0 mg cholesterol
0 mg sodium
14 g total carbohydrate
0 g dietary fiber
0 g protein

Sweet citrus marmalade made from scratch is fat-free breakfast fare that's well worth the effort when you make it yourself. Put a jar or two in a cloth-lined basket with a loaf of crusty, whole-grain bread, and it becomes a perfect way of saying "welcome" or "thank you" to friends and neighbors.

PREP TIME 40 min. + overnight | **COOK TIME 5 min.** | **4 HALF-PINTS**

- 2 large navel or Valencia oranges
- 1 large thick-skinned lemon
- 2 cups water
- 4 cups sugar

Cook's Clue

Jars with rubber seals made for home canning are the safest. They can be reused if they are in perfect condition. Don't reuse two-part metal vacuum lids; they will not make an air-tight seal.

Round Out the Meal

To complement your homemade marmalade, spread it on a toasted whole-wheat English muffin or a piece of whole-wheat toast. You can also brew a hot cup of orange-peel tea.

HEALTH HINT

The rind and white pith of oranges, grapefruits, and lem-ons contain many dis-ease-fighting antioxidants and phytochemicals.

1 Peel the oranges and lemon, cutting away the rind and white pith about ⅜-inch thick. Cut into slivers ¾-inch long and ⅛-inch wide. (Discard excess pith and fiber.) Tie the seeds in a small piece of cheesecloth. Chop the fruit coarsely, reserving the juice.

2 Simmer the rind, chopped fruit, reserved juice, seed bag, and the water in an 8-quart, nonreactive saucepot over medium-high heat, uncovered, for 10 minutes. Remove and discard the seed bag. Pour into a large, heatproof glass bowl. Cover and refrigerate overnight.

3 Wash and rinse the 4 half-pint canning jars, lids, and sealing rings. Place the jars in a large pot, cover with water, bring to a boil, and boil 10 minutes. Remove the jars with tongs to a baking sheet in a 250° oven to keep warm and dry. Sterilize the lids and sealing rings in boiling water or according to the manufacturer.

4 Return the fruit mixture to the pot, add sugar, and place over medium heat. Insert a candy thermometer and bring to a boil, stirring until the sugar dissolves. Continue boiling, stirring occasionally, until the thermometer registers around 218°F to 220°F.

5 Remove from the heat, skim off the foam, and ladle the marmalade into the sterilized jars, leaving ¼-inch head space. Wipe the rims with a clean cloth and seal as directed by the manufacturer. After cooling, the sealed caps should be slightly concave. If a lid fails to seal, the marmalade can be safely refrigerated for two weeks. Label the jars and store in a cool dark place for up to a year.

STEP 1 *Wash the fruit. Slice rind into ¾-inch-long slivers.*

STEPS 4–5 *Cook until the mixture reaches 220°F. Remove from heat and skim off foam.*

STEP 5 *Ladle marmalade into the sterilized jars, stirring to make sure rind is evenly distributed.*

Tropical Smoothie

No, we're not talking about some Caribbean-born Casanova—this is an energizing breakfast drink made with mango, banana, pineapple, and kiwifruit. (Okay, we cheated—kiwi isn't a tropical fruit. But it is a superb source of vitamin C.) Delicious as it is in the morning, this smoothie also goes down nicely at other times of the day.

PER SERVING

164 calories / 11% from fat

1 g saturated fat, 2 g total fat

4 mg cholesterol

45 mg sodium

33 g total carbohydrate

4 g dietary fiber

6 g protein

PREP TIME 15 min.	COOK TIME 0 min.	SERVES 4

- 1 mango
- 1 banana, cut into large chunks
- 1 cup pineapple chunks
- 2 kiwifruits, peeled and sliced
- 1 cup plain low-fat yogurt
- 3 tablespoons toasted wheat germ
- 1 cup ice cubes

1 Cube mango (*see photos, right*).

2 Combine the mango, banana, pineapple, kiwis, yogurt, wheat germ, and ice cubes in a blender. Puree until smooth and thick.

3 Pour into 4 tall glasses. (Mango, pineapple, and kiwifruit can be cut several hours ahead of time. Peel and cut the banana just before preparing the smoothie.) Garnish with skewered cubes of extra fruit, if you like.

How to Prepare a Mango

Make a vertical cut on either side of the mango's large, flat pit.

With the tip of a sharp knife, score the mango in a diamond pattern, cutting to, but not through, the skin.

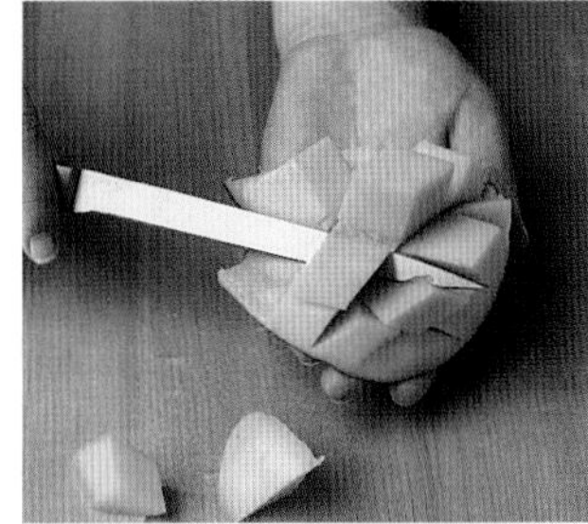

Flip mango skin outward and cut off pieces of fruit.

secret to success

The wheat germ in this velvety blend thickens the smoothie and sneaks in a good helping of B vitamins. If you like, sprinkle a little more wheat germ on top when you serve the drink.

Round Out the Meal

While the smoothie contains plenty of vitamins, add a nut or grain cereal with low-fat milk for additional protein.

HEALTH HINT

Fiber-filled wheat germ is an unusually and exceptionally concentrated food source of the antioxidant vitamin E and provides cardioprotective omega fats as well. Because its heart-healthy oils deteriorate quickly, be sure to store wheat germ in an airtight container in the refrigerator.

Cook's Clue

If you happen to find golden kiwis, which are more fragrant and tart than the green ones, substitute them in this recipe for a change. You don't need to peel the golden kiwis—rather than a "furry" skin, they have a peel like that of a Bosc pear. You can also use 2 nectarines instead of the mango.

Appetizers, Soups and Sandwiches

Guacamole with a Kick

You'll get a fiesta in every bite of this zesty dip: Chunks of onion, tomato, and jalapeño peppers add so much zing, your mouth will sing! Low-fat yogurt and nonfat sour cream lighten the mix and stretch two avocados to feed a horde of hungry dunkers. To keep a lid on the fat, serve baked, not fried, tortilla chips for a slimmed-down snack.

PER SERVING

72 calories / 50% from fat

0.75 g saturated fat, 4 g total fat

0 mg cholesterol

124 mg sodium

8 g total carbohydrate

2 g dietary fiber

2 g protein

PREP TIME 20 min. + standing | **COOK TIME** 0 min. | **SERVES** 16

- ½ cup low-fat plain yogurt
- 2 small jalapeño peppers, seeded
- 2 plum tomatoes, finely chopped
- 1 small white onion, finely chopped
- 2 tablespoons minced cilantro
- ½ teaspoon salt
- ½ cup nonfat sour cream
- 2 large avocados
- 2 tablespoons fresh lime juice
- 3 ounces baked tortilla chips

1 Line bottom of strainer with cheesecloth, coffee filter, or paper towel and set over medium bowl (strainer should not touch bottom of bowl). Spoon in yogurt, cover, and refrigerate 8 hours or overnight, until yogurt cheese is thick and creamy.

2 Remove seeds and ribs from jalapeños with melon baller (wear gloves when handling, as the peppers can burn); mince. Mix jalapeños, tomatoes, onion, cilantro, and salt in large bowl. Fold in yogurt cheese and sour cream.

3 Halve, pit, and peel avocados. Mash with potato masher and sprinkle with lime juice. Quickly fold into tomato mixture. Serve with baked tortilla chips. Makes 3 cups guacamole.

STEP 1 *Yogurt cheese should have the consistency of sour cream.*

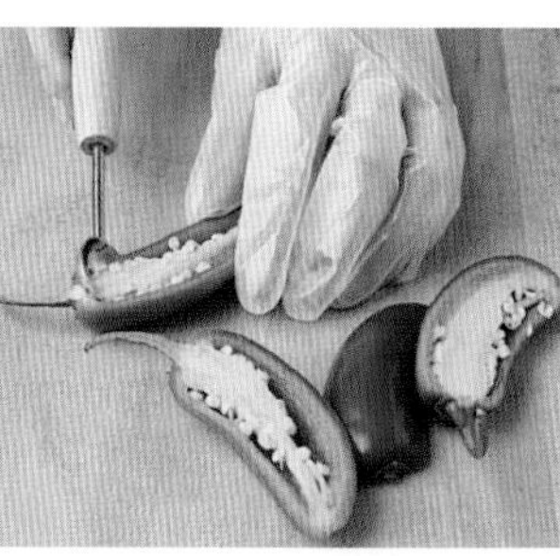

STEP 2 *Remove seeds and ribs from peppers with melon baller.*

STEP 3 *In a bowl, mash avocados until almost smooth but still a little chunky.*

Round Out the Meal

Spoon guacamole on an individual tortilla shell, then top off with a small steamed shrimp; each one is a meal in itself. Serve with a healthy frozen smoothie of papaya and garnish with fresh cilantro leaves.

Cook's Clue

When buying yogurt to make yogurt cheese, read the labels carefully. For a creamy consistency, pick a yogurt that does not contain gelatin, as this holds onto the whey, hampering the draining process.

way back when... Avocados, also known as alligator pears (because of their rough skins), first appeared in print in the American colonies as early as 1690. Because of their bland taste, they did not become popular until the 1950s, when they showed up in salads.

(Source: The Encyclopedia of American Food and Drink, by John F. Mariani, Lebhar-Friedman Books, NY, 1999.)

HEALTH HINT

Avocados are high in monounsaturated fat, the same kind found in olive oil, canola oil, and nut oils. Monounsaturated fats appear to have a protective effect on the heart.

Roasted-Vegetable Wraps with Chive Sauce

PER SERVING
120 calories / 15% from fat
0.5 g saturated fat, 2 g total fat
1 mg cholesterol
435 mg sodium
24 g total carbohydrate
7 g dietary fiber
5 g protein

Wraps became a huge trend in sandwiches a few years ago, but they've been around forever—think crêpes or burritos. Now they're showing up as appetizers too, like this flavorsome roasted-veggie-and-tangy-sauce combination that's destined to disappear fast from an hors d'oeuvre tray.

PREP TIME 20 min. **COOK TIME 30 min.** **SERVES 8**

- 1 tablespoon olive oil
- 1 tablespoon rice vinegar
- 1 teaspoon chopped fresh rosemary
- 1 garlic clove, minced
- ¼ teaspoon salt
- 2 medium zucchini (8 ounces each)
- 2 large red bell peppers, seeded
- 1 large red onion
- 8 flour tortillas, 98% fat free (7 inches)
- ¾ cup plain low-fat yogurt, drained
- ¼ teaspoon onion salt
- 1 tablespoon snipped fresh chives

1 Place oven rack in upper third of oven and preheat oven to 450°F. Lightly coat jelly-roll pan with nonstick cooking spray. Whisk oil, vinegar, rosemary, garlic, and salt in small bowl. Cut each zucchini crosswise in half, then lengthwise into đ-inch slices. Cut each red pepper into 8 strips. Cut onion into 16 wedges.

2 Toss vegetables and oil mixture in pan. Roast, tossing frequently, until brown and tender, about 30 minutes. Sprinkle tortillas with a little water, wrap in foil, and place in oven with the vegetables during the last 5 minutes.

3 Combine yogurt, onion salt, and chives in small bowl. Spread chive sauce evenly on tortillas and top with vegetables.

4 Fold in sides of tortillas and roll up. Cut each wrap into 3 pieces on the diagonal.

STEP 3 *Spread chive sauce on the tortilla and arrange vegetables on top.*

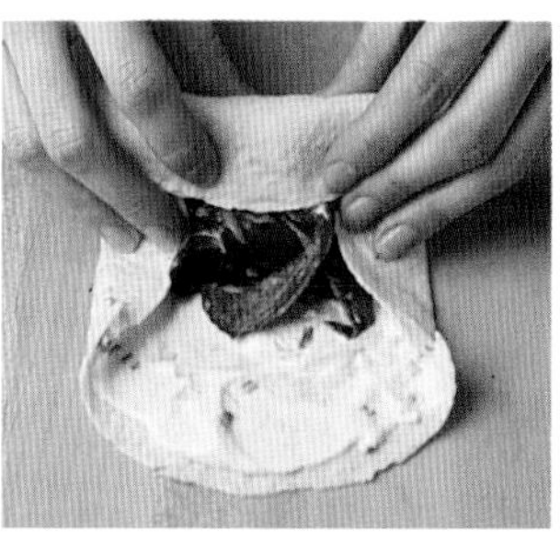

STEP 4 *Fold in sides and roll up tortilla, enclosing vegetables.*

secret to success

Drained yogurt is an excellent stand-in for sour cream. To make, spoon ¾ cup plain nonfat or low-fat yogurt into a strainer lined with a coffee filter, paper towel, or cheesecloth. Set the strainer over a bowl, cover with plastic wrap, and refrigerate for at least 8 hours.

HEALTH HINT

These vegetables provide one-fourth of the Recommended Daily Value for dietary fiber. To get all the valuable fiber that vegetables and fruits can supply, leave their peels on.

Cook's Clue

Roasting vegetables at high heat caramelizes them: It enhances their flavor by concentrating their sugars. For best results, use a shallow pan, arrange the vegetables in a single layer, and put the pan in the hottest part of the oven (usually the top third). To ensure even browning, toss vegetables frequently until they turn a deep caramel color.

Round Out the Meal

Serve wraps on a bed of baby alfalfa sprouts with toasted pine nuts, and finish with a light lemon sorbet.

Chinese Dumplings

Kick off your next party with a platter of succulent dumplings filled with super-lean ground turkey and partnered with a tangy soy-citrus dipping sauce. Once you've mastered the technique, you'll find that it takes just minutes to make a double (or triple) batch for a big crowd. You can buy wonton wrappers at Asian grocery stores, but they're also sold at many supermarkets.

PER DUMPLING

97 calories / 14% from fat
0.5 g saturated fat, 1.5 g total fat
11 mg cholesterol
349 mg sodium
17 g total carbohydrate
1 g dietary fiber
5 g protein

PREP TIME 25 min.	COOK TIME 10 min.	24 DUMPLINGS

- 3 tablespoons reduced-sodium soy sauce
- ½ teaspoon cornstarch
- ½ teaspoon ground ginger
- 3 ounces lean ground turkey
- ⅓ cup chopped cilantro
- 3 scallions, minced
- ¼ cup sliced water chestnuts, minced
- 24 round wonton wrappers (3½ inches)
- 3 tablespoons fresh lime juice
- 1 teaspoon sugar

Cook's Clue

If you can't find wonton wrappers, make your own: Combine 1 cup flour and ¼ cup cold water in a small bowl. Mix and knead until a smooth, stiff dough forms, adding a few drops more water if necessary. Wrap in plastic wrap and let stand 30 minutes. Divide dough into three equal pieces. Cut each piece into 8 pieces and roll each into a ball. Roll each ball to a 3½-inch round. If made a day ahead, store, loosely stacked, in a plastic bag in the refrigerator.

1 Combine 1 tablespoon soy sauce, cornstarch, and ground ginger in medium bowl. Add ground turkey, cilantro, scallions, and water chestnuts and mix well.

2 Place wonton wrappers on work surface. Spoon a rounded teaspoon of turkey mixture onto center of each wrapper. Moisten edges with water. Fold wrapper over and pleat to seal (see photos, right).

3 Spray large heatproof plate with cooking spray. Place 12 dumplings on plate. Place round cake rack in large skillet and pour in water to come just to bottom of rack. Cover and bring to a boil over medium heat. Place plate of dumplings on rack, cover, and steam until filling is firm and cooked through, about 5 minutes. Remove and keep warm. Repeat with remaining dumplings.

4 Meanwhile, combine remaining 2 tablespoons soy sauce, lime juice, and sugar in small skillet over low heat and cook just until sugar has melted, about 1 minute. Serve dumplings with dipping sauce.

Round Out the Meal

Julienne some Napa cabbage, shiitake mushrooms, carrots and green onions and toss with an Asian vinaigrette for a crunchy side salad.

way back when... Chinese Dumpling is called Jiaozi in China. It is a traditional Chinese food, served in Northern China during the holidays. The dumpling is shaped like an ancient Chinese gold or silver ingot, which symbolizes wealth. During Chinese New Year, the dumpling is one of the key foods. Dumplings are made New Year's Eve, and a coin is hidden in one of the dumplings. Whoever finds the coin in the dumpling is expected to have good fortune in the New Year.

(Source: www.chineseculture.about.com/library/weekly/aa020298.htm)

Making Dumplings

Place some filling in center of wonton wrapper and brush the edges of wrapper with water.

Fold wonton wrapper over filling and pinch edges together by making small pleats.

Place dumplings pleat-side up on the counter and press down gently to flatten out the bottom of the dumpling.

Chicken Quesadilla Stack

Bueno! A simple flour tortilla never had it so good. This stack is far from traditional quesadillas, which are fried in vats of oil and stuffed with high-fat cheeses. It stands up high with chicken, chiles, and cheese, plus just the right amount of salsa from south of the border, down Mexico way. Double or triple the recipe and have a fiesta!

PER SERVING

241 calories / 26% from fat

2.5 g saturated fat, 7 g total fat

39 mg cholesterol

643 mg sodium

25 g total carbohydrate

2 g dietary fiber

60 g protein

PREP TIME 20 min. | COOK TIME 20 min. | SERVES 6

- 4 flour tortillas, 98% fat-free (8 inches)
- ¾ cup fat-free refried beans
- 1½ cups chopped, cooked boneless skinless chicken breasts
- 1 can (4½ ounces) chopped green chiles, drained
- ¼ cup chopped fresh cilantro
- ¾ cup shredded low-fat Mexican cheese blend
- ¼ cup reduced-fat sour cream
- ¼ cup salsa

1 Preheat oven to 425°F. Lightly coat baking sheet with nonstick cooking spray. Place one tortilla on baking sheet and spread ¼ cup refried beans on top. Sprinkle with ½ cup chicken, 2½ tablespoons chiles, 1 tablespoon cilantro, and 3 tablespoons cheese. Repeat layering twice. Top with remaining tortilla, pressing down slightly to help hold layers together.

2 Cover top tortilla loosely with foil and bake stack until heated through, about 15 minutes. Remove foil, sprinkle with remaining cheese.

3 Bake until cheese melts, about 5 minutes longer.

4 Meanwhile, combine sour cream and remaining cilantro in small bowl. Cut quesadilla into 6 wedges, but do not separate them. Spread cilantro sour cream over top and spoon salsa in center.

STEP 1 *Complete each layer by sprinkling with cheese.*

STEP 2 *Cover with foil for first 15 minutes of baking.*

STEP 3 *Bake until cheese is golden and melted.*

secret to success

This recipe skims down the fat content even more by using fat-free refried beans, reduced-fat sour cream, and low-fat cheese.

Round Out the Meal

Chayote is a wonderful crisp fruit from Mexico and tastes like a cross between apples and pears. Toss a salad of sliced chayote and watercress with a spicy lime vinaigrette. Finish the meal with mango slices and fresh cilantro.

HEALTH HINT

Chicken breasts are low in fat, and at the same time, an excellent source of protein, which every cell in our bodies needs for growth and repair. Beans and low-fat cheese also contribute protein. Plus beans are high in soluble fiber, which helps reduce cholesterol absorption.

Cook's Clue

Because reduced-fat cheeses are lower in fat and moisture and higher in protein and carbohydrates than full-fat cheeses, they need to be protected from overbrowning and drying out in the oven. Cover with foil during the first part of baking, then uncover and let the cheese melt.

Double Cheese Pizza Bites

What a delicious way to welcome your guests! These personal-size pizzas are loaded with fresh tomato slices and jazzed up with two kinds of cheese, black olives, and fresh herbs. Because these healthy nibbles are on the light side, everyone will still have room for dinner.

PER SERVING

89 calories / 30% from fat

1 g saturated fat, 3 g total fat

6 mg cholesterol

132 mg sodium

13 g total carbohydrate

1 g dietary fiber

3 g protein

PREP TIME 30 min. + rising	COOK TIME 10 min.	SERVES 24

- 2¾ to 3 cups all-purpose flour
- 1 teaspoon sugar
- 1 packet rapid-rise yeast
- 1 cup very warm water (120°F to 130°F)
- 1 tablespoon extra-virgin olive oil
- ½ teaspoon salt
- 1 pint cherry tomatoes
- 4 ounces fontina cheese, shredded (1 cup)
- 3 tablespoons freshly grated Parmesan cheese
- 12 kalamata olives, pitted
- Fresh oregano leaves

1 Mix 1 cup flour, sugar, and yeast in bowl. Stir in the water and oil until blended. Pulse 1¾ cups flour and salt in food processor to mix. Add yeast mixture and pulse until blended. With motor running, add remaining flour, 1 tablespoon at a time, until soft dough forms (you will need to process about 2 minutes).

2 Dust work surface lightly with flour. Turn out dough and knead until smooth, 1 to 2 minutes. Shape into ball. Cover with clean kitchen towel; let rest 10 minutes.

3 Preheat oven to 450°F. Line two baking sheets with parchment paper. Divide dough into 4 pieces. Wrap 3 in plastic; refrigerate. Cut remaining dough into 12 equal pieces; shape each into 1½-inch ball. Arrange on baking sheets; flatten into 3-inch rounds. Lightly coat with nonstick cooking spray.

4 Thinly slice tomatoes; fan out slices. Top each pizza with 2 or 3 slices. Sprinkle with 1 teaspoon fontina, a little Parmesan, plus a few olives and oregano leaves. Bake until bubbly and crust is golden, about 10 minutes. Repeat with remaining dough. Serve 2 pizza bites per person.

STEP 1 *Dough is ready when it comes together in a ball.*

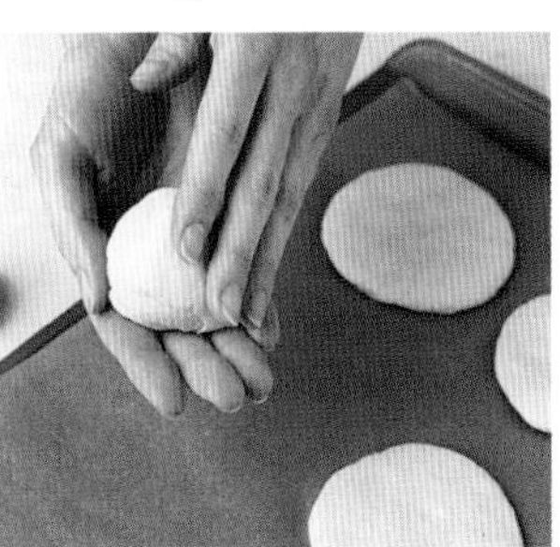

STEP 3 *Roll dough into 1g-inch balls in your hands. Then flatten into 3-inch rounds.*

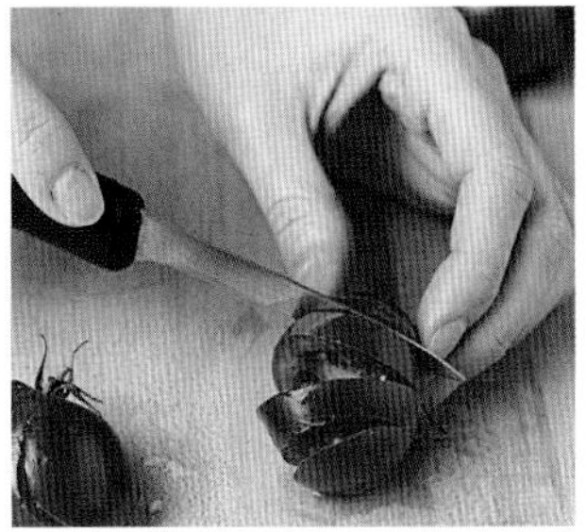

STEP 4 *Cut tomatoes into thin slices, then fan out slices.*

secret to success

When working with yeast, it is important not to have the water too hot, or it will kill the yeast, giving you non-lustier dough.

Cook's Clue

To keep dough from sticking to the food processor, lightly coat the inside of the bowl with non-stick cooking spray.

HEALTH HINT

Olives have healthful monounsaturated fat, which tends to lower LDLs (the "bad" cholesterol); thus helping prevent formation of artery-clogging plaque, which increases the risk of heart disease.

Baked Spinach-Stuffed Clams

Clams, like other kinds of shellfish, are a low-fat source of high-quality protein, as well as minerals such as potassium, iron, and zinc and vitamins such as A, C, and riboflavin. They are also delicious cooked in a variety of ways—steamed and dipped in a sauce, simmered in chowders, or baked with a savory seasoned stuffing, as this appetizer recipe attests.

PER SERVING

150 calories / 30% from fat
1 g saturated fat, 5 g total fat
16 mg cholesterol
330 mg sodium
16 g total carbohydrate
1 g dietary fiber
9 g protein

PREP TIME 15 min. | COOK TIME 25 min. | SERVES 4

- 1 dozen cherrystone or other medium-size hard-shell clams
- 3 teaspoons olive oil
- ¼ cup finely chopped onion
- 2 garlic cloves, minced
- 4 teaspoons all-purpose flour
- ⅔ cup fat-free half-and-half
- ¼ teaspoon salt
- ⅛ teaspoon cayenne pepper
- ⅓ cup thawed, frozen chopped spinach, well drained
- ⅓ cup fresh bread crumbs
- 4 teaspoons grated Parmesan cheese

1 Place clams in large skillet with ½-inch water. Bring to boil, cover, and cook until clams open, about 4 minutes. (Start checking after 2 minutes, and remove clams as they open; discard any that do not open.) Transfer clams to bowl; when cool enough to handle, remove top shell halves and discard. Place shell bottoms with clams attached on baking sheet.

2 Preheat oven to 450°F. In small saucepan, heat 2 teaspoons of oil over low heat. Add onion and garlic and sauté until soft, about 5 minutes. Whisk in flour and cook for 1 minute. Whisk in half-and-half, salt, and cayenne pepper and cook until lightly thickened, about 3 minutes. Stir in spinach. Spoon spinach mixture over clams.

3 In small bowl, stir together bread crumbs and Parmesan cheese. Sprinkle bread crumb mixture over top of spinach mixture and drizzle with remaining teaspoon oil. Bake until clams are bubbly and hot, about 5 minutes. Turn oven to broil, and broil clams until crumbs are lightly browned and crisped, about 1 to 2 minutes.

How to Check Clams

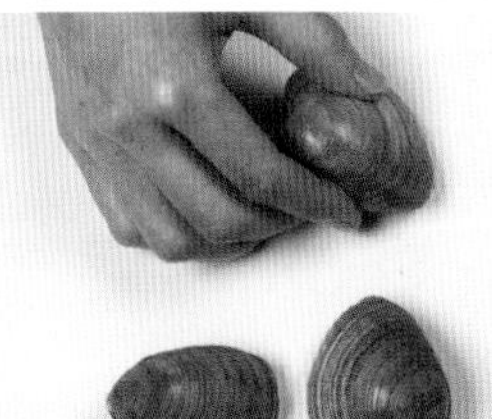

Before cooking live clams, rap them on the counter. Live ones will snap shut. Discard any that don't.

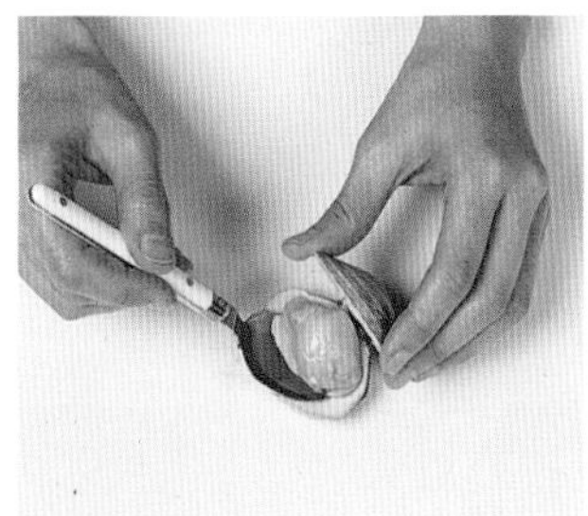

Once cooked, clam meat can be easily scooped from the shell: Use the edge of a spoon to sever the muscle.

secret to success

The work preparing fresh clams is worth it—not only do they taste better, but they are much lower in sodium than canned clams.

Round Out the Meal

Cook up some low carbohydrate whole-wheat pasta and toss with sundried tomatoes and fresh basil. To complete the meal, add sliced nectarines tossed with spearmint for dessert.

Cook's Clue

Clams live buried in the sand. To purge them of their grit, place them in a large bowl of cold salted water with cornmeal, about ¼ cup per gallon of water. Set aside in the refrigerator for at least 2 hours before cooking and they will expel the sand.

way back when... The Americans introduced the clam to the French in 1917. Clams are gathered from the east coast of the United States in muddy estuaries. Clams can also be found in the Charente region of France.

(Source: Larousse Gastronomique, edited by Jenifer Harvey Lang, Crown Publishers, Inc. Reprinted 1998.)

Heart-Healthy Trail Mix

On a hike, in a lunch box, or as a party snack, this toss of crunchies and chewies supplies quick energy and a good amount of protein—but far less fat than traditional trail mixes or "party mixes." Grated Parmesan gives the cereal squares, pretzels, and sunflower seeds a baked-in savory snap that plays off the sweetness of the dried fruit.

PER ½ CUP

126 calories / 20% from fat
1 g saturated fat, 3 g total fat
3 mg cholesterol
342 mg sodium
22 g total carbohydrate
1 g dietary fiber
3 g protein

PREP TIME 5 min.	COOK TIME 15 min.	6 CUPS

- 3 cups corn cereal squares
- 1½ cups fat-free thin pretzel sticks
- ¼ cup hulled sunflower seeds
- ½ teaspoon salt
- Nonstick cooking spray
- ½ cup grated Parmesan cheese
- 1½ cups dried cranberries or currants, coarsely chopped

1 Preheat oven to 350°F. Combine cereal, pretzels, sunflower seeds, and salt in large bowl. Lightly spray with nonstick cooking spray. Add Parmesan cheese and toss to combine.

2 Transfer mixture to jelly-roll pan and bake, stirring occasionally, until crisp and slightly crusty, about 15 minutes.

3 Let cool to room temperature. Transfer to large bowl. Add dried cranberries and toss to combine. Store in the refrigerator.

STEP 1 *Sprinkle Parmesan cheese evenly over trail mix ingredients.*

STEP 2 *Spread mixture in an even layer on a jelly-roll pan.*

STEP 3 *After toasting mix, transfer to a bowl and add dried cranberries.*

secret to success

Always buy cheese in a solid form, if possible, and grate the cheese yourself. Freshly grated cheese will enhance the recipe immensely.

HEALTH HINT

Though sunflower seeds are small, their nutritional benefits are huge: They are packed with fiber, folate, magnesium, vitamin B_6, essential fatty acids, selenium, and vitamin E, all of which help keep your heart in good shape.

Cook's Clue

Jars of trail mix make great gifts—just double or triple the recipe and work in batches. Be sure the trail mix is completely cool before scooping it into attractive containers. If it's not going to be eaten right away, store the mix in the refrigerator or freezer so the sunflower seeds stay fresh. (Make a note of this on the labels when you give this to friends.)

living smart
FOR A HEALTHY HEART

LOOK FOR THE HEART CHECK

When shopping for food, look on the label for the Heart Check. It's the symbol that indicates the American Heart Association certifies that food is low in fat, saturated fat, salt, and cholesterol. Of course, not all heart-healthy foods carry the Heart Check symbol, since some food producers choose not to take part in the program. Also, food companies owned by tobacco corporations are automatically excluded. The bottom line: Helpful as the Heart Check symbol may be, reading the Nutrition Facts panel on the package label is the best way to be sure you're buying foods that are good for your heart.

Creamy Corn Chowder

When it's blustery and cold outside, nothing's more warming inside than a bowlful of chowder. This one is as good as it gets: thick, rich, and creamy with plenty of fresh kernels of corn, chunks of potatoes, and smoky bites of bacon floating throughout. It's so hearty and delicious that no one will ever believe it's low in fat and cholesterol, too.

PER SERVING

293 calories / 18% from fat
2 g saturated fat, 6 g total fat
13 mg cholesterol
534 mg sodium
52 g total carbohydrate
5 g dietary fiber
12 g protein

PREP TIME 20 min. | COOK TIME 45 min. | SERVES 6

- 3 slices turkey bacon
- 1 large onion, chopped
- 1 pound small red-skinned potatoes, quartered
- 2½ cups reduced-sodium chicken broth
- 6 large ears corn, shucked, or 2 packages (10 ounces each) frozen corn kernels
- 18 (2-inch-square) soda crackers, crumbled (1 cup)
- 2½ cups reduced-fat milk (2%)
- ½ teaspoon salt
- ¼ to ½ teaspoon hot red pepper sauce
- 1 tablespoon minced parsley

1 Cook bacon in large heavy nonstick saucepan over medium-high heat until crisp. Transfer to paper towels with slotted spatula to drain; crumble. Sauté onion in pan drippings until soft, about 5 minutes. Stir in potatoes and broth and bring to a boil. Reduce heat to medium and simmer until potatoes are tender, about 20 minutes.

2 If using fresh ears of corn, stand cobs upright and cut off kernels with serrated knife (you need 3 cups). If using frozen corn, put kernels in colander and rinse with warm water; drain.

3 Put cracker crumbs into medium bowl; stir in milk. Let stand until crackers are soft, about 5 minutes.

4 Meanwhile, use an immersion blender to puree about half of potato mixture while still in saucepan on range. Or, transfer half of potato mixture to food processor and puree; return to saucepan. Stir in cracker mixture, corn, salt, and red pepper sauce. Cook until flavors are blended, about 10 minutes. Top with parsley and bacon.

STEP 2 *Stand corn upright and cut off kernels.*

STEP 3 *Pour milk over cracker crumbs. Soak until soft.*

STEP 4 *Avoid splatters by holding blender below surface.*

HEALTH HINT

Yellow corn is a good source of soluble fiber, vitamin C, and the B vitamin folate—three nutrients that help protect your heart.

Round Out the Meal

Serve with a slice of dark rye bread and marinated cucumber-tomato salad. Poach peaches and top with crunchy cinnamon granola for dessert.

Cook's Clue

To thicken chowders without adding cream, puree up to half of the vegetables (no more!) right in the saucepan or in a food processor.

Country Vegetable Soup with Pesto

Fragrant basil pesto lends a taste of summer's bounty to this lightened rendition of a classic French soup. Aromatic vegetables add great flavor and plenty of vitamins while keeping the fat in check. What a wonderful way to eat your vegetables!

PER SERVING
110 calories / 29% from fat
0 g saturated fat, 3.5 g total fat
0 mg cholesterol
523 mg sodium
18 g total carbohydrate
5 g dietary fiber
5 g protein

PREP TIME 25 min. | COOK TIME 35 min. | SERVES 4

- 1 pound plum tomatoes
- 1 onion, chopped
- 1 carrot, chopped
- 1 celery stalk, sliced
- 2 garlic cloves, finely chopped
- 1 medium yellow squash, sliced
- 1 medium zucchini, sliced
- 1 can (14½ ounces) reduced-sodium chicken broth
- 1 can (14½ ounces) vegetable broth
- 1 cup loosely packed fresh basil leaves
- 2½ tablespoons prepared pesto sauce

1 Peel, seed, and chop tomatoes.

2 Coat large saucepan with nonstick cooking spray and set over medium-high heat. Sauté onion, carrot, celery, and garlic until soft, about 5 minutes. Add tomatoes, yellow squash, and zucchini. Sauté until soft, about 8 minutes. Stir in chicken broth and vegetable broth and bring to a boil. Reduce heat and simmer, uncovered, until flavors are blended, about 20 minutes.

3 Put basil and pesto sauce in food processor and pulse until basil is chopped. Process until pesto is thick and creamy.

4 Ladle soup into bowls and top with pesto.

Round Out the Meal

Serve with reduced-fat cheese melted on crusty French bread and a green salad with fresh strawberries for dessert.

How to Peel a Tomato

Cut a shallow X in bottom of each tomato.

Blanch in boiling water until skin begins to shrivel, about 1 minute.

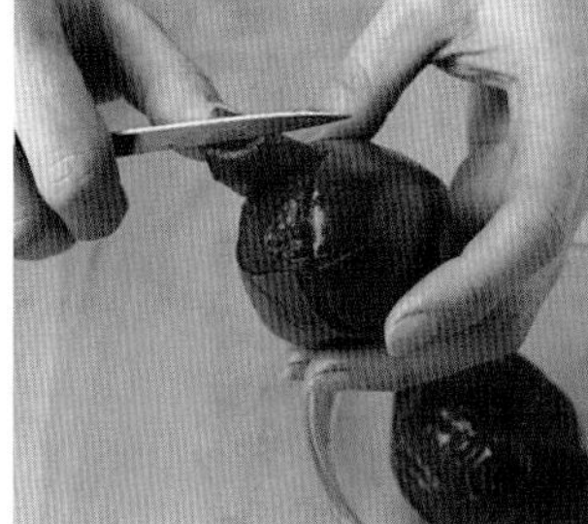

Remove skin with paring knife or your fingers.

secret to success

Buy basil from a farmer's market, or grow it in a window box if you do not have room for a garden. Basil grows relatively easy. Make your own pestos and freeze for fast fabulous meals. A plethora of ingredients can morph a dish into what you desire.

Cook's Clue

For vegetarian vegetable soup, substitute another can of vegetable broth for the chicken broth. You can vary the vegetables according to what's fresh and bountiful at the market. Always start with sautéed onion, carrot, celery, and garlic to give the soup a full-flavored base. In the spring, add a handful of fresh green peas during the last 10 minutes. During the summer, team the tomatoes with corn and green beans from the farmer's market.

HEALTH HINT

When you cook veggies, some vitamins leach into the cooking water. In this soup, the nutrients are not lost because you consume the broth.

Meatless Chili Pots con Queso

Cowboy cooks used to let chili simmer for hours on the chuck-wagon stove, but our "bowl of red" takes less time than a shoot-out at the OK Corral! Chunks of vegetables, a bounty of beans, and low-fat cheddar make it healthier but just as hearty. Skillful spicing provides the perfect bit of heat.

PER SERVING

240 calories / 13% from fat
1 g saturated fat, 3.5 g total fat
4 mg cholesterol
400 mg sodium
45 g total carbohydrate
16 g dietary fiber
19 g protein

PREP TIME 10 min. | COOK TIME 11 min. | SERVES 4

- 1 large green bell pepper, seeded and finely chopped
- 1 large onion, finely chopped
- 2 large garlic cloves, minced
- 2 cans (15 ounces each) red kidney beans, drained and rinsed
- 1 can (28 ounces) no-salt-added crushed tomatoes in puree
- ½ teaspoon chili powder
- ½ teaspoon black pepper
- ½ teaspoon ground cumin
- ¼ teaspoon ground cinnamon
- ¾ cup shredded low-sodium, low-fat cheddar cheese

1 Lightly coat large nonstick skillet with nonstick cooking spray and set over medium-high heat. Sauté green pepper, onion, and garlic until onion is browned, about 5 minutes. Stir in beans, tomatoes and puree, chili powder, black pepper, cumin, and ground cinnamon. Simmer 5 minutes.

2 Preheat broiler. Line broiler pan with foil. Divide chili among four 2-cup broilerproof bowls and set bowls on broiler pan. Mound 2 tablespoons cheese in center of each bowl.

3 Broil 6 inches from heat until cheese melts, about 1 minute (watch closely!).

STEP 1 *Stir vegetable mixture, breaking up tomatoes.*

STEP 2 *Mound cheese on chili in center; do not spread.*

STEP 3 *Broil until cheese melts; be careful not to brown.*

Round Out the Meal

Serve this easy chili with a warmed flour tortilla and a mixed green salad. Offer sliced watermelon or pineapple for dessert.

HEALTH HINT

This chili, naturally low in fat, is full of good stuff: soluble fiber in the beans, lycopene in the canned tomatoes, and calcium in the cheese.

way back when... Queso is the Spanish word for cheese. In Spain and Latin America, many cheeses are called queso, followed by an adjective. For example in Mexico there is a dry, crumbly cheese made from cow or goat milk called "queso anejo".

(Source: Larousse Gastronomique, edited by Jenifer Harvey Lang, Crown Publishers, Inc. Reprinted 1998.)

Cook's Clue

If you don't have broilerproof bowls, place chili in a broilerproof casserole, sprinkle cheese in center, and broil. Or, ladle hot chili into individual bowls; top with cheese (heat from chili melts cheese).

Hungarian Pork Goulash and Noodles

With less saturated fat than skinless chicken legs, pork tenderloin is a great choice for heart-healthy meals. It wouldn't be goulash without sour cream, but the fat-free kind makes a perfectly delicious, rosy-pink sauce. Use imported Hungarian sweet paprika for the most authentic flavor.

PER SERVING

471 calories / 16% from fat

2 g saturated fat, 8.5 g total fat

74 mg cholesterol

521 mg sodium

59 g total carbohydrate

7 g dietary fiber

37 g protein

PREP TIME 15 min. | COOK TIME 45 min. | SERVES 4

- 1 tablespoon olive oil
- 1 pound pork tenderloin, cut into 1-inch chunks
- 1 large onion, halved and thinly sliced
- 4 cloves garlic, slivered
- 1 tablespoon sweet paprika
- 1 teaspoon caraway seeds
- ½ teaspoon salt
- 2 cups water
- 1 cup frozen peas
- 8 ounces wide yolkless noodles
- ½ cup bottled roasted red peppers, seeded, rinsed, and drained
- ¼ cup fat-free sour cream
- 2 tablespoons tomato paste
- 2 tablespoons all-purpose flour

1 Preheat oven to 350°F. Heat oil in medium non-stick Dutch oven over medium heat. Add pork and sauté until lightly browned, about 4 minutes. With slotted spoon, transfer pork to plate.

2 Add onion and garlic to pan and cook, stirring until onion is tender, about 5 minutes. Stir in paprika and cook 1 minute until fragrant.

3 Add caraway seeds, salt, and water to pan and bring to a boil. Return pork to pan. Cover, transfer to oven, and bake 30 minutes, until pork is tender. (Recipe can be made ahead to this point. Reheat in 325°F oven before proceeding.) Remove pan from oven and stir in peas.

4 Meanwhile, cook noodles according to package directions. Drain.

5 Combine red peppers, sour cream, tomato paste, and flour in food processor and puree until smooth. Stir into pan with pork mixture and cook over medium heat until slightly thickened, about 2 minutes. Serve over noodles.

STEP 2 *Stir paprika into sautéed onions and coat evenly.*

STEP 3 *Add peas to goulash toward the end of cooking time.*

STEP 5 *Add red pepper–sour cream mixture to stew.*

Round Out the Meal

Serve with carrot-and-apple slaw, and warm dried-apricot compote with a dollop of nonfat yogurt for dessert.

Cook's Clue

Make sure to cook out the flour at the end of the recipe, by stirring constantly. Raw flour is a less than appropriate flavor in a stew.

HEALTH HINT

Using vegetables to make sauces, such as the pureed red peppers in this stew, is another way to get your five-a-day.

Pot-au-Feu

PER SERVING
337 calories / 24% from fat
2.5 g saturated fat, 9 g total fat
79 mg cholesterol
723 mg sodium
32 g total carbohydrate
7 g dietary fiber
33 g protein

Enjoy this classic French country recipe on a heart-healthy diet without losing one bit of its homey goodness and fabulous flavor. Lean beef tenderloin, plump chicken, country root vegetables, and wedges of cabbage combine to create a dish you'll savor on a cold winter's eve. Truly, it's simmering with satisfaction—a bountiful meal-in-a-bowl.

PREP TIME 20 min. | COOK TIME 1 hr. | SERVES 2

- 4 medium leeks
- 6 sprigs flat-leaf parsley plus ¼ cup chopped
- 6 sprigs fresh thyme
- 1 bay leaf
- 3 pounds bone-in chicken pieces
- 1 head garlic, separated into cloves and peeled
- 1 teaspoon salt
- 1 teaspoon freshly ground black pepper
- 5 cans (14½ ounces each) reduced-sodium chicken broth
- 1 medium green cabbage (about 2 pounds), cut into 8 wedges
- 1 pound carrots, peeled and cut into 2-inch pieces
- 1 pound small red-skinned potatoes, scrubbed and halved
- 1 pound beef tenderloin, tied with string

1 Cut off roots and dark green tops from leeks. Cut white parts lengthwise in half. Rinse leeks well, swishing to remove sand. Tie leek tops, parsley sprigs, thyme, and bay leaf into a bouquet with kitchen string.

2 Put chicken, herb bouquet, white parts of leeks, garlic, and half of salt and black pepper in large soup pot. Pour in broth and add enough water to cover. Bring to a boil over high heat. Reduce heat to medium-low and simmer, uncovered, 30 minutes.

3 Submerge cabbage, carrots, potatoes, and tenderloin in liquid. Simmer until beef is done to taste, about 30 to 35 minutes, or 135°F to 140°F for medium-rare. Season with remaining salt and pepper.

4 Discard herb bouquet and skim off fat from broth. Transfer beef to cutting board, remove string, cover with foil, and let stand 5 minutes. Cut beef across grain into thin slices. Discard skin from chicken. Divide chicken, beef, and vegetables among 8 large soup bowls and ladle in the hot broth. Sprinkle with chopped parsley.

STEP 1 *Tie leek tops, parsley, thyme, and bay leaf together.*

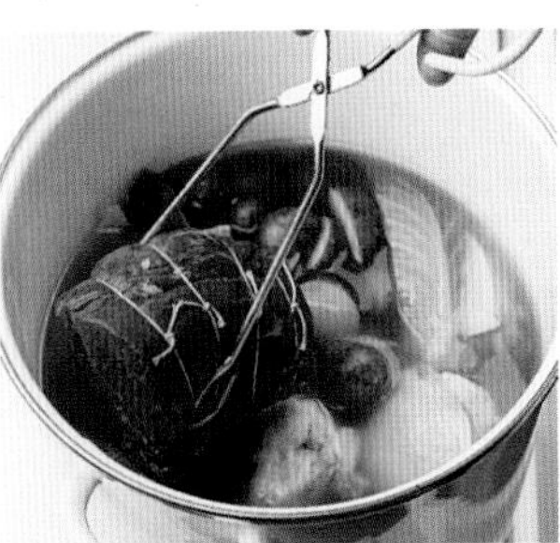

STEP 3 *Submerge beef tenderloin in cooking liquid.*

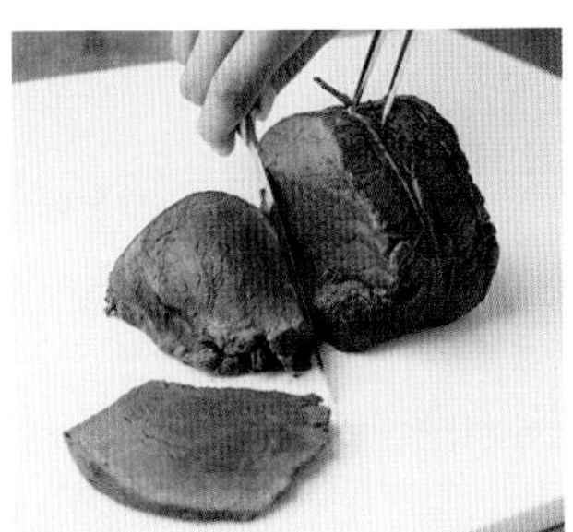

STEP 4 *Slice beef across grain.*

Round Out the Meal

Serve a salad of mustard greens and beet tops with a fresh horseradish dressing. Finish the meal off with caramelized bananas.

Cook's Clue

Add other root vegetables to the broth, such as, parsnips, salsify, or turnips to jazz up the recipe.

way back when... Pot-au-feu, literally "pot on fire" or "pot in the fire," is an ancient dish in France, often referred to as "the foundation of empires." It's a multicourse meal—all cooked slowly in water. First, the broth is skimmed off and served with toasted croutons, sprinkled with cheese. Then the boiled beef, sometimes chicken, and both root and leaf vegetables are served as the main course, usually with accompaniments of gherkins, grated horseradish, various mustards, and pickled onions.

(Source: Larousse Gastronomique, edited by Jenifer Harvey Lang, Crown Publishers, Inc., NY, 1998.)

Sloppy Joes

Get this old-time favorite sandwich off to a healthy start by choosing ground beef that's labeled "95% lean." Then perk up the flavor with a tasty trio of onions, peppers, and zesty chili sauce. You'll have a sandwich that's high in flavor and good for your heart, too.

PER SERVING

396 calories / 25% from fat

3 g saturated fat, 11 g total fat

51 mg cholesterol

767 mg sodium

42 g total carbohydrate

5 g dietary fiber

31 g protein

PREP TIME 10 min. | COOK TIME 15 min. | SERVES 4

- 1 tablespoon vegetable oil
- 1 medium onion, finely chopped
- 1 celery stalk, finely chopped
- 1 small green bell pepper, seeded and finely chopped
- 1 pound lean (95%) ground beef
- 4 sandwich buns, split
- 1 can (14½ ounces) no-salt-added stewed tomatoes
- ½ cup chili sauce
- 2 teaspoons Worcestershire sauce
- ½ teaspoon black pepper
- 2 teaspoons cider vinegar
- 1 large carrot, cut into very thin matchsticks
- ¼ small head cabbage, slivered

1 Put rack in middle of oven and preheat to 350°F. Heat oil in large nonstick skillet over medium-high heat. Sauté onion, celery, and green pepper until tender, about 5 minutes. Add ground beef and cook, breaking up meat with spoon, until meat is no longer pink, about 4 minutes.

2 Meanwhile, put buns cut-side up on baking sheet and heat in oven until toasted, about 4 minutes.

3 Add tomatoes with their juice, chili sauce, Worcestershire, and black pepper to skillet. Cook, stirring often, until flavors blend, about 4 minutes longer. Stir in vinegar.

4 Transfer buns to 4 plates; spoon the Sloppy Joe mixture on bottom of each bun. Top with several strips of carrot and cabbage; cover with top of bun.

Round Out the Meal

Serve with coleslaw and have an oatmeal–raisin cookie for dessert.

secret to success

With a slotted spoon, press meat and vegetable mixture to one side of skillet to release any excess grease from the beef. Discard this grease, thus making an even leaner dish.

Cook's Clue

Stirring vinegar into this meat mixture at the end perks up the flavors, eliminating the need to add extra salt.

HEALTH HINT

A Harvard Medical School study found that eating tomatoes more than twice a week was linked to a reduced risk of prostate cancer. Researchers at the University of North Carolina found that high levels of lycopene (a bioflavonoid in tomatoes) protect against heart disease. Cooking tomatoes helps release the lycopene.

STEP 2 *Remove toasted buns from oven with tongs.*

STEP 3 *Stir vinegar into simmering beef to spark flavor.*

STEP 4 *Spoon about 1 cup Sloppy Joe mixture on bottom of each bun.*

Turkey Cobb Salad Sandwiches

Robert Cobb of Hollywood's famous Brown Derby restaurant invented the salad that inspired these satisfying sandwiches. Layered with all the traditional ingredients, they're hearty enough to please the hungriest and healthful enough to suit sensible diets.

PER SERVING

433 calories / 25% from fat

3 g saturated fat, 12 g total fat

67 mg cholesterol

1,072 mg sodium

46 g total carbohydrate

5 g dietary fiber

36 g protein

PREP TIME 15 min. | COOK TIME 5 min. | SERVES 4

- ¼ cup nonfat mayonnaise
- 1 ounce blue cheese, crumbled (¼ cup)
- 2 tablespoons snipped fresh chives
- 4 slices lean bacon
- 1 small avocado
- 8 slices multigrain or sourdough bread, toasted
- 4 ounces watercress, tough stems trimmed
- 12 ounces fresh-roasted turkey breast slices
- 3 medium tomatoes, sliced
- 4 scallions, thinly sliced

1 Combine mayonnaise, blue cheese, and chives in small bowl.

2 Cook bacon in medium skillet over medium-high heat until crisp. Transfer to paper towels to drain, then tear into small pieces. Pit, peel, and thinly slice avocado.

3 Spread blue cheese mixture evenly on bread. Layer 4 slices with watercress, turkey, tomatoes, scallions, avocado, and bacon. Top with remaining bread, and cut sandwiches diagonally in half.

HEALTH HINT

Many people avoid eating avocados because they are high in fat. While that's true—a medium Hass avocado has about 30 grams of fat—most of it is monounsaturated. Recent studies suggest that monounsaturated fat can lower LDLs ("bad" cholesterol). In addition, avocados provide a good amount of dietary fiber, potassium, and folate.

Cook's Clue

Like the tomato, the avocado is a fruit used as a vegetable. Hass and Fuerte avocados are the two most common in supermarkets. Hass are smaller with dark, pebbly skins; they have a richer, creamier texture than Fuerte avocados. Fuertes have smooth, bright green skins and a milder flavor. Buy avocados that are heavy for their size and free of bruises and soft spots. Usually, avocados are sold unripe. To speed the ripening process, put them in a brown paper bag and store at room temperature. When they yield to gentle pressure, they are ripe.

living smart
FOR A HEALTHY HEART

ARGININE MAY PREVENT HEART DISEASE

Arginine (pronounced AR-ji-neen) is an amino acid believed to enhance circulation and strengthen blood flow around the heart. Arginine-rich foods include dairy foods, fish, poultry, grains, and nuts. Make sure to select low-fat or fat-free dairy foods, and remove the skin from poultry to reduce fat intake.

Preparing Avocados

Cut avocado in half lengthwise, and twist halves in opposite directions to separate.

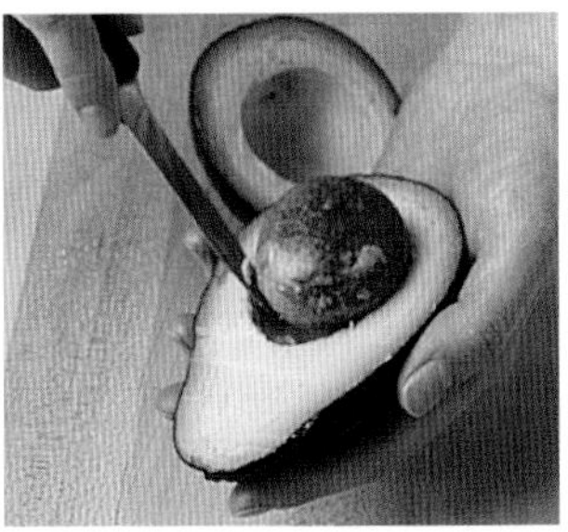

Release seed with the tip of a knife and lift out.

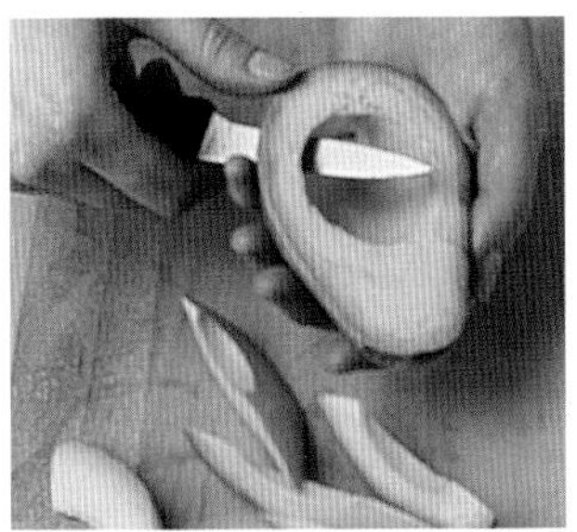

Peel avocado, then cut lengthwise into thin slices.

Cuban Sandwich

"El sandwich Cubano" *is built on a loaf of bread and filled with cheese, meat, and tangy peppers. This one's a relative lightweight (in fat, but not in flavor), with its reduced-fat cheese and lean ham. Cuban sandwiches are made in a press that resembles a waffle iron, but you can cook them on the stove, pressed with a heavy skillet.*

PER SERVING

241 calories / 21% from fat
2 g saturated fat, 5.5 g total fat
19 mg cholesterol
843 mg sodium
34 g total carbohydrate
2 g dietary fiber
14 g protein

PREP TIME 10 min. | COOK TIME 5 min. | SERVES 4

- ⅓ cup fat-free mayonnaise
- 2 tablespoons fresh lime juice
- 1 loaf whole-wheat Italian bread (8 ounces), halved horizontally
- ½ cup shredded reduced-fat Monterey Jack cheese (2 ounces)
- 3 pickled cherry peppers, sliced thick, seeded
- 3 ounces thinly sliced lean smoked ham

1 Combine mayonnaise and lime juice in small bowl. Spread mixture on cut sides of bread.

2 Sprinkle cheese on bottom piece of bread. Scatter pepper slices over cheese. Top with ham. Close the sandwich up and cut in half crosswise.

3 Spray a nonstick skillet or griddle with nonstick cooking spray and heat over low heat. Put sandwiches in pan, cover with foil, and place a small heavy skillet on top, pressing down gently to compress the sandwich slightly. Cook until bottoms of sandwiches are golden brown, about 2 minutes.

4 Remove small skillet, turn sandwiches over, and replace foil and skillet. Cook until bread is golden brown and cheese has melted, about 2 minutes. Cut each sandwich in half and serve.

STEP 2 *Layer ham on top of cherry peppers and Jack cheese.*

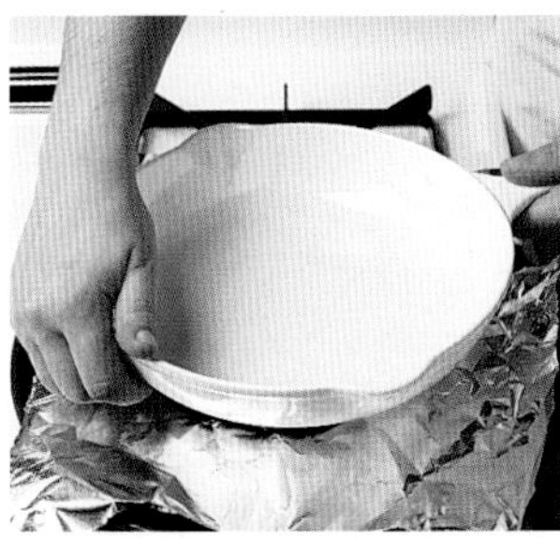

STEP 3 *Cover sandwiches with foil and weight with small, heavy skillet.*

STEP 4 *After browning on one side, turn sandwiches over, cover with foil and weight again, and brown on second side.*

secret to success

Do not purchase prepackaged sliced ham. The amount of sodium and preservatives simply markets them out of the running with respect to healthy eating. Find a reputable deli counter and order freshly sliced smoked ham.

Round Out the Meal

Serve with green salad tossed in a spicy lime vinaigrette and mango sorbet for dessert.

way back when... After the 1959 Cuban revolution, many Cubans fled to Little Havana, a community in Miami that keeps the culinary traditions of Cuba alive. The Cuban sandwich is a Miami favorite. You can find them in all the restaurants, but the best place to purchase a Cuban sandwich is from the loncherias, which are street corner snack bars.

(Source: whatscookingamerica.net/history/sandwichhistory.htm)

Cook's Clue

We've used pickled cherry peppers in our Cuban sandwich, but you can use any type of pickle or pepper you want. Try pickled jalapeños, sweet pickles, canned mild green chilies, or dill pickle chips. You can even use roasted pepper slices.

Tuna Provençale on a Baguette

PER SERVING

325 calories / 28% from fat
2 g saturated fat, 10 g total fat
36 mg cholesterol
795 mg sodium
34 g total carbohydrate
4 g dietary fiber
26 g protein

Picture yourself on a picnic in southern France. Flavorful, savory, and full of heart-smart nutrients, this sandwich is sure to become a favorite. The special today: a variation of the classic pan bagnat, *a baguette bursting with tuna, olives, and garden-fresh veggies.*

PREP TIME 20 min. + standing | COOK TIME 0 min. | SERVES 4

- 2 large tomatoes, peeled and chopped
- 5 ripe olives, pitted and finely chopped
- ¼ teaspoon salt
- 1 baguette (6 ounces, about 24 inches long)
- 1½ tablespoons extra-virgin olive oil
- 1 large onion
- 1 large green bell pepper, seeded
- 2 cans (6 ounces each) water-packed albacore tuna, drained
- 2 tablespoons white wine vinegar
- 2 garlic cloves, minced
- ¼ teaspoon anchovy paste

1 Mix tomatoes, olives, and salt in medium bowl, and let stand until juicy, about 15 minutes.

2 Meanwhile, cut bread almost in half, lengthwise (do not slice completely through). Open like a book, being careful not to separate bread. Pull out about ½ cup of soft bready center with your hands. Using ½ tablespoon oil, brush cut sides of bread. Then spread on tomato mixture and any juices that have collected in bowl.

3 Cut onion in half through stem end, then cut crosswise into thin semicircles. Cut green pepper in half and seed, then cut crosswise into thin semicircles. Layer onion, green pepper, and tuna over tomato mixture. Whisk vinegar, garlic, anchovy paste, and remaining oil in small bowl. Drizzle over tuna.

4 Wrap stuffed loaf tightly in plastic wrap. Weigh it down with heavy skillet, and let stand at room temperature until ingredients have soaked into bread, about 30 minutes. Cut diagonally into 4 equal sandwiches.

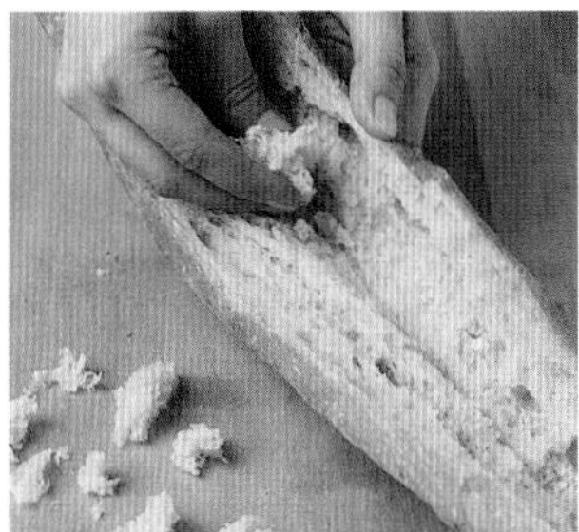

STEP 2 *Pull out enough bread to make room for filling.*

STEP 3 *Put tuna into sandwich last, letting some peek out.*

STEP 4 *Weigh down sandwich until ingredients have soaked into bread, about 30 minutes.*

Round Out the Meal

Serve with a cucumber and onion salad sprinkled with fresh dill and doused with rice vinegar. For dessert, serve a low-fat biscotti with decaffeinated vanilla soy cappuccino.

secret to success

Albacore tuna packed in spring water has only 1.5 grams of fat per serving, compared with tuna packed in oil, which has three times more fat.

Cook's Clue

To make this sandwich ahead of time, weigh it down with a heavy skillet at room temperature for 30 minutes. Remove the skillet and refrigerate the sandwich up to 24 hours.

Salads and Vegetables

Warm Lentil and Roasted Pepper Salad

PER SERVING

250 calories / 29% from fat
1 g saturated fat, 8 g total fat
0 mg cholesterol
253 mg sodium
34 g total carbohydrate
8 g dietary fiber
15 g protein

You've heard of lentil soup, so why not lentil salad? Health experts say everyone should routinely include vegetarian meals in their diets to help reduce saturated fat and cholesterol. This hearty, Mediterranean-style dish is a satisfying and delicious way to do just that.

PREP TIME 45 min. | **COOK TIME 35 min.** | **SERVES 4**

- 3 cups water
- 1 cup brown lentils
- 1 teaspoon salt
- ¼ cup chopped parsley
- ½ cup diced, drained, and rinsed canned roasted sweet red pepper
- 1 medium stalk celery, diced
- ½ cup diced red onion
- 1 cup diced and seeded plum tomatoes
- 2 garlic cloves, minced
- 2 tablespoons lemon juice
- 2 tablespoons olive oil
- ¼ teaspoon black pepper

1 Bring water, lentils, and ½ teaspoon of the salt to boil in 3-quart saucepan over high heat. Reduce heat to medium-low and simmer, covered, until lentils are firm but fully cooked, 20 to 30 minutes.

2 Meanwhile, mix parsley, sweet pepper, celery, onion, tomatoes, garlic, lemon juice, oil, black pepper, and remaining ½ teaspoon salt in large serving bowl.

3 Drain lentils, add to serving bowl, and toss. Serve warm. Makes 4 servings.

Round Out the Meal

Serve with leafy lettuce, goat cheese, and flat bread. For dessert, a baked apple topped with vanilla frozen yogurt.

Cook's Clue

Unlike most dried beans and other legumes, lentils require no soaking before cooking and in fact, if soaked first, will become mushy when cooked. However, you should always rinse lentils lightly in a sieve or colander before cooking, and pick through with your fingers to be sure there are no stones or other debris in the batch.

way back when... Cultivated since ancient times, for many centuries, the lentil became central Asia's diet for the poor, and Egypt exported large shiploads of lentils to ancient Rome. Several varieties exist: green puy lentil, green lentil, champagne brown lentil, and blonde lentil. The tasty green puy lentil is dark green with blue marbling. The small green lentil has a thick skin; the champagne brown lentil is reddish. The blonde lentil is flat and oval.

(Source: Larousse Gastronomique, edited by Jenifer Harvey Lang, Crown Publishers, Inc. 1990)

HEALTH HINT

If you use enough of it, parsley not only adds its own earthy flavor to dishes, it contributes a significant amount of antioxidants such as vitamin C and beta-carotene.

How to Dice a Red Onion

Cut onion in half lengthwise, lay one half on its flat side, and cut lengthwise into thin slices.

Turn stack of slices 90 degrees, and make equally spaced cuts perpendicular to the first.

German Potato Salad with Dijon Vinaigrette

PER SERVING
190 calories / 14% from fat
1 g saturated fat, 3 g total fat
7 mg cholesterol
597 mg sodium
36 g total carbohydrate
3 g dietary fiber
5 g protein

Kartoffelsalat—potato salad made the German way, can also be heart-healthy. Start with red-skinned new potatoes, slice them, then sprinkle with bacon, add onion and peppers, and season with a slimmed-down version of the authentic warm vinegar dressing.

PREP TIME 10 min. | COOK TIME 18 min. | SERVES 6

- 1½ pounds small red-skinned potatoes, scrubbed and quartered
- ½ teaspoon salt
- 4 slices turkey bacon
- 1 small onion, chopped
- ¼ cup cider vinegar
- 2 tablespoons sugar
- 1 tablespoon country-style Dijon mustard
- 1 teaspoon olive oil
- ½ teaspoon black pepper
- ¼ cup finely chopped sweet pickles
- ¼ cup finely chopped red bell pepper
- ¼ cup minced parsley

1 Bring potatoes, enough water to cover, and ¼ teaspoon salt to a boil in large saucepan over high heat. Reduce heat to medium, and cook until potatoes are tender, about 10 minutes. Drain and keep warm.

2 Meanwhile, cut bacon in half crosswise, and cook in large nonstick deep skillet until crisp; transfer to paper towels to drain. Crumble. Sauté onion in pan drippings until golden, about 7 minutes.

3 Shake vinegar, sugar, mustard, oil, black pepper, and remaining salt in a jar, then whisk into skillet. Bring to a simmer and cook until fragrant, about 2 minutes.

4 Add potatoes, half of bacon, pickles, and red pepper and cook; stir until potatoes are evenly coated and heated through, about 2 minutes. Sprinkle with parsley and remaining bacon. Serve warm or at room temperature.

STEP 2 *By frying half-strips of bacon (instead of whole strips), it cooks faster and more evenly.*

STEP 3 *Pour dressing from jar over sautéed onions.*

STEP 4 *Add potatoes to hot dressing. Toss to coat evenly.*

secret to success

Avoid storing potatoes anywhere too cold, and do not boil them in aluminum or iron pots. Use stainless steel only.

Round Out the Meal

Serve with grilled reduced-fat turkey-beef kielbasa and a tomato salad. End with mango cubes and raspberries.

HEALTH HINT

Potatoes are excellent sources of vitamin C and good sources of the B vitamin, niacin. Be sure to leave on the skin for extra iron and fiber—the soluble, cholesterol-lowering kind.

Cook's Clue

Turn this salad into a main dish by adding 1 cup of roasted chicken strips, grilled beef strips, or cooked pork tenderloin strips with the potatoes in Step 4.

Fruit Boats with Orange-Balsamic Glaze

PER SERVING
180 calories / 5% from fat
0 g saturated fat, 1 g total fat
0 mg cholesterol
24 mg sodium
43 g total carbohydrate
8 g dietary fiber
3 g protein

Fresh melon boats, carved in only minutes and overflowing with tart kiwis, ripe berries, and juicy melon balls, are the perfect refresher. A sweet-and-sour glaze gives the fruits unexpected zest and dresses them up for a summery lunch. They're low in calories and have only one gram of fat per serving.

PREP TIME 20 min. | **COOK TIME 5 min.** | **SERVES 4**

- ¼ cup balsamic vinegar
- ¼ teaspoon grated orange zest
- 2 tablespoons fresh orange juice
- 2 teaspoons brown sugar
- 1 large cantaloupe
- 1 pint strawberries, hulled and quartered
- ½ pint blueberries
- ½ pint raspberries
- 2 kiwifruits, peeled, halved, and cut into thin wedges

1 Combine balsamic vinegar, orange zest and juice, and brown sugar in microwavable dish. Microwave on high until syrupy, 2 to 3 minutes. Or cook over medium-high heat in a small saucepan, 4 to 5 minutes. Set glaze aside.

2 Make melon balls and prepare cantaloupe boats *(see photos, right)*. Put cantaloupe balls, strawberries, blueberries, raspberries, and kiwis in large bowl.

3 Drizzle fruit with glaze. Toss to coat evenly. Spoon into cantaloupe boats and serve immediately.

Round Out the Meal

Serve with a sandwich of datenut bread with light cream cheese and layers of watercress. Offer iced tea with fresh mint, and end the meal with macaroons.

Cook's Clue

To keep the juice of dark fruits (such as blueberries and raspberries) from coloring paler fruits (including melons, pears, and peaches), wait to mix until just before serving.

way back when... Balsamic vinegar dates back to 1046, when a bottle was given to Emperor Enrico III of Franconia as a gift. In the Middle Ages, it was used as a disinfectant and considered a miracle cure for sore throats and labor pains.

(Source: www.whatscookingamerica.net)

HEALTH HINT

Like all yellow and orange fruits and vegetables, cantaloupe is rich in beta-carotene, an antioxidant converted by the body to vitamin A. Beta-carotene may provide protection against heart disease by preventing LDLs (low-density lipoproteins, known as the "bad" cholesterol) from oxidizing and promoting the development of artery-clogging plaque.

Making Melon Balls and Boats

Cut cantaloupe lengthwise in half.

Cut each melon half crosswise to form four triangular "boats." Discard seeds.

Scoop out cantaloupe with a melon baller, leaving a thin layer of flesh on the rind.

Mango and Shrimp Salad

PER SERVING
365 calories / 15% from fat
1 g saturated fat, 6 g total fat
172 mg cholesterol
700 mg sodium
57 g total carbohydrate
6 g dietary fiber
26 g protein

A simple and elegant salad is also a powerhouse of nutrients. A mango's golden-orange flesh tips you off to the fruit's stellar beta-carotene content. This tropical delight also supplies lots of vitamin A and C and even some vitamin E, all heart-saving antioxidents. The red peppers add more vitamins A and C. Finally, the shrimp is a high source of low-fat protein, B vitamins, and minerals.

PREP TIME 20 min. | **COOK TIME 5 min.** | **SERVES 4**

- ⅓ cup lemon juice
- 1 bay leaf
- ¼ teaspoon crushed red pepper flakes
- ¼ teaspoon salt
- 1 pound medium shrimp, peeled and deveined
- ¼ cup chili sauce
- 1 tablespoon olive oil
- 1 red bell pepper, seeded and slivered
- 1 cup cherry tomatoes, halved
- 1 cucumber, halved lengthwise, seeded, and cut into half-rounds
- 2 mangoes (2¼ pounds total), peeled and cut into ¼-inch cubes
- 8 lettuce leaves
- Cilantro sprigs, for garnish

1 In large skillet, combine 2 cups water, 1 tablespoon lemon juice, bay leaf, red pepper flakes, and salt. Bring to boil over moderate heat. Add shrimp, reduce to simmer, cover, and cook until pink and firm, about 4 minutes. Drain shrimp and set aside, cooling at room temperature.

2 In large bowl, whisk together chili sauce, olive oil, and remaining lemon juice. Add shrimp, bell pepper, tomatoes, cucumber, and mangoes, tossing gently to combine. Line plates with lettuce and top with shrimp mixture. Garnish with cilantro.

secret to success

Eat shrimp the day it's bought for the best flavor, and make sure the shrimp is practically see-through. Selecting fresh shrimp can be tricky, but watch for these signs: Avoid shrimp that has a slight ammonia aroma or shrimp with spots.

HEALTH HINT

Much of the dietary fiber in mangoes is pectin, a form of soluble fiber shown to help reduce blood cholesterol.

Cook's Clue

Ripe mangoes usually have a red "blush," but Evergreen, a new variety, is green skinned when ripe. You can tell it is ripe by its flowery fragrance. Its flesh—like that of other mangoes—is deep orange and rich in vitamins C and E as well as beta-carotene.

How to Cube a Mango

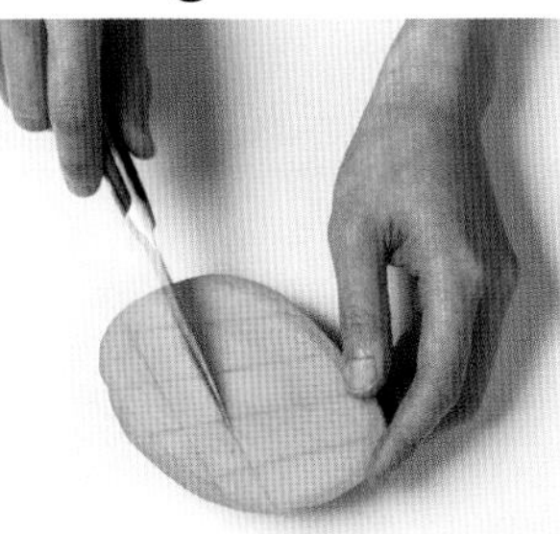

Cut fruit lengthwise on both sides of pit. Cut each piece of mango in a lattice without cutting through peel.

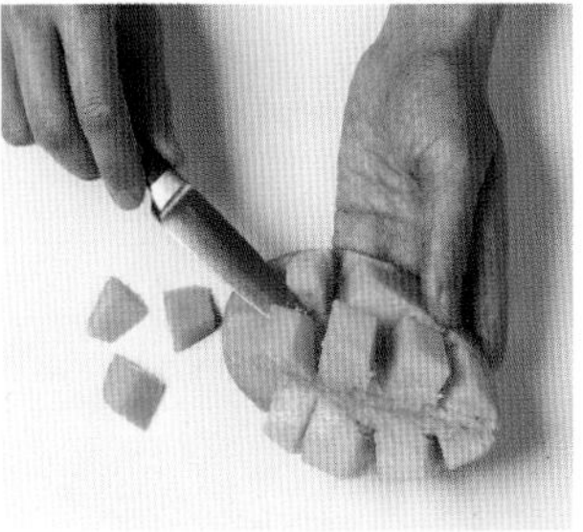

Push peel to turn each piece out, then scrape cubes from peel.

Stacked-Up Vegetable Salad

A vegetable lover's dream—eight layers of garden goodness, crowned with a creamy chive dressing. The result not only looks lovely but has such an array of ingredients it's sure to please everyone. This layered salad is also a powerhouse of vitamins and fiber, which play important roles in keeping your heart strong.

PER SERVING

155 calories / 29% from fat
2 g saturated fat, 5 g total fat
11 mg cholesterol
660 mg sodium
24 g total carbohydrate
5 g dietary fiber
5 g protein

PREP TIME 45 min. | **COOK TIME 22 min. + chilling** | **SERVES 12**

- 4 slices turkey bacon
- 8 ounces red-skinned potatoes, cut into ½-inch pieces
- 1 package (10 ounces) frozen green peas
- 6 ounces snow peas (2 cups)
- 8 ounces baby carrots, halved lengthwise
- 2 cups corn kernels
- 2 cups shredded red cabbage
- 1 pint cherry tomatoes, halved
- 1 large red bell pepper, seeded and cut into thin strips
- 2 cups nonfat mayonnaise
- 1 cup reduced-fat sour cream
- ¼ cup chopped fresh chives
- Chive pieces for garnish

1 Cook bacon in medium skillet until crisp. Drain on paper towels, then crumble and refrigerate.

2 Bring potatoes and water to a boil in large saucepan. Cook until tender, about 5 minutes. With slotted spoon, transfer potatoes to colander, rinse under cold water, and let cool in colander.

3 Set out large bowl of ice water. Blanch vegetables separately in same saucepan of boiling water: green peas and snow peas, 2 minutes each; carrots and corn, 3 minutes each.

4 Immediately plunge vegetables into ice water, then drain and place in separate piles on double layer of paper towels.

5 Layer vegetables in straight-sided 6-quart glass bowl: cabbage, green peas, tomatoes, potatoes, carrots, snow peas, corn, and red pepper.

6 Blend mayonnaise, sour cream, and chopped chives to make dressing. Spread over salad, then cover and refrigerate up to 4 hours. Garnish salad with chive pieces and bacon.

STEP 3 *Lower strainer with peas into boiling water.*

STEP 4 *Plunge peas, still in strainer, into ice water.*

STEP 5 *Layer vegetables, starting in center of bowl and working to the edge.*

HEALTH HINT

In addition to folate, vitamin C, beta-carotene, and fiber, the vegetables in this salad provide a host of phytochemicals that work together to fight disease.

way back when... Native to Asia and Europe, chives have been around for over 5,000 years. The botanical name for chive is derived from the Greek meaning *reedlike leek*. The Latin name for chive is *cepa*, which means onion. Unlike the onion, which has a bulb, chives grow like a clump of grass. Edible lavender flowers grow on top, and the chives become harsher in flavor after flowering.

(Source: www.homecooking.about.com/library)

Cook's Clue

To blanch means to cook food, usually vegetables, briefly in boiling water and then immerse them immediately in ice water to stop the cooking.

Wilted Spinach, White Bean and Bacon Salad

PER SERVING
264 calories / 22% from fat
1 g saturated fat, 6.5 g total fat
9 mg cholesterol
835 mg sodium
37 g total carbohydrate
12 g dietary fiber
17 g protein

There's a magical moment in the life of a leaf of spinach when it's neither raw nor cooked—just wilted by a warm dressing. In the race against heart disease, this salad is a real winner, with lean turkey bacon, beans for a healthy helping of low-fat protein, and plenty of vitamin-rich vegetables.

PREP TIME 15 min. | **COOK TIME 15 min.** | **SERVES 4**

- 1 tablespoon olive oil
- 3 slices turkey bacon, cut crosswise into ½-inch-wide strips
- 12 ounces fresh shiitake mushrooms, stems removed and caps thinly sliced
- 1 can (19 ounces) white beans, rinsed and drained
- ½ cup low-sodium, mixed vegetable juice
- 2 tablespoons red wine vinegar
- 1 tablespoon Dijon mustard
- ½ teaspoon salt
- ¼ teaspoon black pepper
- 12 cups spinach leaves
- 1 yellow bell pepper, seeded and cut into small squares
- 1 large red onion, halved and thinly sliced

1 Heat oil in large nonstick skillet over medium heat. Add bacon and cook until crisp, about 5 minutes. With slotted spoon, transfer bacon to paper towels to drain.

2 Add shiitake mushrooms to skillet and cook until tender, about 5 minutes. Add beans and cook until heated through, about 3 minutes.

3 Whisk vegetable juice, vinegar, mustard, salt, and black pepper in small bowl. Add to mushroom mixture in skillet and bring to a boil.

4 Meanwhile, combine spinach, bell pepper, red onion, and bacon in large bowl. Add hot mushroom mixture to bowl and toss to combine.

Round Out the Meal

Serve with seeded flatbreads. Offer vanilla frozen yogurt topped with crushed amaretti cookies for dessert.

STEP 2 *Sauté sliced shiitake mushrooms until tender.*

STEP 3 *Add dressing mixture to mushrooms and beans in skillet.*

STEP 4 *Pour hot mushroom mixture over vegetables in salad bowl.*

secret to success

Never forget to wash fruits and vegetables, especially spinach. Because spinach grows in sandy soil, it could contain grains of sand–a texture less than desirable in your salad or your teeth.

way back when... Persia is where spinach originated. In the Middle Ages, spinach was sold fresh or cooked. It was also sold chopped and pressed into balls or *espinoche*. In the 17th century, spinach became fashionable, especially cooked with sugar. Spinach is rich in vitamins and minerals, and the iron gives spinach a pronounced flavor.

(Source: Larousse Gastronomique, *edited by Jenifer Harvey Lang, Crown Publishers, Inc. 1990)*

HEALTH HINT

Fiber is important for heart health, and thanks to the beans, spinach, mushrooms, and bell pepper in this recipe, you'll get half of your daily fiber requirement in just a single serving. The white beans are especially high in soluble fiber, which helps to lower LDL ("bad") cholesterol while not affecting the protective HDL cholesterol levels.

Beefy Pasta Salad

This satisfying salad makes a fine summer supper or buffet offering. The pasta, broccoli, tomatoes, and strips of sirloin are lavished with a light dressing based on fat-free yogurt, not a gloppy mayonnaise mixture. Corkscrew-shaped pasta (rotelle or fusilli) is just one option for this dish; you could use any other short pasta shape, such as radiatore, penne rigate, or medium shells.

PER SERVING

471 calories / 29% from fat

4.5 g saturated fat, 15 g total fat

50 mg cholesterol

781 mg sodium

58 g total carbohydrate

7 g dietary fiber

29 g protein

PREP TIME 25 min. | **COOK TIME 20 min.** | **SERVES 4**

- 8 ounces rotelle or other small pasta shape
- 6 cups broccoli spears
- 10 ounces well-trimmed sirloin steak
- 1¼ cups plain fat-free yogurt
- 3 tablespoons light mayonnaise
- 1 tablespoon balsamic vinegar
- ¾ cup basil leaves
- 1 teaspoon salt
- 1 pound plum tomatoes, quartered
- 1 medium red onion, halved and thinly sliced

secret to success

Oil is overrated when it comes to pasta. It prevents sticking, but the pasta itself becomes oily and does not absorb the sauce. For an interesting flavor, don't use olive oil. Instead, add 1 to 2 tablespoons of sea salt to rapidly boiling water.

1 Cook pasta in large pot of boiling water according to package directions. Add broccoli spears during last 2 minutes of cooking; drain.

2 Meanwhile, preheat broiler. Broil steak 4 inches from heat for 4 minutes per side for medium or until done to taste. Transfer steak to cutting board and thinly slice across the grain, on the diagonal.

3 Combine yogurt, mayonnaise, vinegar, basil, and salt in food processor and process until smooth. Transfer dressing to large serving bowl.

4 Add steak and any juices accumulated on cutting board and toss to coat. Add pasta, broccoli, tomatoes, and onion to bowl and toss again. (Recipe can be made ahead and refrigerated. Bring back to room temperature before serving.)

Round Out the Meal

Serve with crisp whole-grain breadsticks and a mixture of fresh blueberries and strawberries.

HEALTH HINT

Enriched pastas and other grain foods are great sources of folate, a B vitamin essential for a healthy heart.

Cook's Clue

Sirloin is a relatively lean cut of meat. Lean cuts should not be broiled past the "medium" stage, or they'll toughen. Slicing the meat thinly across the grain also helps enhance its tenderness.

STEP 1 *To avoid having another pot of boiling water, cook broccoli in same pot with pasta.*

STEP 2 *After slicing steak, save any juices that accumulate on cutting board.*

STEP 4 *Add onions and toss ingredients gently to coat with dressing.*

Succotash

The word "succotash" comes from the American Indian word msickquatash, *which simply means "boiled kernels of corn." The dish itself is a creamy combination of corn and lima beans. In this heart-smart version, fat-free half-and-half provides the creaminess, and olive oil stands in for the more traditional butter.*

PER SERVING

154 calories / 18% from fat

0 g saturated fat, 3 g total fat

0 mg cholesterol

332 mg sodium

26 g total carbohydrate

5 g dietary fiber

6 g protein

PREP TIME 30 min. **COOK TIME 12 min.** **SERVES 6**

2 cups fresh or frozen baby lima beans

2 cups fresh or frozen corn kernels

1 cup fat-free half-and-half

1 tablespoon light olive oil

¾ teaspoon salt

3 tablespoons chopped chives

¼ teaspoon black pepper

1 Bring lima beans, corn, half-and-half, olive oil, and salt to boil in large saucepan over high heat.

2 Reduce heat to medium, cover, and cook until tender—10 to 12 minutes. Remove from heat and stir in chives and black pepper.

Round Out the Meal

Get your protein from sautéed chicken smothered in caramelized onions. Add a salad of marinated cucumbers, and end the meal with fresh orange and pineapple slices.

HEALTH HINT

When it comes to fiber content, lima beans are at the top of the list. Limas are also a good source of iron, magnesium, and other essential minerals. Corn is also a good source of fiber, as well as the B vitamins, thiamin and folate.

way back when... Over 7,000 years ago, lima beans were cultivated in Peru. Some historians believe that lima beans could have also originated in Guatemala. Once Columbus discovered America, Spanish explorers noticed lima beans in other varieties growing throughout South and Central America and the Caribbean, and they introduced lima beans to Asia and Europe. Portuguese explorers introduced lima beans to Africa. Because lima beans can handle tropical and humid weather better than most beans, they are an important crop in areas of Asia.

(Source: www.whfoods.com)

Cook's Clue

To make green bean succotash, substitute 2 cups trimmed green beans for lima beans and 2 tablespoons fresh chopped thyme or ½ teaspoon dried thyme for chives.

Preparing Fresh Corn

Pull off husks and silks from cob and trim stem. Brush off remaining silks with fingers.

Stand cob on stem and hold firmly. Working downward, slice off kernels with large, sharp knife.

Diner-Style Hash Browns

Craving the flavor of sizzling-hot hash browns? Well, dig in—and don't feel guilty for a minute! Potatoes are a powerhouse of nutrients, and smart cooking techniques keep them extra crisp and full of good taste, not grease from the griddle. Seconds, anyone?

PER SERVING

240 calories / 30% from fat

2 g saturated fat, 8 g total fat

8 mg cholesterol

558 mg sodium

35 g total carbohydrate

4 g dietary fiber

7 g protein

PREP TIME 15 min.	COOK TIME 35 min.	SERVES 4

- 1½ pounds all-purpose potatoes, peeled
- 3 slices turkey bacon, chopped
- 1 medium onion, chopped
- 1 medium green bell pepper, seeded and chopped
- ½ teaspoon paprika
- ½ teaspoon salt
- ¼ teaspoon freshly ground black pepper
- 2 tablespoons margarine

1 Coarsely grate potatoes into large bowl of ice water. Let stand 10 minutes.

2 Meanwhile, cook bacon in large nonstick skillet over medium-high heat until crisp, 5 minutes. Transfer to paper towels to drain, leaving drippings in skillet.

3 Sauté onion and green pepper in skillet until soft, about 5 minutes. Transfer with slotted spoon to paper towel.

4 Drain potatoes, squeezing out as much water as possible. Transfer to kitchen towel and pat dry. Combine potatoes, bacon, onion, green pepper, paprika, salt, and black pepper in large bowl.

5 Add margarine to drippings and melt over medium heat. Spread potato mixture evenly in skillet and cook, without stirring, until golden brown and crispy on bottom, about 15 minutes. Place large plate over skillet and invert. Slide potatoes back into skillet. Cook until golden brown and crispy on second side, about 10 minutes longer.

STEP 1 *Grate potatoes into bowl of ice water.*

STEP 4 *Squeeze out water and pat potatoes dry on clean kitchen towel.*

secret to success

Turkey bacon gives you all the flavor of the traditional recipe with a fraction of its fat and cholesterol.

HEALTH HINT

Advocates of high-protein, low-carbohydrate diets have given potatoes a bad reputation. In fact, the humble tuber is very good for you. It's low in calories (as long as it's not deep-fried or topped with butter and sour cream), high in complex carbohydrates (your body's main source of energy), and loaded with vitamin C.

Cook's Clue

Soaking the potatoes may seem like extra work, but it's crucial to crisp hash browns. The ice water converts some of the starch to sugar, which helps the spuds brown faster and absorb less fat. Squeezing them dry ensures that they fry when they hit the pan. If they are wet, they'll steam, and you'll end up with soggy, not crispy, hash browns.

Round Out the Meal

Finish off the meal with a chilled cantaloupe soup with strawberry compote.

Summer Ratatouille

This classic dish hails from Provence, a region in the south of France. Simmer lots of fresh vegetables in a splash of olive oil just long enough to bring out their natural flavors. You'll be eating as they do along the Mediterranean—an area known for its low incidence of heart disease.

PER SERVING

132 calories / 27% from fat
0.5 g saturated fat, 4 g total fat
0 mg cholesterol
698 mg sodium
24 g total carbohydrate
8 g dietary fiber
4 g protein

PREP TIME 25 min. | **COOK TIME 35 min.** | **SERVES 6**

- 1 large eggplant (about 2 pounds)
- 1 teaspoon salt
- 1 small fennel bulb
- 4 teaspoons olive oil
- 2 medium yellow squash (8 ounces each), chopped
- 1 medium onion, cut into thin wedges
- 3 tablespoons reduced-sodium chicken broth
- 3 large garlic cloves, minced
- 1 can (28 ounces) no-salt-added whole tomatoes
- 2 tablespoons chopped fresh oregano
- 1 teaspoon chopped fresh rosemary, plus sprigs for garnish
- 1 green bell pepper, seeded and chopped

1 Slice eggplant crosswise (*see photo, right*).

2 Sprinkle both sides with ½ teaspoon salt. Set on double layer of paper towels. Let stand 15 minutes. Rinse off eggplant, pat dry with paper towels, and cut into cubes.

3 Trim and chop fennel bulb.

4 Heat 2 teaspoons oil in large nonstick skillet over medium-high heat. Sauté squash and onion until onion is soft, about 5 minutes. Transfer to large bowl. Add 1 teaspoon oil and broth to skillet. Stir in eggplant and reduce heat to medium. Cover and cook, stirring occasionally, until eggplant is tender, about 12 minutes. Add to vegetables in bowl.

5 Add remaining oil and garlic to skillet and cook 30 seconds. Stir in tomatoes, fennel, oregano, and chopped rosemary, breaking up tomatoes with spoon. Cover and simmer 5 minutes. Stir in green pepper. Cover and simmer 7 minutes longer. Return vegetables to skillet. Sprinkle with remaining salt and bring to a boil. Cook, uncovered, 3 minutes, stirring occasionally. Serve warm or at room temperature, garnished with sprigs of rosemary.

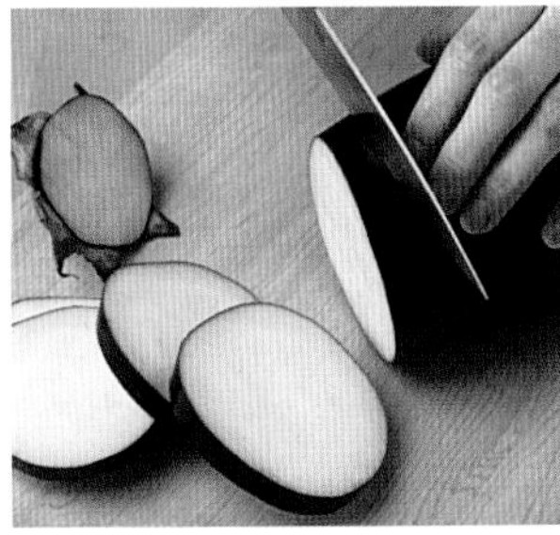

STEP 1 *Cut eggplant crosswise into 3/8-inch slices.*

STEP 2 *Place slices on paper towels. Salt both sides and let stand 15 minutes.*

Round Out the Meal

Sauté lean lamb tenderloins and serve sliced over the ratatouille and garnish with light feta cheese. Serve fresh figs with balsamic syrup for dessert.

Cook's Clue

Eggplant is very porous and absorbs oil like a sponge, so it typically cooks in plenty of oil. To slash fat, cook the eggplant in a combination of chicken broth and olive oil—a chef's trick that imparts flavor while reducing fat.

HEALTH HINT

People living throughout the Mediterranean have a notably low occurrence of heart disease. Their diets are high in vegetables, fruits, and grains, and their main source of fat is olive oil. Olive oil contains heart-healthy monounsaturated fats, which can help reduce cholesterol levels in individuals whose diets are low in fat overall.

Butternut Gratin

A perfect butternut squash, with its graceful pear shape and satiny golden skin, could almost get by on its looks. But hiding inside is dense, mildly sweet, orange flesh that's an excellent source of disease-battling beta-carotene. A big butternut can be a bit tricky to cut up; you'll do best with a large, sturdy chef's knife.

PER SERVING

181 calories / 25% from fat
1.5 g saturated fat, 5 g total fat
5 mg cholesterol
561 mg sodium
32 g total carbohydrate
6 g dietary fiber
6 g protein

PREP TIME 10 min. | **COOK TIME 45 min.** | **SERVES 4**

- 1 butternut squash (about 2 pounds), halved crosswise, then lengthwise, seeded, and peeled
- 1 medium red onion, halved and thinly sliced
- 1½ cups frozen corn kernels, thawed
- 2¼ teaspoons olive oil
- ¾ teaspoon salt
- ⅓ cup grated Parmesan cheese

1 Preheat oven to 400°F. Quarter butternut squash pieces lengthwise and cut each piece crosswise into ½-inch-thick chunks. Combine squash, onion, corn, oil, and salt in large bowl, tossing to coat.

2 Arrange vegetables in 9 x 13-inch baking dish. Bake until butternut squash is tender, about 40 minutes, stirring halfway through cooking time.

3 Sprinkle Parmesan cheese over vegetables and bake until melted and golden, about 5 minutes.

Round Out the Meal

Serve with roast chicken and a salad of fresh fennel with shaved Parmesan. For dessert, serve broiled pear halves topped with vanilla frozen yogurt.

Cook's Clue

For an unusual pasta dish, bake the vegetables for 40 minutes, but stop short of adding the Parmesan. Instead, chop the vegetables, and stir them into a good-quality bottled tomato sauce. Toss the sauce with hot cooked pasta.

way back when... Gratin refers to the golden crust that forms on the surface of a dish after it is put under the grill or in the oven. Gratin formerly referred to the crust adhering to the cooking receptacle. The crust was scraped off (*graff* in French) and eaten. Today, the term refers to a method of cooking. The preparation is reheated in the oven and a protective layer forms. The surface is covered with a crust, preventing the food from drying out, which improves the taste.

(Source: Larousse Gastronomique, edited by Jenifer Harvey Lang, Crown Publishers, Inc. 1990)

HEALTH HINT

Butternut squash and corn contain soluble fiber, which may help reduce LDL ("bad") cholesterol by blocking its absorption into the body.

How to Cut up a Butternut Squash

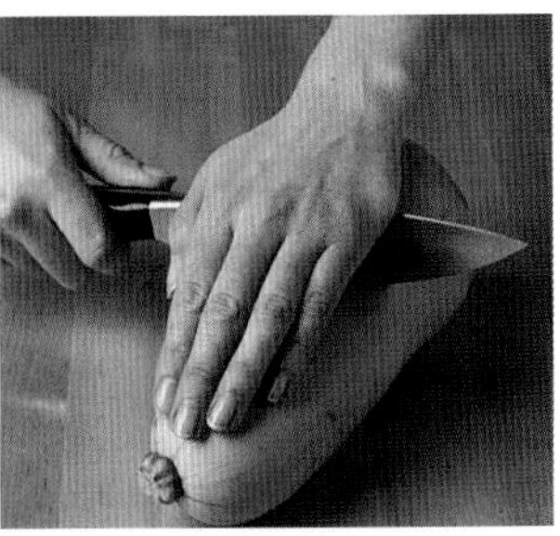

With large, sturdy knife, cut squash crosswise at its natural "waistline."

Cut bulbous piece of squash in half lengthwise and scoop out seeds.

Peel squash and cut according to recipe instructions.

Country-Style Mashed Potatoes

PER SERVING
196 calories / 28% from fat
1 g saturated fat, 6 g total fat
8 mg cholesterol
423 mg sodium
31 g total carbohydrate
3 g dietary fiber
5 g protein

A timeless side dish you can say yes to frequently because it's made for heart-smart eaters. These mashed potatoes deliver all the rich and creamy satisfaction you want—but without the fat you don't want. To give potatoes extra personality, crown them with bacon and frizzled onions.

PREP TIME 20 min. | **COOK TIME 20 min.** | **SERVES 6**

- ½ teaspoon salt
- 1½ pounds Russet or Eastern potatoes
- ⅓ cup reduced-fat milk (2%)
- 2 tablespoons margarine, cut into pieces
- ⅛ teaspoon black pepper
- 2 scallions (green parts only), very thinly sliced
- 4 slices turkey bacon, coarsely chopped
- 1 small red onion, chopped
- 1 teaspoon chopped fresh thyme

1 Half-fill a medium saucepan with water; add ¼ teaspoon salt and bring to a boil over high heat. Meanwhile, peel potatoes and cut each into 8 pieces. Add potatoes to boiling water, reduce heat to medium, and simmer until potatoes are tender, about 10 minutes. Drain. Shake potatoes in pan over low heat until dry. Remove from heat, cover, and keep hot.

2 Heat milk and margarine in small saucepan over medium heat until margarine has melted and milk is hot and begins to bubble, about 3 minutes. Pour over potatoes. Add black pepper and remaining salt and mash to a chunky puree with a potato masher (not mixer or food processor). Stir in scallions and keep hot.

3 Meanwhile, sauté bacon and onion in medium nonstick skillet over medium-high heat until bacon is crisp and onions are browned, about 7 minutes. Stir in thyme. Spoon on top of potatoes.

STEP 1 *Shake cooked potatoes over low heat until dry.*

STEP 2 *When mashing potatoes, be sure to mash gently—leaving a few lumps is fine!*

Cook's Clue

No more gluey mashed potatoes! Pick spuds high in starch such as Russet (Idaho) or all-purpose (Eastern). Simmer, don't boil, potatoes. Gently hand mash them; don't use a food processor or electric mixer. Excess heat and overbeating potatoes break down the starch, turning them tough and gluey.

way back when... Because the potato was unknown to them, Europeans initially considered potatoes poisonous and evil due to their similarities to the nightshade family. Some members of the nightshade family include mandrake and belladonna, both used for medicinal purposes. Germany's King Frederick William realized potatoes were a good food source and ordered his peasants to plant and eat potatoes or their noses would be cut off!

(Source: www.healthypotato.com)

HEALTH HINT

To keep more fiber, iron, and phosphorus in this dish, scrub the potatoes instead of peeling them.

secret to success

Instead of adding rich cream, cheese, or butter, try reduced-fat milk, some of the potato cooking water, buttermilk, beef or chicken broth, nonfat sour cream, or nonfat plain yogurt. Spice up the cooking water by adding cloves of garlic, fresh thyme sprigs, slivers of onion, or a dash of black pepper.

Vegetable Stir-Fry with Spicy Garlic Sauce

Has your passion for vegetables faded lately? This lively stir-fry will make the sparks fly again! Fresh, crisp broccoli, bright red bell peppers, and tender baby corn are flash-fried with tantalizing Asian seasonings for a speedy, healthful side dish.

PER SERVING

140 calories / 29% from fat
1 g saturated fat, 4.5 g total fat
0 mg cholesterol
345 mg sodium
21 g total carbohydrate
7 g dietary fiber
5 g protein

PREP TIME 15 min.	COOK TIME 14 min.	SERVES 4

- 1½ cups reduced-sodium chicken broth
- 2 tablespoons light soy sauce, or to taste
- 2 tablespoons cornstarch
- ½ teaspoon Thai chili paste (optional)
- 2 garlic cloves
- 1½ teaspoons peanut or vegetable oil
- 3 tablespoons minced peeled fresh ginger
- 2 cups broccoli florets
- 1 can (15 ounces) baby corn, drained
- 1 large red bell pepper, seeded and cut into thin strips
- 1 can (8 ounces) sliced water chestnuts, drained
- 1 tablespoon sesame seeds, toasted

1 Combine ¼ cup broth, soy sauce, cornstarch, and chili paste (if using) in small bowl until smooth. Set aside. Crush garlic cloves by smashing with side of chef's knife and remove peels.

2 Coat large nonstick wok or deep skillet with nonstick cooking spray. Add oil and set wok over high heat until hot but not smoking. Stir-fry ginger and garlic until fragrant, about 1 minute. Remove with slotted spoon and set aside.

3 Add broccoli to wok and stir-fry just until it begins to soften, about 4 minutes. Transfer to bowl. Add corn, red pepper, and water chestnuts; stir-fry just until they begin to soften, about 3 minutes. Return broccoli to wok and add remaining broth.

4 Cover and cook until vegetables are crisp-tender, about 3 minutes. Whisk cornstarch mixture again and add to wok with ginger and garlic. Stir-fry just until sauce thickens and boils, about 1 minute. Sprinkle with sesame seeds.

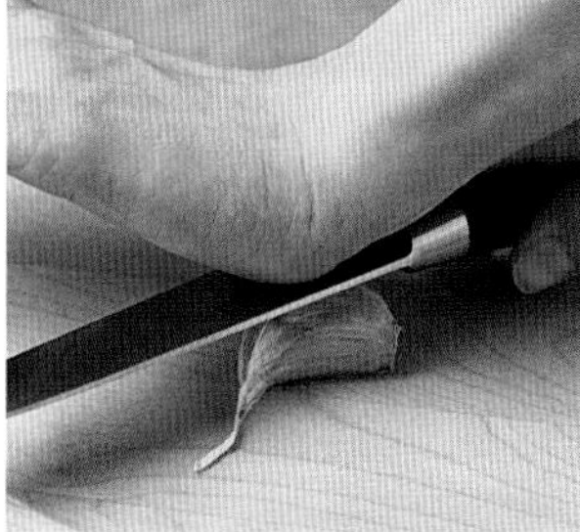

STEP 1 *Smash unpeeled cloves with chef's knife. Remove peels.*

STEP 3 *Briskly stir-fry vegetables over high heat.*

STEP 4 *When sauce thickens, boils, and turns clear, it's done.*

Round Out the Meal

For a simple Asian-style supper, serve this stir-fry with grilled shrimp and steamed brown rice. A scoop of orange sorbet with a vanilla wafer makes a lovely dessert.

secret to success

Choose broccoli that has a "bloom." A bloom is a purple hue—tight crowns that are not yellow. By selecting the proper broccoli, the dish will have a fresh, crisp taste and texture.

Cook's Clue

Stir-frying is a fast, easy, and healthful way to cook, but it pays to be prepared. Cut up and measure ingredients before you heat the wok. Make sure all vegetables are cut into similar-size pieces so they cook evenly. Stir-fry vegetables with similar cook times together. Most of all, don't crowd the pan: If you add too many vegetables, they will steam rather than fry, and you'll end up with soggy results. Stir-fry in several batches, if necessary, to keep veggies crisp.

Santa Fe Stuffed Peppers

Peter Piper never picked a pepper as tasty as these! They're roasted whole bell peppers, packed with a southwestern medley of rice, beef, beans, and salsa, and topped with a little melted cheese. They're spiced up, just like chiles rellenos—without the fuss or fat—and a whole lot better than Peter's peck of pickled peppers.

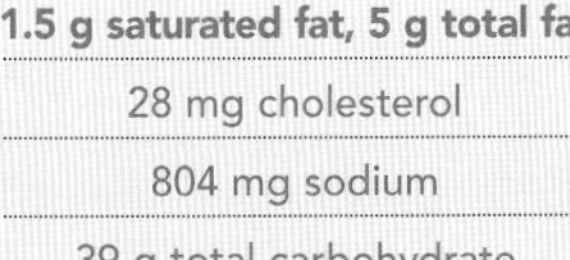

PER SERVING

284 calories / 16% from fat

1.5 g saturated fat, 5 g total fat

28 mg cholesterol

804 mg sodium

39 g total carbohydrate

7 g dietary fiber

23 g protein

PREP TIME 20 min.	COOK TIME 21 min. + standing	SERVES 4

- 4 large red, yellow, or green bell peppers, seeded
- 1 cup reduced-sodium chicken broth
- 1 cup instant brown rice
- 1 large onion, chopped
- 8 ounces lean (95%) ground beef
- 1 cup chunky salsa
- ½ cup drained, rinsed canned black beans
- ¼ teaspoon freshly ground black pepper
- ⅓ cup shredded nonfat cheddar cheese

1 Preheat broiler. Line broiler pan with foil, leaving 2-inch overhang. Fit with slotted rack. Arrange bell peppers on rack and place about 8 inches from heat. Broil, turning about every 4 minutes, until skin is charred and blistered on all sides, about 10 minutes. Slide peppers onto foil; crimp tightly to close. Let stand until tender, about 10 minutes.

2 Peel off dark skin from peppers with small paring knife, keeping stems intact. Make a slit along one side of peppers, and carefully remove seeds with small spoon.

3 Meanwhile, bring broth to a boil in a small saucepan over high heat. Stir in rice and simmer 5 minutes. Remove from heat, cover, and let stand 5 minutes. If any liquid remains, drain off. Keep rice warm.

4 Set large nonstick skillet over medium-high heat. Sauté onion and beef until onion is soft and beef is no longer pink, about 7 minutes. Stir in rice, salsa, beans, and black pepper. Spoon rice mixture into bell peppers. Return peppers to broiler pan. Sprinkle with cheddar and broil until cheese melts, about 1 minute.

STEP 1 *Roast peppers on broiler pan lined with foil until skins are charred and blistered.*

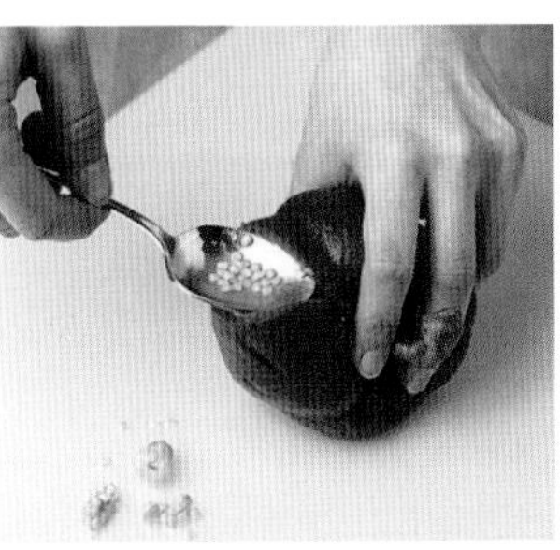

STEP 2 *Make slit in side of roasted pepper, and carefully scoop out seeds.*

STEP 4 *Gently spoon stuffing into pepper through slit. (Be careful not to tear it!)*

Round Out the Meal

Serve with a salad of crisp romaine lettuce with avocado slices and Bermuda onion laced with cumin vinaigrette, and offer fresh pineapple and mango tossed with fresh cilantro for dessert.

HEALTH HINT

The water-soluble fiber in this dish makes it especially heart-smart. Fiber binds with bile acids, which the liver synthesizes out of cholesterol. This action withdraws cholesterol from the blood and converts it back into bile acids, reducing the risk of heart disease.

Cook's Clue

Use a serrated grapefruit spoon to clean the membrane and seeds out of a bell pepper.

Balsamic Baked Tomatoes with Parmesan Crumbs

Choose firm, deep-red tomatoes for this recipe: Good color signals an abundance of lycopene, a carotenoid that may fight heart disease as well as cancer. The tomatoes are baked with a topping of whole-grain bread crumbs and Parmesan and served with a lively balsamic-vinegar glaze.

PER SERVING

76 calories / 24% from fat

0.5 g saturated fat, 2 g total fat

2 mg cholesterol

240 mg sodium

13 g total carbohydrate

2 g dietary fiber

3 g protein

PREP TIME 5 min. | **COOK TIME 25 min.** | **SERVES 8**

- 4 large tomatoes (8 ounces each)
- ½ teaspoon salt
- 2 slices whole-grain bread (2 ounces)
- 3 tablespoons Parmesan cheese
- 1 teaspoon olive oil
- ⅓ cup balsamic vinegar
- 2 tablespoons light brown sugar
- 2 tablespoons water

1 Preheat the oven to 400°F. Core tomatoes and cut in half horizontally. Place tomatoes, cut-side up, in ceramic or glass baking dish large enough to hold them in a single layer. Sprinkle tomato halves with salt.

STEP 1 *With small knife, cut the core out of the stem end of tomatoes.*

2 Place bread in food processor and pulse to fine crumbs. Combine crumbs, Parmesan, and oil in small bowl. Sprinkle tomatoes with crumb mixture.

STEP 2 *Sprinkle bread crumb-Parmesan mixture over tomatoes in baking dish.*

3 Bake, uncovered, until topping begins to brown and tomatoes are heated through, about 25 minutes.

4 Meanwhile, combine balsamic vinegar, brown sugar, and water in small skillet. Bring to a boil over high heat and cook until syrupy, about 3 minutes. Drizzle over baked tomatoes.

STEP 4 *In small skillet, cook balsamic vinegar with brown sugar and water to make a glaze.*

Round Out the Meal

Serve string beans sautéed with pine nuts or fresh oregano and strawberries tossed with balsamic vinegar and a light dusting of sugar (or sugar substitute) for dessert.

Cook's Clue

When cooking tomatoes, never use aluminum cookware. The high acid in the tomatoes causes the aluminum to migrate into the food, resulting in an altered, unpleasant taste. New studies show that aluminum might also have negative effects on the nervous system.

HEALTH HINT

By making your own whole-grain bread crumbs, you'll not only reap the nutritional advantages of the whole grains, you'll also avoid the additives found in many commercially processed bread crumbs.

secret to success

To keep the saturated fat levels in this dish low, the proportions of a typical cheese-and-crumb topping are shifted from mostly cheese to mostly bread crumbs. By using the sharp flavors and fine texture of grated Parmesan cheese, you can make a little go a long way.

Lemony Sugar Snaps

The very essence of early summer, emerald-green sugar snaps are so tender you can eat them up pods and all. No fussy sauces, ruffles, or flourishes are needed. These sweetest of sweet peas shine in a simple stir-fry accented with shallots, garlic, and lemon zest. For a simple, heart-smart meal, serve the sugar snaps with grilled chicken and steamed new potatoes—another early summer delicacy.

PER SERVING

99 calories / 23% from fat

0.5 g saturated fat, 2.5 g total fat

0 mg cholesterol

454 mg sodium

15 g total carbohydrate

5 g dietary fiber

4 g protein

PREP TIME 10 min.	COOK TIME 10 min.	SERVES 4

1½ pounds sugar snap peas

2 teaspoons olive oil

3 shallots, thinly sliced

1 garlic clove, minced

1 tablespoon grated lemon zest

¾ teaspoon salt

1 Remove strings from both sides of sugar snap peas.

2 Heat oil in large nonstick skillet over medium heat. Add shallots and garlic and cook, stirring, until shallots are softened, about 3 minutes.

3 Add sugar snaps, lemon zest, and salt to skillet and cook, stirring, until peas are just tender, about 4 minutes.

STEP 1 *Remove strings from sugar snaps. Large peas will have tough strings on both sides that need removing.*

STEP 2 *Sauté minced garlic and sliced shallots in skillet.*

STEP 3 *Add lemon zest to sugar snap peas in skillet.*

secret to success

In heart-smart cooking, anytime the recipe calls for a liquid fat—as in the melted butter that might traditionally have been used on these sugar snaps—you can safely, and healthfully, substitute olive oil.

HEALTH HINT

Sugar snap peas and other edible-podded peas (such as snow peas) supply three times as much vitamin C as shelled peas. The antioxidant properties of vitamin C help to prevent LDL ("bad") cholesterol from sticking to artery walls. To get the most vitamin C, eat the peas raw or cook them very briefly, as in this recipe.

Cook's Clue

You can simply grate the lemon zest for this recipe on a box grater, but for a more attractive presentation, try making very fine tendrils of lemon zest. To do this, you can use either a tool called a zester or a vegetable peeler. Remove wide strips of lemon zest with the peeler; then, with a paring knife, cut the strips into very fine slivers.

way back when... Archeologists found peas in ancient Egyptian tombs, suggesting that dried peas were eaten by ancient civilizations. Europeans ate dried peas until the Italian Renaissance, when Italians developed *piselli novelli*, a type of pea eaten fresh and unripe. As early as the 16th century in France and England, fresh peas were served during the season of Lent. The Dutch and English developed the edible pod peas, called *mangetout* (eat-all) in the early 17th century. The sugar snap pea did not become available until the 1970s. The sugar snap pea is a cross between an English pea and a snow pea.

(Source: www.enquirer.com)

Spinach with Garlic and Sun-Dried Tomatoes

This speedy side dish will enliven whatever it's paired with. The vegetables' vivid colors (signaling the presence of heart-saving phytochemicals) and lively flavors perk up simple grilled chicken or poached fish. To keep that brilliant emerald green hue, heat the spinach just long enough to wilt it.

PER SERVING

144 calories / 31% from fat

0.5 g saturated fat, 5 g total fat

0 mg cholesterol

500 mg sodium

22 g total carbohydrate

8 g dietary fiber

9 g protein

PREP TIME 10 min.	COOK TIME 10 min.	SERVES 4

- ½ cup sun-dried tomatoes (not oil-packed)
- 1½ cups boiling water
- 1 tablespoon olive oil
- 2 medium onions, cut into ¼-inch slices
- 4 cloves garlic, minced
- 1 tablespoon sugar
- 2 pounds spinach leaves
- 1½ tablespoons imitation bacon bits
- ½ teaspoon salt

1 Combine tomatoes and boiling water in small heatproof bowl and set aside to soften, about 10 minutes. Drain, reserving ⅓ cup of soaking liquid. Thinly slice tomatoes.

2 Meanwhile, heat oil in large nonstick saucepan or Dutch oven over medium heat. Add onions, garlic, and sugar to pan and cook, stirring frequently, until onions are golden brown, about 7 minutes.

3 Add tomato-soaking liquid, tomatoes, spinach, bacon bits, and salt.

4 Cover and cook until spinach has wilted, about 2 minutes.

STEP 1 *Once softened in hot water, sun-dried tomatoes are easily sliced.*

STEP 3 *Add spinach to pan. If it doesn't all fit, wait a couple seconds for first layer to wilt a bit.*

STEP 4 *After 1 or 2 minutes spinach will be fully wilted.*

secret to success

Imitation bacon bits are a healthful way to fool your taste buds into thinking that your spinach (or salad, or sandwich) is topped with freshly fried morsels of fatty bacon. The fat count goes way down (and the saturated fat disappears completely), plus you get the benefit of soy protein and soy oil, the main ingredients in "fake bacon."

HEALTH HINT

Spinach supplies an extraordinary wealth of vitamins and minerals and a host of phytochemicals that work to protect your heart and blood vessels from disease. The B vitamin folate, plentiful in spinach, lowers blood levels of homocysteine, an amino acid associated with higher risk of heart disease. Spinach is also rich in beta-carotene, lutein, and cholesterol-lowering plant sterols. The vitamin C in spinach can help prevent stroke.

Round Out the Meal

Toss some whole-wheat pasta into this dish, and serve a frozen orange granita for dessert.

Pasta and Grains

Spanish Rice

The Spaniards brought rice to the New World in the 16th century, so it's no wonder many American rice dishes have a Spanish flair. Traditional versions of this red-rice skillet dish often begin with spicy (and extremely fatty) chorizo sausage. This healthy adaptation forgoes the sausage and the fat it contributes and boosts the flavors with extra vegetables. Serve as is, or toss in shrimp or chicken for a main attraction!

PER SERVING

162 calories / 6% from fat

0 g saturated fat, 1 g total fat

0 mg cholesterol

226 mg sodium

35 g total carbohydrate

3 g dietary fiber

5 g protein

PREP TIME 20 min. | **COOK TIME 33 min.** | **SERVES 6**

- 1 medium onion, finely chopped
- 1 large green bell pepper, seeded and finely chopped
- 1 celery stalk, finely chopped
- 2 garlic cloves, minced
- 4 ounces white mushrooms, sliced
- 1 cup long-grain white rice
- 1½ cups no-salt-added tomato juice
- 1 cup reduced-sodium chicken broth
- ½ teaspoon salt
- ¼ teaspoon black pepper
- 1 bay leaf
- 6 plum tomatoes, halved, seeded, and diced

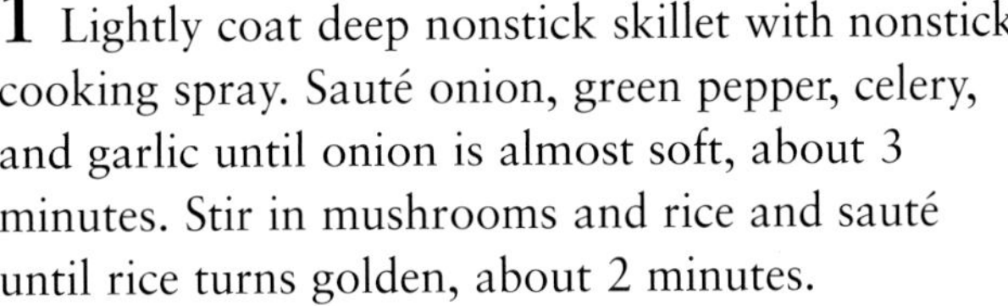

1 Lightly coat deep nonstick skillet with nonstick cooking spray. Sauté onion, green pepper, celery, and garlic until onion is almost soft, about 3 minutes. Stir in mushrooms and rice and sauté until rice turns golden, about 2 minutes.

2 Stir in tomato juice, broth, salt, black pepper, and bay leaf. Bring to a boil over medium-high heat. Cover, reduce heat, and simmer, stirring occasionally, 15 minutes. Stir in tomatoes.

3 Cover and cook until the rice is tender and liquid is absorbed, about 10 minutes longer. Fluff with fork to test for doneness and to keep rice from sticking together. Remove from heat and discard bay leaf.

secret to success

Many recipes for Spanish rice exist—and most begin with drippings from cooked salt pork, smoked bacon, fatback, or chorizo sausage. Skip all that saturated fat, and add flavor with onion, garlic, and spices. Keep the salt level in check by using no-salt-added tomato juice and reduced-sodium chicken broth. The dish is just as good, but twice as healthful!

STEP 1 *Add rice to sautéed vegetables and cook until golden.*

STEP 2 *Stir diced tomatoes to distribute evenly.*

STEP 3 *Fluff rice with fork to test for doneness.*

Cook's Clue

For a hearty paella, prepare this recipe, adding 1½ pounds shelled, deveined, large shrimp and 2 cups peas in Step 3 during the last 8 minutes of cooking.

HEALTH HINT

Diets high in refined carbohydrates appear to increase the risk of heart attack. Switch to whole grains—less processed, complex carbohydrates that contain high amounts of insoluble fiber. Studies show that people who consume whole grains are less likely to develop lymphomas and many different cancers.

Salsa Chicken and Rice

There are hundreds of ways to serve chicken and rice, a mainstay in cuisines around the world. Here's a Latin American–influenced recipe, made with fiber-rich brown rice and plenty of cholesterol-lowering garlic. Keep this recipe in mind when you have leftover chicken.

PER SERVING

326 calories / 21% from fat
1.5 g saturated fat, 7.5 g total fat
48 mg cholesterol
699 mg sodium
41 g total carbohydrate
3 g dietary fiber
23 g protein

PREP TIME 20 min. | COOK TIME 50 min. | SERVES 4

- 2 teaspoons olive oil
- 6 scallions, thinly sliced
- 4 garlic cloves, minced
- 1 cup brown rice
- 1½ cups water
- 1 cup reduced-sodium, fat-free chicken broth
- ¾ teaspoon salt
- 6 Kalamata olives, pitted and coarsely chopped
- 2 large tomatoes, cut into large wedges
- 8 ounces cooked chicken breast, cut into bite-size pieces
- 1 cup chopped cilantro
- 1 tablespoon white wine vinegar

1 Heat oil in medium saucepan over low heat. Add scallions and garlic, and cook until scallions are tender, about 3 minutes.

2 Stir in brown rice, water, broth, and salt. Bring to a boil. Reduce to a simmer, cover, and cook until rice is tender and all liquid has been absorbed, about 45 minutes.

3 Just before serving, stir olives, tomatoes, chicken, cilantro, and vinegar into rice.

Round Out the Meal

Start the meal with low-fat guacamole. Accompany the rice and chicken dish with a green bean salad. For dessert, enjoy pineapple sorbet.

HEALTH HINT

Brown rice contains a healthful phytochemical called oryzanol, thought to help guard against cardiovascular disease. There is also an abundance of the heart-helping B vitamins folate and B_6 and the mineral magnesium in brown rice. Because brown rice is a whole grain with its bran intact, it is an exceptional source of fiber, furnishing about three times more fiber than white rice.

secret to success

Always follow package directions when cooking pasta or rice. Test colored rice for doneness by tasting a bite or squeezing a few grains between your fingers. If you feel a hard center in the rice, additional time on the stove is necessary.

How to Mince Leafy Herbs

When chopping leafy herbs with stems, such as cilantro, begin by folding washed and drained sprigs into a compact ball.

Keeping the herbs in a tight ball, use a chef's knife to cut them crosswise into coarse shreds.

Then rock the chef's knife across the coarse shreds to cut into smaller pieces.

Green Rice with Lime and Cilantro

Herbs are not just for flavor: When used in copious quantities, fresh green herbs are good sources of vitamin C and beta-carotene. In this recipe, scallions, cilantro, basil, and parsley bring their emerald color to fiber-rich brown rice. Lightly-cooked peas add more green, plus folate.

PER SERVING

182 calories / 22% from fat
0.5 g saturated fat, 4.5 g total fat
0 mg cholesterol
465 mg sodium
31 g total carbohydrate
3 g dietary fiber
4 g protein

PREP TIME 20 min. | **COOK TIME 50 min.** | **SERVES 4**

- 1 tablespoon olive oil
- 4 scallions, thinly sliced
- 3 garlic cloves, minced
- ¾ cup brown rice
- ½ cup chopped cilantro
- ¼ cup chopped basil
- ¼ cup chopped parsley
- 1 teaspoon grated lime zest
- 1¾ cups water
- ¾ teaspoon salt
- ½ cup frozen peas
- 1 tablespoon fresh lime juice

1 Heat oil in medium saucepan over medium heat. Add scallions and garlic, and cook until scallions have wilted, about 2 minutes.

2 Add rice, ¼ cup cilantro, basil, parsley, and lime zest, stirring to coat. Add water and salt, and bring to a boil. Reduce to a simmer, cover, and cook until rice is tender, about 45 minutes.

3 Stir in peas and cook until heated through, about 1 minute. Remove from heat and stir in remaining ¼ cup cilantro and lime juice.

STEP 1 *Sauté scallions and garlic in medium saucepan.*

STEP 2 *Add rice and stir to coat grains with herbs.*

STEP 3 *Add peas and cook just to heat them through.*

way back when... Limes were used in the 18th century to help soldiers fight scurvy, a disease caused by a lack of vitamin C, which threatened to wipe out the ranks of the British navy. The lime juice dramatically reduced their mortality rate. Aside from their daily portion of rum, they were required to drink the juice, and sailors were given the nickname "limeys."

(Source: www.homecooking.about.com)

Cook's Clue

For a cool, tasty variation on Middle Eastern tabbouleh, replace the brown rice with bulgur. Soak 1 cup of bulgur in boiling water according to package directions until tender. Transfer the bulgur to a large serving bowl, and stir in the oil, scallions, garlic, herbs, and lime zest and juice.

HEALTH HINT

When herbs such as cilantro, basil, and parsley are dried, they lose some important nutrients, notably vitamin C, B vitamins, and some of their natural oils. Use fresh green herbs to get the benefit of their nutrients in addition to more immediate and refreshing flavor.

Lemon Orzo with Chicken

Funny thing about the small pasta shape called orzo: Although the word means "barley," the pasta actually looks a lot more like rice. And it's fun to use orzo in recipes that would ordinarily be made with rice. Orzo is a common ingredient in Greek dishes, and you'll detect Greek flavors in this speedy dinner dish: lots of fresh lemon, feta cheese, and fresh mint.

PER SERVING

380 calories / 19% from fat
2.5 g saturated fat, 8 g total fat
44 mg cholesterol
514 mg sodium
52 g total carbohydrate
4 g dietary fiber
25 g protein

PREP TIME 15 min. | COOK TIME 15 min. | SERVES 4

- 8 ounces orzo
- 1 cup frozen peas
- 1 tablespoon olive oil
- 2 shallots, minced
- 3 garlic cloves, minced
- 8 ounces boneless, skinless chicken breast, cut into ½-inch pieces
- ½ teaspoon salt
- 2 teaspoons grated lemon zest
- 3 tablespoons fresh lemon juice
- ½ teaspoon black pepper
- ¼ cup chopped fresh mint
- ⅓ cup crumbled feta cheese

1 In large pot of boiling water, cook orzo according to package directions. Add peas during final 10 seconds of cooking. Drain.

2 Meanwhile, heat oil in large nonstick skillet over medium heat. Add shallots and garlic to skillet and cook, stirring frequently, until shallots are tender, about 2 minutes. Add chicken and ¼ teaspoon of salt, and sauté until chicken is just cooked through, about 4 minutes.

3 Remove from heat. Add remaining ¼ teaspoon salt, lemon zest, lemon juice, and black pepper to skillet, stirring to coat chicken. Add drained orzo with peas, mint, and feta cheese and toss gently to combine. Recipe can be served hot, at room temperature, or chilled.

STEP 1 *Add frozen peas to orzo for last 10 seconds of cooking to heat them through.*

STEP 2 *Cook chicken in skillet with sautéed shallots and garlic.*

STEP 3 *With the heat off, add feta cheese to orzo–chicken mixture in skillet.*

Round Out the Meal

Serve with arugula and sliced tomatoes sprinkled with cracked black pepper and extra-virgin olive oil. For dessert, try pineapple sorbet and sugar cookies.

Cook's Clue

Never rinse pasta after it has been cooked. It is unnecessary because the starch that remains on the surface of the pasta acts as a natural thickener once the sauce is added. Rinsing the pasta can cause it to stick together.

HEALTH HINT

Substituting beans or lentils for some of the pasta in a dish has the added benefit of providing low-fat protein, heart-protective vitamins and minerals, and dietary fiber. The soluble fiber found in beans and lentils helps reduce harmful LDL blood cholesterol levels.

Quinoa Pilaf with Cherries and Walnuts

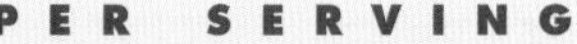

Grainlike quinoa (pronounced KEEN-wah) is not a grain at all, but the seed of a plant related to Swiss chard. This staple food of the ancient Incas was "rediscovered" in recent times. Today we know it as a real nutritional powerhouse—a super source of protein, potassium, magnesium, and iron.

PER SERVING

190 calories / 24% from fat

0.5 g saturated fat, 5 g total fat

0 mg cholesterol

300 mg sodium

31 g total carbohydrate

3 g dietary fiber

5 g protein

PREP TIME 10 min. | **COOK TIME 30 min.** | **SERVES 12**

- 2 teaspoons olive oil
- 1 large onion, finely chopped
- 2 cups quinoa
- 2 cups boiling water
- 1½ teaspoons salt
- 1 teaspoon black pepper
- ½ teaspoon thyme
- 1 cup dried cherries
- ½ cup walnuts, toasted and coarsely chopped

1 Heat oil in nonstick Dutch oven over medium heat. Add onion and cook, stirring frequently, until golden brown, about 7 minutes.

2 Meanwhile, place quinoa in large ungreased skillet over medium heat and cook, stirring often, until lightly toasted, about 5 minutes.

3 Add quinoa to onion in Dutch oven. Stir in boiling water, salt, black pepper, and thyme. Return to a boil, cover, and gently boil 10 minutes. Uncover and cook, stirring occasionally, until liquid has been absorbed and quinoa is tender, 10 to 12 minutes.

4 Remove from heat and stir in cherries and walnuts. Serve hot, at room temperature, or chilled.

STEP 1 *Cook onions in Dutch oven until golden brown.*

STEP 2 *Toast quinoa in skillet, stirring often for even color.*

STEP 4 *After quinoa is cooked, add cherries and walnuts.*

Round Out the Meal

Serve as a side dish with roast turkey breast and arugula salad. For dessert, try vanilla frozen yogurt topped with shaved chocolate.

Cook's Clue

To turn this side dish into a meaty meal, just add some leftover shredded chicken breast, strips of roast pork tenderloin, or cubes of cooked lean beef.

HEALTH HINT

High-protein quinoa is full of substances that keep you in good shape. When plant protein replaces protein from animal foods high in saturated fat, studies show that dangerous LDL ("bad") cholesterol levels are diminished. In quinoa, this heart-healthy effect may be amplified by substantial amounts of cholesterol-lowering substances called saponins.

secret to success

Because of quinoa's high oil content, always store it in the refrigerator. Before cooking, rinse thoroughly since it has a bitter and soapy flavor.

Barley Pilaf with Herbs

If you've ever made the classic Italian dish risotto, you know that stirring rice frequently as it cooks produces a smooth, creamy texture rather than fluffy, separate kernels. You can also use this method to cook barley, creating a similar dish high in cholesterol-cutting soluble fiber, so it's healthier for your heart.

PER SERVING

153 calories / 24% from fat
1 g saturated fat, 4 g total fat
7 mg cholesterol
538 mg sodium
25 g total carbohydrate
5 g dietary fiber
6 g protein

PREP TIME 10 min. | COOK TIME 55 min. | SERVES 6

- 2 teaspoons olive oil
- 2 slices turkey bacon, coarsely chopped
- 1 medium onion, finely chopped
- 3 garlic cloves, minced
- 2 carrots, thinly sliced
- ¾ cup pearled barley
- 1 teaspoon salt
- ¾ teaspoon rubbed sage
- ¾ teaspoon thyme
- 3¼ cups water
- 1 teaspoon slivered lemon zest
- ¾ teaspoon black pepper
- ¼ cup grated Parmesan cheese

secret to success

Always keep an eye on bacon as it's frying—it burns quickly! Older bacon burns about twice as fast as fresh bacon.

1 Heat oil in medium saucepan over medium heat. Add bacon and cook for 2 minutes. Add onion and garlic to pan, and cook until onion is tender and golden brown, about 5 minutes.

2 Add carrots to pan and cook until tender, about 5 minutes.

3 Add barley, stirring to combine. Add salt, sage, thyme, and water to pan and bring to a boil. Reduce to a simmer and cook, stirring frequently, until barley is tender, about 45 minutes.

4 Stir in lemon zest, black pepper, and Parmesan until evenly combined.

HEALTH HINT

Along with heart-healthy fiber, barley also has lignans, phytochemicals that help lower cholesterol. Other phytochemicals in barley, plant sterols, may also assist in reducing total and LDL ("bad") cholesterol levels. In addition, the cardioprotective antioxidant mineral selenium is plentiful in barley, and it teams with vitamin E to shield your heart from damage caused by free radicals.

Cook's Clue

Barley comes in different forms, including pearl or pearled (hulled, but with the bran layer intact) and scotch, or "pot" barley, which has some bran removed. There is also quick-cooking or instant barley, which has the same nutritional value as pearl barley but is presteamed so it cooks faster. If you use it here, check the package for the amount of water required.

STEP 2 *Add sliced carrots to browned onions and bacon.*

STEP 3 *Add barley to cooked vegetables and stir to coat.*

STEP 4 *When barley is tender, stir in lemon zest and Parmesan.*

Golden Risotto with Peas

Risotto—the crowning glory of all rice cookery—is conjured up from Italian Arborio rice, broth, and Parmesan cheese. The rice, stirred as it cooks, yields its starch to the hot broth, turning tender and creamy. Risotto Milanese, the most famous version of the dish, is tinted with saffron, but here, carrot juice contributes color and a helping of health-promoting beta-carotene.

PER SERVING

237 calories / 15% from fat
2 g saturated fat, 4 g total fat
8 mg cholesterol
635 mg sodium
38 g total carbohydrate
2 g dietary fiber
9 g protein

PREP TIME 10 min.	COOK TIME 45 min.	SERVES 6

- 2 teaspoons olive oil
- 1 small onion, finely chopped
- 1 garlic clove, minced
- 1 cup Arborio rice
- 1 cup carrot juice
- 2½ cups reduced-sodium, fat-free chicken broth
- 1 teaspoon salt
- ½ teaspoon black pepper
- 1 cup frozen peas
- ½ cup grated Parmesan cheese

1 Heat oil in a medium nonstick saucepan over low heat. Add onion and garlic and cook until onion is tender, about 7 minutes. Add rice, stirring to coat.

2 Add ½ cup carrot juice and cook, stirring frequently, until liquid has been absorbed, 2 to 3 minutes. Add remaining ½ cup carrot juice and cook, stirring frequently, until liquid has been absorbed, about 5 minutes.

3 Continue cooking, adding 2 cups chicken broth, ½ cup at a time, stirring after each addition until liquid has been absorbed, about 20 minutes total.

4 Add remaining ½ cup broth, salt, black pepper, and peas and cook, stirring, until rice is tender and creamy, about 8 minutes. Remove from heat and stir in Parmesan.

Round Out the Meal

Serve with thin slices of deli ham and beefsteak tomato sprinkled with shredded fresh basil and balsamic vinegar. For dessert, offer fresh figs.

STEP 2 *Add carrot juice to rice, ½ cup at a time.*

STEP 3 *Also add broth, ½ cup at a time. This allows rice to gradually swell and absorb liquids.*

STEP 4 *Off heat, stir in Parmesan. The residual heat of the rice will melt the cheese.*

secret to success

Frozen green peas hold their color, flavor, and nutrients better than canned and have less sodium. To keep the flavor, add a teaspoon of sugar to the water.

HEALTH HINT

If you have access to fresh carrot juice from a health-food store or juice bar, use it in this recipe because it maintains more of the carrot's nutritional benefits than canned or bottled juice.

Cook's Clue

Arborio is a short-grain (almost round) rice. It is one of several Italian-grown rices traditionally used for risotto. Because risotto rices are starchy and absorb up to five times their weight in liquid as they cook, they produce a very creamy dish.

Linguine with No-Cook Sauce

Of the hundreds of ways to dress linguine, this quick and easy sauce is bound to become the most requested pasta topper in your house. Bursting with fresh-from-the-garden flavor, it's full of tomatoes and olive oil—foods that keep your heart pumping strong.

PER SERVING

545 calories / 30% from fat

3 g saturated fat, 18 g total fat

5 mg cholesterol

447 mg sodium

81 g total carbohydrate

7 g dietary fiber

17 g protein

PREP TIME 20 min. + standing | COOK TIME 12 min. | SERVES 4

- 3 pounds plum tomatoes, seeded and chopped
- ⅔ cup chopped fresh basil
- ¼ cup extra-virgin olive oil
- ¼ cup chopped flat-leaf parsley
- 2 tablespoons chopped fresh mint
- 2 teaspoons grated orange zest
- 3 garlic cloves, minced
- ½ teaspoon salt
- ½ teaspoon black pepper
- 12 ounces linguine
- ¼ cup Parmesan cheese

1 Mix tomatoes, basil, oil, parsley, mint, orange zest, garlic, salt, and black pepper in bowl. Let stand at least 30 minutes or up to 2 hours at room temperature.

2 Cook pasta according to package directions. Drain well and put into a large pasta bowl. Top with sauce and sprinkle with Parmesan.

Round Out the Meal

Serve this dish on a sultry summer evening with a simple green salad, low-fat balsamic dressing, and a slice of Italian bread.

way back when... Over the centuries, the tomato has been called a variety of names: the Peruvian apple or acacia apple in Spain, the love apple in southern France, and the golden apple in Italy, because the first varieties seen there were yellow. Until the mid-19th century, tomatoes were cooked cautiously and eaten sparingly. In America, Eliza Leslie, in her *Directions for Cookery* (1848), advised readers to cook tomatoes at least three hours so they would lose their raw taste.

(*Source:* The Encyclopedia of American Food and Drink, by John F. Mariani, Lebhar-Friedman Books, NY, 1999)

HEALTH HINT

The fresh tomatoes in this dish supply more than a full day's requirement of vitamin C in each serving. Vitamin C helps form the protein collagen, which gives structure to bones, cartilage, muscle, and blood vessels; helps maintain capillaries, bones, and teeth; and aids in the absorption of iron. Serving tomatoes (and all fruits and vegetables) raw preserves their vitamin C content.

How to Seed a Tomato

Halve tomatoes lengthwise.

Scrape out seeds with the tip of a small spoon. Discard seeds.

Angel Hair Pasta with Basil-and-Walnut Pesto

In the Italian seaport of Genoa, pesto is made the classic way—from basil, pine nuts, two cheeses, and lots of oil. But this recipe adds the extra health boost of spinach and the peppery surprise of arugula. And in true heart-healthy style, it skimps on the oil, but not the flavor. Buon appetito!

PER SERVING

446 calories / 24% from fat

2 g saturated fat, 12 g total fat

3 mg cholesterol

673 mg sodium

70 g total carbohydrate

4 g dietary fiber

15 g protein

PREP TIME 15 min. | **COOK TIME 9 min.** | **SERVES 4**

- 4 ounces fresh basil leaves (2 cups)
- 4 ounces trimmed fresh spinach (2 cups)
- 2 ounces trimmed fresh arugula (1 cup)
- ⅓ cup walnut pieces
- 3 tablespoons grated Parmesan cheese
- 3 garlic cloves, peeled
- 1 teaspoon salt
- 1 tablespoon olive oil
- 12 ounces angel hair pasta (capellini)
- Fresh basil sprigs
- 1 large lemon, halved

1 Put basil, spinach, and arugula in colander. Wash with cold running water. Shake to dry. Transfer to food processor.

2 Add walnuts, Parmesan, garlic, and salt and pulse until finely chopped. With machine running, slowly drizzle oil through feed tube, processing until thick.

3 Meanwhile, cook pasta according to package directions; drain. Toss pasta with pesto in large serving bowl until evenly coated. Garnish with basil sprigs. Squeeze lemon juice over pasta.

secret to success

Classic pesto uses ½ cup of oil and 10 tablespoons of cheese (Parmesan and Pecorino Romano), to 2 cups of basil or greens. This rendition triples the greens and uses only 3 tablespoons of cheese and just a tablespoon of oil.

HEALTH HINT

Walnuts are a great source of omega-3 essential fatty acids, and it doesn't take a giant serving to gain the health benefits. They are especially healthy for your heart.

Cook's Clue

Take a tip from the Italians, who really know their pasta! Never add pasta to boiling water until everyone's nearly ready to eat. That avoids the dreaded state of *scotta,* or overcooked pasta—definitely not acceptable in a respectable Italian household. Whether you're cooking fresh or dried pasta, read the package directions (cooking times differ greatly). Start timing *after* you've added the pasta and the water has returned to a rolling boil.

STEP 1 *Shake washed basil, spinach, and arugula in colander to dry thoroughly.*

STEP 2 *With processor running, drizzle 1 tablespoon oil through feed tube.*

STEP 3 *Squeeze lemon over pasta right before serving.*

Fusilli and Meatballs

Hearty, healthy, and everyone's favorite Italian dish—don't you want pasta and meatballs for dinner tonight? Unlike traditional recipes, these meatballs are low in fat, yet they're full of the terrific taste you crave. Long curls of pasta add a fun twist. For a casual supper with friends, just double or triple the recipe.

PER SERVING

412 calories / 13% from fat

2 g saturated fat, 6 g total fat

69 mg cholesterol

331 mg sodium

61 g total carbohydrate

5 g dietary fiber

28 g protein

PREP TIME 30 min.	COOK TIME 1 hr. 20 min.	SERVES 6

- 1 large onion, chopped
- 2 garlic cloves, minced
- 1 can (28 ounces) no-salt-added Italian tomatoes
- 1 can (28 ounces) no-salt-added whole tomatoes in puree
- ¼ cup chopped fresh basil
- 1 tablespoon fresh oregano or 1 teaspoon dried
- 2 slices firm-textured white bread
- 1 pound lean (93%) ground beef
- 1 large egg
- 2 tablespoons reduced-fat milk (2%)
- ½ teaspoon salt
- ½ teaspoon black pepper
- 12 ounces long fusilli

1 Coat large saucepan with nonstick cooking spray and set over medium-high heat. Sauté onion and garlic until soft, about 5 minutes. Transfer 2 tablespoons onion mixture to large bowl.

2 Process Italian and whole tomatoes in food processor until fairly smooth. Add to saucepan. Bring to a boil over medium-high heat. Reduce heat to medium-low. Cover and simmer, stirring often, 30 minutes. Add basil and oregano during the last 15 minutes.

3 Process bread until crumbs form. Add crumbs, beef, egg, milk, salt, and black pepper to onion mixture and mix just until blended. Shape into twenty 1-inch meatballs. Coat medium skillet with nonstick cooking spray and set over medium-high heat. Cook meatballs in batches until browned on all sides, about 8 minutes.

4 Drain on paper towels. Add meatballs to sauce. Cover and cook, stirring occasionally, 20 minutes.

5 Meanwhile, cook pasta according to package directions. Drain and toss with 1½ cups sauce in large heated serving bowl. Spoon 1 cup sauce over pasta. Serve meatballs and remaining sauce alongside.

STEP 3 *Turn meatballs frequently so they brown evenly.*

STEP 4 *Transfer meatballs to paper towels to soak up fat.*

STEP 5 *Toss fusilli with some sauce in bowl to flavor pasta.*

Cook's Clue

Fusilli means twisted spaghetti, and it has many culinary uses. Mix with different types of sauces, add to soups, or make into a salad.

HEALTH HINT

Lycopenes—phytochemicals closely related to beta-carotene—are natural cancer-fighting agents in tomatoes. Studies have shown that lycopene is best absorbed by the body if the tomatoes are cooked—as in tomato sauce.

secret to success

By making the meatballs with very lean ground beef, you can dive into this satisfying bowl of pasta without feeling any guilt.

Vegetable Fettuccine Alfredo

PER SERVING
540 calories / 17% from fat
4 g saturated fat, 10 g total fat
17 mg cholesterol
661 mg sodium
87 g total carbohydrate
7 g dietary fiber
24 g protein

When public-health watchdogs called fettuccine Alfredo a "heart attack on a plate," they weren't talking about this recipe. It delivers all the cheesy-rich flavor and creamy texture you'd expect from the classic, but it skimps on the fat. Toss in some fresh vegetables, and you've made a good-for-you Alfredo dish no one can refuse.

PREP TIME 10 min. | **COOK TIME 18 min.** | **SERVES 4**

- 12 ounces fettuccine
- 2 cups broccoli florets
- 8 ounces baby carrots, cut in half lengthwise
- 1 cup fresh or frozen green peas
- 1 large red bell pepper, seeded and cut into thin strips
- 1 tablespoon margarine
- 1 small garlic clove, minced
- 2 tablespoons all-purpose flour
- ½ teaspoon salt
- 1½ cups reduced-fat milk (2%)
- ½ cup nonfat half-and-half
- ½ cup freshly grated Parmesan cheese

1 Cook pasta according to package directions. Drain.

2 Meanwhile, cook broccoli and carrots in large saucepan of boiling water, 5 minutes. Add peas and red pepper and cook them 3 minutes longer. Drain and keep warm.

3 Melt margarine in medium saucepan over medium heat. Sauté garlic until golden, about 2 minutes. Whisk in flour and salt and cook until bubbling, about 2 minutes longer.

4 Gradually whisk in milk and half-and-half and bring to a boil. Reduce heat and simmer, whisking, until sauce thickens, 1 to 2 minutes.

5 Reduce heat to low. Stir in cheese until melted and smooth. Toss pasta, vegetables, and sauce in large serving bowl.

STEP 3 *Sauté garlic in melted margarine and whisk in flour.*

STEP 4 *Gradually whisk in milk and nonfat half-and-half, then whisk and cook till smooth and thickened.*

STEP 5 *Blend in cheese until melted.*

secret to success

Have you discovered nonfat half-and-half? It's an ideal stand-in for the heavy cream typically used in this dish. Lots of vegetables add a healthful dose of vitamins. The result? A rich and satisfying dish that keeps the fat content in check.

HEALTH HINT

The broccoli and red bell pepper make this dish exceptionally high in vitamin C, which strengthens blood-vessel walls and promotes the healing of wounds. Vitamin C also may help control blood cholesterol and prevent atherosclerosis.

living smart
FOR A HEALTHY HEART

FILL UP ON FIBER

High-fiber foods like oats, legumes (beans and peas), and myriad vegetables and fruits are rich in soluble fiber–the type that help lower blood cholesterol. Most nutrition experts recommend 25 to 30 grams each day. Not only will eating more fiber-rich foods help your heart and keep your blood sugar steady, but they are filling and low in calories, therefore great if you're watching your weight.

Sausage and Herb Lasagna

No need to shy away from lasagna just because you're eating heart smart! This recipe has plenty of everything you love: layers of creamy cheese, chunks of sausage in a savory sauce, and oodles of noodles. How can anything this luscious be good for your heart? Don't ask—just have another bite!

PER SERVING

381 calories / 23% from fat

5 g saturated fat, 10 g total fat

43 mg cholesterol

722 mg sodium

46 g total carbohydrate

4 g dietary fiber

29 g protein

PREP TIME 30 min. | COOK TIME 1 hr. + standing | SERVES 8

- 15 lasagna noodles (12 ounces)
- 1 container (15 ounces) 50%-less-fat ricotta cheese
- ⅓ cup freshly grated Parmesan cheese
- ½ cup chopped fresh basil
- ¼ cup fat-free egg substitute
- ¼ teaspoon black pepper
- 8 ounces lean sweet Italian turkey sausage, casings removed
- 3 medium onions, chopped
- 2 cans (14 ounces each) no-salt-added tomato sauce
- ½ teaspoon salt
- 1 package (8 ounces) 50%-less-fat shredded mozzarella cheese

1 Cook noodles according to package directions (or see Cook's Clue below). Drain, then cool in shallow pan of cold water for 5 minutes. Transfer noodles to wire rack set over paper towels. Blend ricotta, 2 tablespoons Parmesan, basil, egg substitute, and black pepper in bowl.

2 Cook sausage and onions in nonstick skillet over medium-high heat until sausage is cooked through, 7–10 minutes, breaking up sausage with spoon. Stir in 1½ cups of tomato sauce and salt.

3 Preheat oven to 350°F. Spread ½ cup tomato sauce in bottom of 13 x 9-inch baking dish. Layer lasagna: Set 3 noodles, side by side, in dish. Spread one-third ricotta mixture over noodles. Top with one-third sausage mixture and sprinkle with ½ cup mozzarella. Repeat layering twice.

4 Weave remaining 6 noodles in lattice pattern on top *(see photo at right)*, trimming them as necessary. Spread remaining tomato sauce over noodles, then top with remaining mozzarella and remaining Parmesan.

5 Loosely cover with foil. Bake 40 minutes. Remove foil and bake until mixture is bubbling around edges, about 20 minutes longer. Let stand 15 minutes before cutting.

STEP 1 *Place cooled lasagna noodles on wire rack to dry.*

STEP 3 *Layer noodles, ricotta mixture, sausage mixture, and then shredded mozzarella.*

STEP 4 *Alternately weave noodles in a lattice pattern.*

Cook's Clue

Don't waste time by cooking or boiling lasagna noodles before making your lasagna, and don't waste money buying the "No Bake" noodles. Simply cover every inch of the noodles with sauce while layering. The sauce actually helps cook the noodles while the lasagna bakes.

HEALTH HINT

Dairy products, including ricotta, Parmesan, and mozzarella cheeses, are high in calcium, magnesium, and potassium—minerals that help regulate blood pressure. High blood pressure (hypertension) is a risk factor for developing heart disease.

Orecchiette with Cannellini Beans and Arugula

"Mamma mia! *Pass the pasta again—I can't remember when it tasted so good!" There's good reason: This dish overflows with goodness and flavor—lots of arugula, tomatoes, and cannellini beans—tossed with little ear-shaped pasta called orecchiette. A sprinkling of Parmesan tops it off.*

PER SERVING

489 calories / 7% from fat

1 g saturated fat, 4 g total fat

4 mg cholesterol

826 mg sodium

91 g total carbohydrate

9 g dietary fiber

21 g protein

PREP TIME 10 min.	COOK TIME 18 min.	SERVES 4

- 12 ounces orecchiette pasta
- 8 ounces arugula
- 1 small carrot, grated
- 1 small red onion, chopped
- 3 garlic cloves, minced
- 1 can (28 ounces) plum tomatoes in puree
- 1 cup reduced-sodium chicken broth
- 1 can (15½ ounces) cannellini beans, rinsed and drained
- ¼ cup chopped basil
- ¼ cup grated Parmesan cheese
- ½ teaspoon salt
- ¼ cup seasoned dry bread crumbs

1 Cook pasta according to package directions. Drain and keep warm.

2 Meanwhile, wash arugula well, remove any tough stems, and tear into bite-size pieces. Lightly coat Dutch oven with nonstick cooking spray and place over medium-high heat. Sauté carrot, onion, and garlic until tender, about 5 minutes.

3 Add tomatoes in puree, broth, beans, 2 tablespoons basil, 2 tablespoons Parmesan, and salt. Simmer, uncovered, 5 minutes. Add arugula and cook until sauce is bubbling, about 4 minutes.

4 Mix in pasta and heat through, about 2 minutes. Transfer to pasta bowl. Sprinkle with bread crumbs and remaining Parmesan and basil.

Round Out the Meal

Serve with roasted peppers and breadsticks, and top off the meal with a fresh fruit salad.

STEP 2 *Remove stems from arugula, then tear leaves into bite-size pieces.*

STEP 3 *Stir arugula into tomato-bean mixture.*

STEP 4 *Mix in orecchiette until heated through.*

secret to success

For the best flavor, both cooks and connoisseurs suggest grating fresh Parmesan just before serving. Once grated, it makes a great addition to any pasta, sauce, soup, or bread. Be creative—it even adds great flavor to grapefruit, apples, mashed potatoes, asparagus, spinach salads, and much more.

HEALTH HINT

Eat pasta—it's good for your heart! Pasta is naturally high in complex carbohydrates, which become a storehouse of energy for the body. These carbohydrates break down slowly in the body, so they keep you going a long time. (No wonder pasta's the choice of athletes.) To get more fiber in your diet, look for whole-wheat versions of your favorite pasta shapes.

Cook's Clue

Experiment with other pastas: cavatappi (spirals), cavatelli (lip-shaped shells), farfalle (butterflies), radiatori (radiators), rotelle (wheels), and rotini (corkscrews).

Cincinnati Chili

A favorite pasta dish of Cincinnatians is "five-way" chili: thick spaghetti topped with beef chili, kidney beans, chopped onions, and finely shredded cheddar. Our lightened version is made with ground top round (rather than a fattier cut), colorful spinach linguine, and so many richly flavorful seasonings, we could skip the cheese.

PER SERVING

489 calories / 15% from fat
2 g saturated fat, 8 g total fat
51 mg cholesterol
929 mg sodium
73 g total carbohydrate
12 g dietary fiber
36 g protein

PREP TIME 15 min. | COOK TIME 25 min. | SERVES 4

- 2 teaspoons olive oil
- 2 large onions, finely chopped
- 3 garlic cloves, minced
- 8 ounces lean ground top round
- 2 tablespoons chili powder
- 1 teaspoon cinnamon
- 1½ cups canned tomatoes, chopped with their juice
- 1 can (15 ounces) red kidney beans, rinsed and drained
- ¼ cup water
- 3 tablespoons tomato paste
- 2 teaspoons brown sugar
- 2 teaspoons unsweetened cocoa powder
- ¾ teaspoon salt
- 8 ounces spinach linguine
- 4 scallions, thinly sliced

1 Heat oil over medium heat in large nonstick skillet. Add onions and garlic and cook, stirring frequently, until onions are golden brown, about 10 minutes.

2 Stir in beef, chili powder, and cinnamon, and cook, breaking up beef with spoon, until no longer pink, about 5 minutes.

3 Stir in tomatoes, beans, water, tomato paste, brown sugar, cocoa, and salt, and simmer until chili sauce is flavorful, about 10 minutes.

4 Meanwhile, in large pot of boiling water, cook pasta according to package directions. Drain and transfer pasta to large bowl. Add chili sauce and scallions and toss to combine.

Round Out the Meal

Serve with whole-wheat sourdough toasts and a crisp green salad. Offer oatmeal cookies and applesauce for dessert.

STEP 1 *Cook garlic and onions until browned and golden.*

STEP 2 *While cooking beef, break up clumps with a spoon.*

STEP 3 *Sprinkle cocoa powder evenly over chili ingredients in the skillet.*

way back when... There are several theories about the origins and inventor of chili. A Macedonian immigrant invented Cincinnati chili in 1922. His hot dog stand, "Empress" was the location where this dish originated. Using Middle Eastern spices, his concoction was a heap of spaghetti, covered in chili, onions, red kidney beans, and shredded cheese, served with oyster crackers. On the side, he served a hot dog with shredded cheese.

(Source: http://southernfood.about.com)

Cook's Clue

Because this chili is much milder than Texas-style (due to the combination of the sweet spices), adventurous chili lovers may mix in some cayenne pepper or hot sauce.

secret to success

It's doubtful that the folks who came up with this recipe in the 1920s were thinking, "Hmmm . . . let's cut fat and cholesterol and add fiber." Still, that's what they did when they added beans to this chili-based pasta sauce. It's a good idea to substitute beans for some of the meat in most any pasta sauce.

Baked Macaroni with Four Cheeses

Do you have fond childhood memories of creamy macaroni and cheese for supper? You can still enjoy it, thanks to this version that's low in fat but still high in flavor. This cheesy pleaser is even a few steps up on the sophistication scale, but it still retains the warm, comfy feeling of the original.

PER SERVING

484 calories / 15% from fat

5 g saturated fat, 8 g total fat

25 mg cholesterol

669 mg sodium

62 g total carbohydrate

2 g dietary fiber

29 g protein

PREP TIME 20 min. | **COOK TIME 50 min.** | **SERVES 8**

- 1 pound elbow macaroni
- 2 large onions, chopped
- 4 cups nonfat half-and-half
- ¼ cup all-purpose flour
- 2 teaspoons dry mustard
- ¼ teaspoon salt
- ½ teaspoon black pepper
- 2 cups shredded reduced-fat cheddar cheese (8 ounces)
- 1½ cups shredded part-skim mozzarella cheese (6 ounces)
- ½ cup shredded reduced-fat Monterey Jack cheese (2 ounces)
- 8 ounces fat-free cream cheese
- 1½ teaspoons paprika

1 Preheat oven to 350°F. Lightly coat 13 x 9-inch baking dish with nonstick cooking spray. Cook macaroni according to package directions; drain and set aside.

2 Meanwhile, coat large saucepan with cooking spray and set over medium-high heat. Sauté onions until soft, about 5 minutes. Put ½ cup half-and-half and flour into jar with tight-fitting lid and shake until blended and smooth. Stir into onions in skillet, then blend in remaining half-and-half. Whisk in dry mustard, salt, and black pepper and bring to a simmer. Continue cooking, whisking constantly, until mixture thickens, about 3 minutes.

3 Add cheddar, mozzarella, Monterey Jack, and cream cheese. Cook, stirring, until cheeses melt. Remove from heat and fold in macaroni.

4 Spoon mixture into baking dish and sprinkle with paprika. Bake until bubbly and lightly browned, about 35 minutes.

STEP 2 *Whisk dry mustard, salt, and pepper into half-and-half in large saucepan.*

STEP 3 *Fold in macaroni (with pot off heat).*

STEP 4 *Spoon macaroni evenly into baking dish.*

Round Out the Meal

Start off with a Mesclun salad with plum tomatoes, a few capers, and a sprig of mint, topped with a light lemon poppyseed dressing. For dessert, enjoy cantaloupe boats topped with fresh raspberries, drizzled with honey.

HEALTH HINT

The mineral calcium helps control high blood pressure—a risk factor for heart disease. Dairy products are a great source of calcium, but they can be high in fat. In this recipe, reduced-fat and fat-free cheeses plus fat-free half-and-half deliver plenty of this bone-building mineral, while keeping fat in check.

Cook's Clue

Since cheese flavors come in a variety of strengths and macaroni and cheese requires a great amount of cheese, most recipes suggest using milder flavors like cheddar or American cheese. Experiment with amount, combinations, and flavors to find your perfect taste.

Cold Sesame Noodles and Vegetables

A longtime favorite at Chinese restaurants, cold sesame noodles make a great side dish (double the portions for a main dish). We've replaced hard-to-find Chinese sesame paste with peanut butter and sesame oil. Whole-wheat noodles and shreds of colorful vegetables make it healthier for your heart.

PER SERVING

200 calories / 25% from fat
1 g saturated fat, 5.5 g total fat
0 mg cholesterol
422 mg sodium
33 g total carbohydrate
6 g dietary fiber
7 g protein

PREP TIME 15 min.	COOK TIME 1 min. + chilling	SERVES 6

- 8 ounces whole-wheat linguine
- ⅓ cup cilantro leaves
- 2 tablespoons peanut butter
- 2 tablespoons reduced-sodium soy sauce
- 2½ teaspoons honey
- 1 tablespoon rice vinegar or cider vinegar
- 1 tablespoon dark sesame oil
- 2 garlic cloves, peeled
- ½ teaspoon salt
- ¼ teaspoon cayenne pepper
- 2 carrots, slivered
- 1 red bell pepper, seeded and slivered
- 1 large stalk celery, slivered
- 2 scallions, slivered

1 Cook linguine in large pot of boiling water according to package directions. Drain, reserving ½ cup cooking water.

2 Meanwhile, combine cilantro, peanut butter, soy sauce, honey, vinegar, sesame oil, garlic, salt, and cayenne pepper in food processor. Puree. Transfer to large bowl.

3 Whisk in reserved pasta cooking water. Add linguine, carrots, bell pepper, celery, and scallions. Toss. Chill at least 1 hour before serving.

Round Out the Meal

Serve alongside grilled turkey burgers. For dessert, try chilled orange slices sprinkled with slivered almonds.

HEALTH HINT

Add vegetables to a pasta or noodle dish whenever possible. It's an easy way to get your five daily servings of vegetables that furnish disease-fighting phytonutrients and an array of heart-healthy benefits. In addition, vegetables add flavor to the recipe without raising the calorie count all that much.

secret to success

The pasta cooking water, which carries some of the pasta's starch, is used here to "stretch" the sauce. This traditional Italian technique for thinning or smoothing a sauce coats the noodles better. And the water replaces what might otherwise be a lot more fat.

living smart
FOR A HEALTHY HEART

GO WITH THE GRAIN

Health experts say to aim for at least three servings of whole-grain foods each day. Studies show that it has many health benefits. Substitute whole-wheat pasta for regular (or use half regular and half whole wheat). Experiment with interesting grains as side dishes in place of rice and pasta, such as quinoa, barley, buckwheat, or wheatberries.

How to Sliver Celery

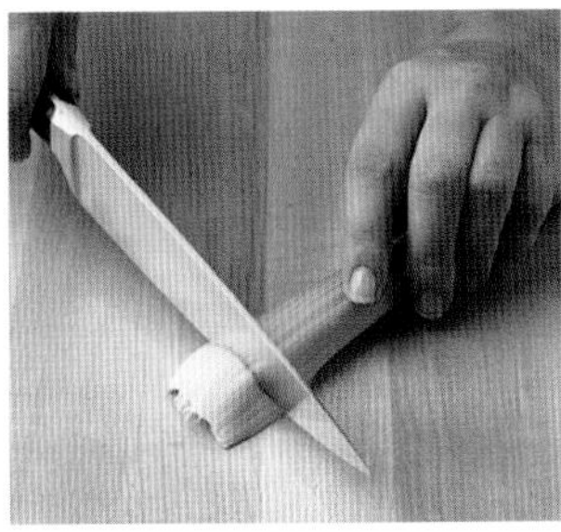

Trim thick white ends from celery stalks.

Cut stalk crosswise into even lengths.

Cut each celery piece into thin slices, then sliver the slices.

Turkey Tetrazzini

Pasta dishes tend to fall into two categories: with tomato sauce or without. Turkey tetrazzini, an all-American favorite, is of the "no-tomato-sauce" type. This noodle, mushroom, and turkey casserole features a creamy, reduced-fat white sauce, with the inspired seasonings of cayenne pepper and nutmeg.

PER SERVING

483 calories / 17% from fat

4 g saturated fat, 9 g total fat

60 mg cholesterol

806 mg sodium

62 g total carbohydrate

3 g dietary fiber

36 g protein

PREP TIME 15 min. | COOK TIME 30 min. | SERVES 4

- 10 ounces fettuccine
- 2 teaspoons olive oil
- 4 scallions, thinly sliced
- 8 ounces mushrooms, thinly sliced
- 2 tablespoons flour
- 1½ cups fat-free half-and-half
- ¾ teaspoon salt
- ¼ teaspoon cayenne pepper
- ⅛ teaspoon nutmeg
- ⅔ cup grated Parmesan cheese
- 8 ounces cooked turkey breast, shredded

1 Preheat oven to 400°F. Cook pasta in large pot of boiling water according to package directions. Drain.

2 Meanwhile, heat oil in large saucepan over medium heat. Add scallions and cook until softened, about 1 minute. Add mushrooms and cook, stirring frequently until tender, about 5 minutes.

3 Add flour to pan and cook, stirring, until mushrooms are evenly coated, about 2 minutes. Add half-and-half, salt, cayenne, and nutmeg to pan and bring to a boil. Reduce to a simmer and cook until slightly thickened, about 5 minutes. Stir in ⅓ cup Parmesan, the pasta, and turkey.

4 Transfer to 7 x 11-inch baking dish. Sprinkle remaining ⅓ cup Parmesan on top. Bake until bubbling and crusty, about 10 minutes.

STEP 3 *Sprinkle cayenne pepper over stew ingredients before stirring it in.*

STEP 4 *Evenly distribute Parmesan cheese over the tetrazzini mixture in baking pan.*

Round Out the Meal

Serve with steamed artichokes, mixed greens salad, and orange segments with red plum slices for dessert.

living smart
FOR A HEALTHY HEART

SPOTLIGHT ON OLIVE OIL

Olive oil is just as versatile as butter or margarine and is better for your health because it contains heart-friendly phytochemicals and monounsaturated fats thought to lower blood levels of LDL cholesterol. Each type of olive oil has its own flavor, but all are equally healthful. Use strongly flavored "extra-virgin" varieties as bread spreads and in salad dressings; regular olive oil for sautéing and broiling meat, poultry, fish or vegetables; and "light" or "extra light" for baking.

HEALTH HINT

Using reduced-fat and fat-free dairy products is key to heart-healthy eating. Take the fat-free half-and-half in this recipe, for example: The same amount of regular half-and-half would add 42 grams of fat, more than 10 grams per serving.

Fish and Shellfish

Shrimp and Vegetable Stir-Fry

PER SERVING

266 calories / 20% from fat

1 g saturated fat, 6 g total fat

172 mg cholesterol

992 mg sodium

23 g total carbohydrate

4 g dietary fiber

29 g protein

A simple skillet supper that's ready in 30 minutes! Fresh shrimp, crisp-yet-tender veggies, a hint of soy, and the zing of ginger—all at only 20 percent of calories from fat. Stir-frying is quick, so it limits nutrient loss. Fast food that's healthful, too—a winning combination!

PREP TIME 20 min. | **COOK TIME 10 min.** | **SERVES 4**

- ⅓ cup light soy sauce
- 3 tablespoons white wine or orange juice
- 2 tablespoons cornstarch
- 1½ teaspoons grated peeled fresh ginger
- 1 tablespoon vegetable oil
- 2 garlic cloves, minced
- 1 pound large shrimp, peeled and deveined
- 4 cups fresh broccoli florets
- 1 large red bell pepper, seeded and cut into strips
- 1 large yellow bell pepper, seeded and cut into strips
- 4 ounces snow peas
- ½ cup drained whole baby corn
- ½ cup sliced water chestnuts
- 4 scallions, cut diagonally into 2-inch pieces

1 Blend ⅔ cup water, soy sauce, wine, cornstarch, and ginger in small bowl until smooth. Set aside.

2 Heat oil in large wok or large deep skillet over medium-high heat until hot. Stir-fry garlic until soft, about 2 minutes. Add shrimp and stir-fry until pink, about 3 minutes. Remove shrimp with a slotted spoon and set aside. Add broccoli to wok and stir-fry until bright green, about 2 minutes. Add red and yellow peppers and snow peas and stir-fry until crisp-tender, about 1 minute longer.

3 Return shrimp to wok. Add corn, water chestnuts, and scallions. Pour in sauce mixture and stir-fry until sauce thickens and boils, about 1 minute.

secret to success

To select fresh shrimp, make sure the bodies are firm and attached to their shells. Black spots indicate that the flesh has begun breaking down. Shells should not be yellow or gritty, as this indicates that chemicals have been used to bleach them. Good quality shrimp should smell of saltwater. If possible, buy shrimp on display instead of prepackaged.

HEALTH HINT

Although shrimp is high in cholesterol, it appears to have little effect on the actual levels circulating in the bloodstream. This may be because shrimp is low in saturated fat, which is more likely to raise blood cholesterol than dietary cholesterol itself. Ounce per ounce, shrimp and other shellfish contain fewer calories than most other animal proteins.

Round Out the Meal

Serve the stir-fry on brown or white rice, and finish the meal with fresh orange sections and a fortune cookie.

Cleaning Shrimp

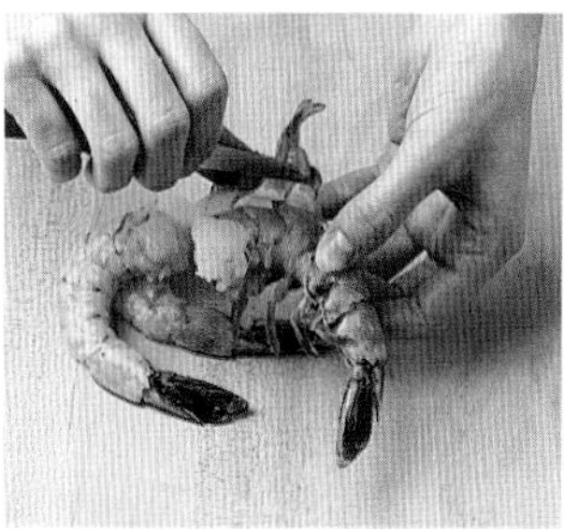

Use a paring knife to peel away shrimp shell and remove legs.

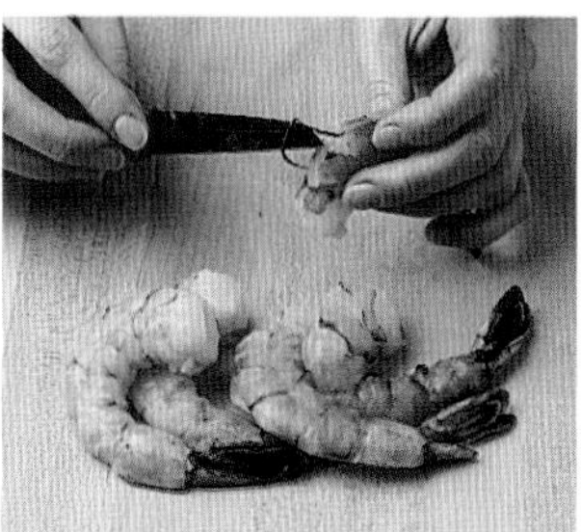

Slit the outside curved edge of shrimp. Lift out dark vein.

Don't overcook shrimp: stir-fry until just opaque and pink.

Cook's Clue

Stir-frying is an ideal method for cooking shrimp. If cooked too long or at too high a temperature, shrimp becomes unpleasantly dry and tough.

Beer-Battered Shrimp

Do you crave the puffy, golden shrimp that star at those all-you-can-eat Friday night buffets? Believe it or not, you can enjoy them occasionally and still do your heart—and waistline—good. The slimming secrets? Whip up a light batter spiced just right, and forget deep-fat frying—sautéing with a fraction of the fat works just as well.

PER SERVING

376 calories / 23% from fat
1.5 g saturated fat, 9.5 g total fat
173 mg cholesterol
680 mg sodium
38 g total carbohydrate
1 g dietary fiber
29 g protein

PREP TIME 30 min. | **COOK TIME 25 min.** | **SERVES 6**

- 1½ pounds large shrimp
- ½ cup fresh lemon juice
- 4 teaspoons Old Bay seasoning
- 2 cups all-purpose flour
- 12 ounces beer (regular or nonalcoholic), room temperature
- 2 scallions, finely chopped
- 2 tablespoons finely chopped parsley
- 3 large egg whites
- Pinch of salt
- 3 tablespoons vegetable oil

1 Peel and devein shrimp, leaving tails on. Mix lemon juice and 1 teaspoon Old Bay seasoning in medium bowl. Add shrimp, tossing to coat, then refrigerate while making batter.

2 Combine flour and remaining Old Bay seasoning in large bowl. Gradually whisk in beer until smooth, then stir in scallions and parsley. Beat egg whites and salt in medium bowl until stiff peaks form. Fold into flour mixture.

3 Preheat oven to 250°F. Set wire cooling rack on baking sheet and place in oven. Heat 2 tablespoons oil in large nonstick skillet over medium-high heat until hot but not smoking.

4 One at a time, dip shrimp into batter, letting excess batter drip off.

5 Slip shrimp into oil. Cook until puffed and golden, about 2 minutes on each side. Transfer shrimp to rack in oven as they are done. Cook remaining shrimp, adding more oil to skillet if necessary.

STEP 1 *Choose large, fresh shrimp. Peel, leaving tails on.*

STEP 4 *Dip shrimp into batter, letting excess drip away.*

STEP 5 *Sauté, turning with tongs—don't crowd the skillet!*

secret to success

Instead of deep-frying shrimp, sauté them in just a few tablespoons of oil. They'll turn out golden, crispy, and crunchy, with much less fat per bite.

HEALTH HINT

Shrimp provide vitamins B_6, B_{12}, and E and niacin. They are a fair source of iron and contain the trace mineral copper, which helps keep your immune system working optimally.

way back when... Babylonian king Hammurabi established a law requiring a daily beer ration, which was dependent on the social rank of individuals. In ancient times, it was exchanged for barley. Beer brewing was a woman's job, and it was taken seriously. Hammurabi had one woman drowned because she accepted silver for her beer. The same punishment applied for serving poor quality beer.

(Source: www.eat-online.net)

Cook's Clue

To tell when shrimp is done, cut into one. It should be opaque throughout. Don't overcook, or it will become dry, tough, and flavorless.

Shrimp Scampi

Ever wondered how some people can give great dinner parties on short notice? They have a secret: fast, "fancy" dishes they've long since mastered. Cook scampi a few times, and you'll have it down pat. Your dazzled guests won't guess (unless you tell them) that you've made the dish heart friendly by leaving out the quarter-cup of butter normally added to the sauce.

PER SERVING

145 calories / 25% from fat

1 g saturated fat, 4 g total fat

173 mg cholesterol

473 mg sodium

3 g total carbohydrate

0 g dietary fiber

23 g protein

PREP TIME 20 min.	COOK TIME 10 min.	SERVES 6

- 1½ pounds large shrimp
- 2 teaspoons olive oil
- 3 garlic cloves, minced
- ⅔ cup bottled clam juice or chicken broth
- 3 tablespoons fresh lemon juice
- ½ teaspoon salt
- ⅛ teaspoon crushed red pepper flakes
- 1 teaspoon cornstarch blended with 1 tablespoon water
- ¼ cup chopped parsley

1 Shell the shrimp (*see photos, right*). If you wish to devein, make a shallow cut along the back of each shrimp and remove the black vein.

2 In very large nonstick skillet, add oil and heat over medium heat. Add garlic and cook until tender, about 2 minutes.

3 Add shrimp and cook, stirring frequently, until almost cooked through, about 3 minutes. Add clam juice, lemon juice, salt, and red pepper flakes and bring to a boil. Cook until shrimp are opaque throughout, about 1 minute.

4 With slotted spoon, transfer shrimp to serving plates. Bring liquid in skillet to a boil, stir in cornstarch mixture and cook, stirring, until sauce is lightly thickened, about 1 minute. Stir in parsley and spoon sauce over shrimp.

Round Out the Meal

Serve with rice, steamed asparagus, and pineapple upside-down cake for dessert.

HEALTH HINT

Bottled clam juice has a significant quantity of vitamin B_{12}, which protects your heart by helping lower levels of homocysteine, a substance that may clog arteries and contribute to heart disease. Shrimp provide an exceptional amount of the mineral selenium, which works as a powerful antioxidant to keep your heart in top shape.

living smart

FOR A HEALTHY HEART

Shrimp are a good choice for your diet. Not only are shrimp rich in heart-healthy omega-3 fatty acids, but they are also low in saturated fat (especially when compared with other sources of animal protein, such as steak). Saturated fat is actually more of a risk than dietary cholesterol.

How to Shell Shrimp

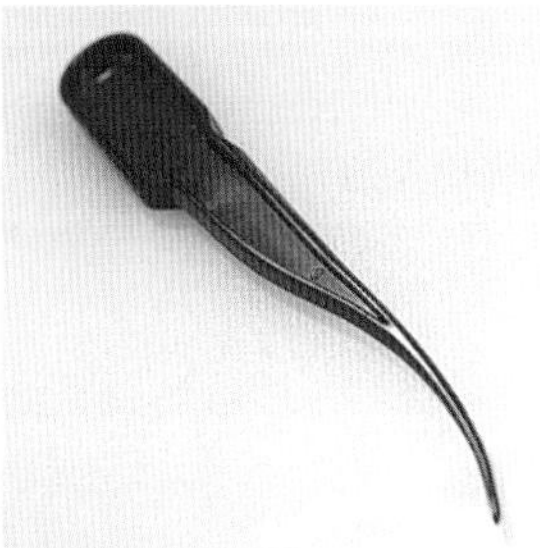

Shrimp-shellers come in a variety of sizes and designs, but all share one feature: One end is pointed and narrow, and the device widens out toward the handle.

To shell the shrimp, insert the pointed end in the space between the shell and the vein that runs down the back of the shrimp.

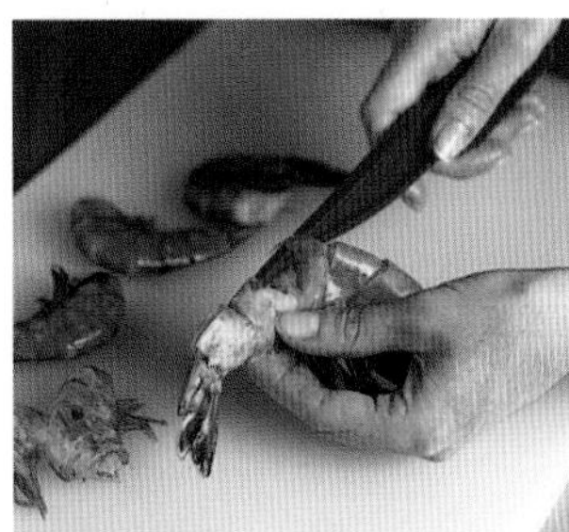

Push the tool toward the tail of the shrimp, following the vein line. When the wider part of the tool is pushed in, it breaks the shrimp shell and pulls it off.

Cajun Shrimp and Crab Jambalaya

Jambalaya, crawfish pie, or filé gumbo—it's time for supper, Cajun style! This recipe brings home many favorites from the bayou country—from fresh-caught shrimp and crab to the toasty roux that flavors it all. Stir up a double recipe for friends, and serve it straight from the skillet, the down-home way.

PER SERVING

363 calories / 15% from fat

1 g saturated fat, 6 g total fat

152 mg cholesterol

687 mg sodium

45 g total carbohydrate

2 g dietary fiber

30 g protein

PREP TIME 20 min. | COOK TIME 42 min. + standing | SERVES 6

- 1 tablespoon vegetable oil
- 2 tablespoons all-purpose flour
- 2 medium onions, chopped
- 1 large green bell pepper, seeded and chopped
- 1 celery stalk, chopped
- 3 ounces Canadian bacon, chopped
- 1 can (28 ounces) chopped tomatoes in puree
- 1 can (14 ounces) reduced-sodium chicken broth
- 1½ cups long-grain white rice
- 2 teaspoons Old Bay seasoning
- 1 pound large shrimp, peeled and deveined
- 8 ounces lump crabmeat, picked through
- 2 tablespoons chopped fresh cilantro

1 Lightly coat a large heavy skillet with nonstick cooking spray and set over medium heat. (Cast iron does not need spray.) Add oil and flour, and stir constantly until roux turns a deep mahogany brown, about 5 minutes. Add onions, green pepper, celery, and bacon; sauté until vegetables are soft, about 5 minutes longer.

2 Stir in tomatoes in puree, broth, rice, and Old Bay seasoning; bring to a boil over high heat. Reduce heat to medium-low, cover, and simmer until most of liquid is absorbed and rice is almost tender, about 20 minutes. Fold in shrimp and cook just until shrimp are pink and firm, about 5 minutes.

3 Gently fold in crab; cover and cook 1 minute. Remove from heat and let stand 3 minutes. Sprinkle with cilantro.

way back when... Most historians believe *jambalaya* comes from *jamon*, the Spanish word for ham. Others say it was created in a New Orleans inn. The owner asked his cook, Jean, to *balayez*, or mix some things together in the Louisiana Acadian dialect. Jean's concoction, named "Jean Balayez," is known as jambalaya today.

(Source: The Encyclopedia of American Food and Drink, *by John F. Mariani, Lebhar-Friedman Books, NY, 1999)*

Cook's Clue

When boiling or steaming shrimp, if it curls to make the letter C, it is cooked to completion; if it curls to form the letter O, it is overdone. Once cooked, it should be firm, pink, and opaque. If you're still in doubt, hold it upside down and pull the tail down. If cooked, it will spring back up, if not, it won't.

STEP 1 *Cook oil and flour, stirring constantly until roux turns a deep mahogany brown.*

STEP 2 *Add tomatoes to sautéed vegetables in roux.*

STEP 3 *Stir in crabmeat and cover skillet.*

secret to success

Substitute Canadian bacon for the high-fat chorizo sausage traditionally used in jambalaya. You'll have a typically Cajun-flavored dish while still keeping the fat in check.

Chesapeake Crab Cakes

Fishing for the crispy goodness of fried seafood but not the grease? You've hooked a winner! These crab cakes are rich in vitamins like A and B_6 as well as minerals like zinc, iron, and magnesium. A treat for your taste buds and your heart! To make in advance, brown the cakes, drain, cover, and refrigerate for up to 8 hours before baking.

PER SERVING

208 calories / 22% from fat
1 g saturated fat, 5 g total fat
68 mg cholesterol
683 mg sodium
16 g total carbohydrate
1 g dietary fiber
24 g protein

PREP TIME 14 min. | **COOK TIME 16 min.** | **SERVES 4**

- ½ cup fresh bread crumbs
- 1 celery stalk with leaves, finely chopped
- ⅓ cup finely chopped and seeded red bell pepper
- 2 tablespoons minced shallot
- 2 tablespoons finely chopped parsley
- 2 tablespoons coarse Dijon mustard
- 2 tablespoons low-fat mayonnaise
- 2 large egg whites
- 1 teaspoon Old Bay seasoning
- 1 pound lump crabmeat, picked through
- ⅓ cup all-purpose flour
- 2 teaspoons vegetable oil

1 Mix bread crumbs, celery, red bell pepper, shallot, parsley, mustard, mayonnaise, egg whites, and Old Bay seasoning in large bowl. Gently fold in crabmeat.

2 Preheat oven to 350°F. Spread flour on waxed paper. Divide crab mixture into 8 mounds, then form into patties with floured hands. Dredge in flour.

3 Lightly coat large nonstick ovenproof skillet with nonstick cooking spray and set over medium-high heat until hot but not smoking. Cook 4 crab cakes until brown, about 2 minutes on each side. Drizzle 1 teaspoon oil around crab cakes, gently shaking pan to spread oil, right after turning crab cakes over. Transfer to plate lined with paper towels. Repeat with remaining crab cakes and oil.

4 Lightly coat baking sheet with nonstick cooking spray, place crab cakes on sheet, and bake until very hot in center, 8 to 10 minutes.

STEP 2 *Form patties with a ⅓-cup dry measure and gently shape with floured hands, then dredge in flour to coat.*

STEP 3 *Turn crab cakes with a slotted spatula.*

Round Out the Meal

Serve the crab cakes with steamed sugar snap peas and roasted new potatoes. End the meal with peach halves sprinkled with amaretti cookie crumbs.

MEDITERRANEAN DIET REVISITED

People who eat traditional cuisines of Mediterranean regions suffer far less heart disease, diabetes, obesity, and certain cancers compared with those who eat the typical American diet. Tomatoes, figs, legumes, olive oil, fish, yogurt, nuts, seeds, red wine, and grains are Mediterranean staples contributing to that region's diet, which is:

- ♥ low in saturated fat and animal protein
- ♥ high in plant-derived protein
- ♥ high in seasonally fresh, locally grown fruit and vegetables
- ♥ rich with olive oil, noted for its cardioprotective monounsaturated fat and phytochemicals
- ♥ abundant in fish, with heart-healthy omega-3 fatty acids

HEALTH HINT

Shellfish are relatively high in cholesterol, but they're low in saturated fat. Recent studies show that for most people, blood cholesterol levels are affected more by the saturated fat, not the cholesterol, in foods. Your doctor can tell you if your blood cholesterol levels are affected by dietary cholesterol.

American Bouillabaisse

Our bouillabaisse is a bit simpler and lower in fat than the French original—but it is still very special and flavorful. When having company, you can prepare this dish ahead of time, right up to the end point of adding the fish. Then, when your guests are about to be seated, you can head back to the kitchen and quickly finish it off.

PER SERVING

232 calories / 16% from fat
1 g saturated fat, 4 g total fat
115 mg cholesterol
798 mg sodium
3 g total carbohydrate
0 g dietary fiber
33 g protein

PREP TIME 20 min.	COOK TIME 50 min.	SERVES 6

- 1 onion, chopped
- 2 carrots, peeled and thinly sliced
- 1 leek, halved lengthwise, washed and thinly sliced
- 2 tomatoes, cored, seeded, and chopped
- 2 garlic cloves, minced
- 1 cup dry white wine
- 4 bottles (8 ounces each) clam juice
- 6 cups fish broth
- 2 pinches saffron threads, crumbled
- 1 dozen clams in shell
- 2 pounds mussels
- ½ pound boneless halibut, cut into 1½-inch pieces
- ½ pound boneless scrod, cut into 1½-inch pieces
- ½ pound bay scallops
- ½ pound large shrimp, peeled and deveined

1 Combine onion, carrots, leek, tomatoes, garlic, wine, clam juice, fish broth, and saffron in 8-quart Dutch oven. Bring to a boil over medium-high heat. Reduce heat to medium-low and simmer, uncovered, for 30 minutes.

2 Strain the broth, discard vegetables, and return broth to the pot. Bring to a full boil.

3 Add clams and mussels, reduce heat to medium-low, cover, and simmer until shells open, about 5 minutes. Discard any mussels and clams that do not open. Add halibut, scrod, scallops, and shrimp. Simmer, uncovered, 5 minutes more.

4 Divide fish and shellfish among 6 large heated soup bowls and ladle in broth.

Round Out the Meal

Serve with crusty bread, broccoli vinaigrette, and chocolate sorbet with strawberries for dessert.

HEALTH HINT

Next time you make this dish, use a half-and-half combination of lean fish such as cod, scrod, halibut, hake, snapper, or tilapia and oily fish such as tuna, salmon, bluefish, sturgeon, or swordfish. Fattier fish contain more omega-3 fatty acids thought to be beneficial to your heart.

secret to success

When purchasing mussels, see that shells are closed tightly—not broken, and without cracks. They should smell of the sea. Do not store in the refrigerator for more than a day. Soak them in water and salt for a few hours to remove sand and dirt.

Cook's Clue

For the best flavor, use a broth made from fresh fish trimmings. Also, use fully ripe tomatoes and good-quality white wine.

Checking Live Clams

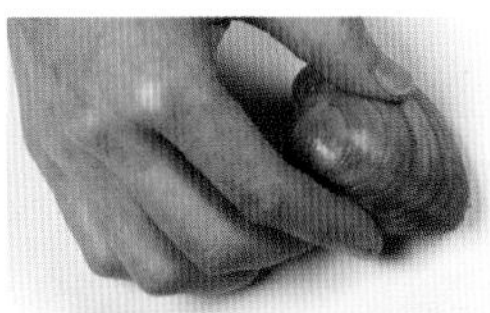

Before cooking clams, check to see if they're still alive by rapping them on the counter. Discard any that don't snap shut.

Debearding Mussels

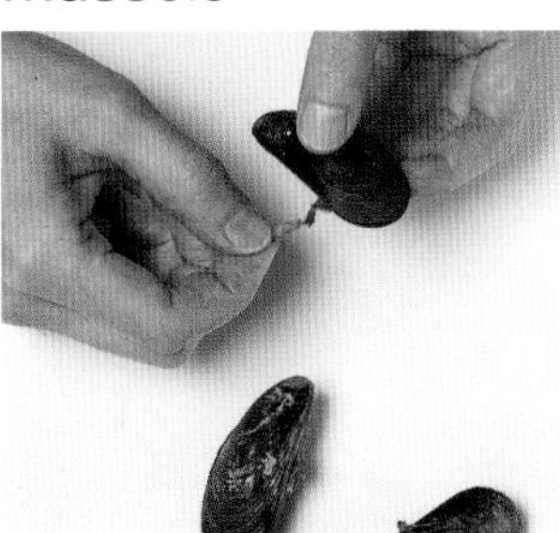

Before cooking mussels, scrub shells under running water with a stiff brush and pull out the hairlike "beards."

Scallop and Cherry Tomato Sauté

Scallops are infinitely adaptable, pleasing when paired with various vegetables and herbs, spices, and sauces. Here, these low-fat, low-cholesterol morsels of succulent seafood are sautéed with cherry tomatoes, seasoned with garlic and basil, and enlivened with a vermouth-based sauce.

PER SERVING

176 calories / 18% from fat

0.5 g saturated fat, 3.5 g total fat

37 mg cholesterol

483 mg sodium

10 g total carbohydrate

1 g dietary fiber

20 g protein

PREP TIME 5 min. | **COOK TIME** 10 min. | **SERVES** 4

- 1 pound sea scallops
- 4 teaspoons cornstarch
- 2 teaspoons olive oil
- 3 garlic cloves, minced
- 1 pint cherry tomatoes
- ⅔ cup dry vermouth, white wine, or chicken broth
- ½ teaspoon salt
- ⅓ cup chopped fresh basil
- 1 tablespoon cold water

1 Dredge scallops in 3 teaspoons cornstarch, shaking off excess. Heat oil in large nonstick skillet over medium heat. Add scallops and sauté until golden brown and cooked through, about 3 minutes. With slotted spoon, transfer scallops to bowl.

2 Add garlic to pan and cook 1 minute. Add tomatoes and cook until they begin to collapse, about 4 minutes.

3 Add vermouth, salt, and basil to pan. Bring to a boil and cook for 1 minute.

4 Meanwhile, stir together remaining 1 teaspoon cornstarch and cold water in small bowl. Add cornstarch mixture to pan and cook, stirring, until sauce is slightly thickened, about 1 minute.

5 Return scallops to pan, reduce to a simmer, and cook just until heated through, about 1 minute.

STEP 1 *Cook the scallops until golden brown on both sides.*

STEP 2 *Cook tomatoes until they start to collapse.*

STEP 3 *Add vermouth, salt, and chopped fresh basil to skillet.*

HEALTH HINT

When a dish is very low in calories (like this one), the percentage of calories from fat can seem high, even though there is a small amount of fat in the recipe. The fat used is heart-friendly olive oil, which is high in monounsaturated fat and protects beneficial HDL cholesterol levels while lowering harmful LDL levels. Moreover, the mineral-rich scallops are naturally low in both saturated and total fat.

Round Out the Meal

Serve with Asian rice vermicelli or brown rice. For dessert, serve chunks of honeydew melon with a dipping sauce of lemon yogurt and orange juice.

way back when... Scallops became popular during the Middle Ages. Pilgrims who went to the St. James shrine used empty shells for eating and begging. Scallops became a symbol of this shrine, and people decorated their homes, doorways, and coats of arms with these shells, which are abundant in the Mediterranean and Atlantic Ocean.

(Source: www.whfoods.com)

Lobster Newburg

Can a dish this decadent get only 3 percent of its calories from fat? You bet! The trick is to make smart substitutions without sacrificing the recipe's luxurious richness. Chicken broth and nonfat half-and-half stand in for the egg yolks, heavy cream, and butter typically used in the creamy sauce. Lemon peel, tarragon, and sherry liven up the flavor. Enjoy every delectable bite!

PER SERVING

387 calories / 3% from fat
.25 g saturated fat, 1.5 g total fat
53 mg cholesterol
509 mg sodium
65 g total carbohydrate
2 g dietary fiber
24 g protein

PREP TIME 25 min. | COOK TIME 38 min. | SERVES 4

- 1⅓ cups long-grain white rice
- ¼ teaspoon salt
- ½ teaspoon black pepper
- 2 live lobsters (1¼ to 1½ pounds each)
- 1 cup reduced-sodium chicken broth
- 3 tablespoons all-purpose flour
- 1 cup nonfat half-and-half
- 2 tablespoons dry sherry
- 2 tablespoons chopped fresh tarragon and sprigs for garnish
- 1 teaspoon grated lemon zest
- 12 ounces small white or cremini mushrooms, sliced

1 Prepare rice according to package directions, adding ⅛ teaspoon salt and ¼ teaspoon black pepper to cooking water. Let stand 5 minutes, covered.

2 Meanwhile, bring 2 inches of water to a vigorous boil in large stockpot fitted with a rack over high heat. Add live lobsters, head first. Cover and steam until shells turn bright red and meat is opaque throughout, 12 to 15 minutes. Remove lobsters from pot and rinse with cold water to stop the cooking. Remove lobster meat from shells and cut into 1½-inch chunks.

3 Put broth and flour in jar with tight-fitting lid and shake until blended and smooth. Pour into small saucepan. Bring to a boil, stirring constantly, and then add half-and-half. Reduce heat to medium-low and simmer sauce until smooth and thickened, about 5 minutes. Stir in sherry, 1 tablespoon chopped tarragon, lemon zest, and remaining salt and black pepper; remove from heat. Lightly coat large nonstick skillet with nonstick cooking spray and set over medium-high heat. Sauté mushrooms until tender, about 5 minutes; stir in sauce and lobster. Cook over medium heat just until heated through, about 4 minutes.

4 Generously coat six 1-cup timbales with cooking spray and pack in rice with spoon. Turn out each timbale of rice onto a dinner plate. Spoon on lobster mixture. Garnish with tarragon sprigs.

Round Out the Meal

Serve with a broiled tomato half. End the meal with a slice of angel food cake topped with raspberries.

STEP 2 *Drop live lobsters into boiling water, head first.*

STEP 3 *Stir lobster meat into creamy white sauce.*

Cook's Clue

To keep live lobsters fresh until cooking time, wrap them in a wet towel or wet newspaper and refrigerate on a bed of ice, or place lobsters on dry ice in an ice chest for toting to a friend's house. Cook within a few hours. If you can't find lobsters, 2 pounds of frozen lobster tails may be substituted. Cook according to package directions.

HEALTH HINT

Eating fish reportedly increases HDL cholesterol and reduces the risk of heart disease. Fish contains little saturated fat, and its oil contains EPA and DHA, omega-3 fatty acids, which protect against heart disease. Lobsters are very low in saturated fat, therefore, good for your heart.

Fish 'n' Chips

Although classic fish 'n' chips has an undeniable appeal, this deep-fried English specialty turns two fundamentally healthful foods into a definite no-no. In this heart-healthy version, we found a way to ditch the frying and keep the crispy coating. As a health bonus, we included fiber-rich plum tomatoes baked with the same cheese-crumb topping as the fish and potatoes.

PER SERVING

495 calories / 14% from fat
2 g saturated fat, 7.5 g total fat
69 mg cholesterol
828 mg sodium
58 g total carbohydrate
6 g dietary fiber
48 g protein

PREP TIME 15 min. | **COOK TIME 30 min.** | **SERVES 4**

- 3 large egg whites
- 1 tablespoon water
- 2 teaspoons olive oil
- ¾ cup plus 1 tablespoon plain dry bread crumbs
- 2 tablespoons grated Parmesan cheese
- 1½ pounds all-purpose potatoes, cut crosswise into ⅓-inch slices
- 8 plum tomatoes, halved lengthwise
- ½ teaspoon black pepper
- 4 skinless, boneless red snapper fillets (6 ounces each)
- 2 teaspoons paprika
- ¾ teaspoon salt

1 Preheat oven to 400°F. Spray a large baking sheet with nonstick cooking spray. Whisk together egg whites, water, and oil in large, shallow bowl. Combine ¾ cup bread crumbs and 1 tablespoon Parmesan cheese in separate shallow bowl. Dip potatoes in egg-white mixture, then in bread-crumb mixture and place on baking sheet. Bake until potatoes are crisp on the outside and cooked through, about 25 minutes, turning them over midway.

2 Meanwhile, place tomatoes, cut-side up, on separate baking pan. In small bowl, combine ¼ teaspoon black pepper and remaining 1 tablespoon bread crumbs and 1 tablespoon Parmesan. Sprinkle tomatoes with bread-crumb mixture and place in oven for final 10 minutes of potato baking time.

3 Spray a broiler pan with nonstick cooking spray. Place fish on broiler pan. Sprinkle fish with paprika, remaining ¼ teaspoon black pepper, and ¼ teaspoon of salt.

4 Remove potatoes and tomatoes from oven and preheat broiler. Sprinkle potatoes with remaining ½ teaspoon salt. Broil fish 4 inches from heat, until golden brown and cooked through, about 5 minutes.

Round Out the Meal

Serve with romaine lettuce hearts drizzled with fat-free ranch dressing and poached pears for dessert.

STEP 1 *Dip potato slices first in egg-white mixture, then in bread-crumb mixture.*

STEP 2 *Sprinkle bread-crumb mixture over tomato halves.*

STEP 3 *Place fish fillets on broiler pan and sprinkle with salt, black pepper, and paprika.*

HEALTH HINT

The potatoes contribute close to two-thirds of the fiber in this dish, with the tomatoes and bread crumbs accounting for the rest. Be sure to leave the potato skin on because that contains most of the potatoes' fiber.

secret to success

When purchasing red snapper, the fresh whole snappers should be deeply buried in ice, and fillets should be on top. Choose fillets whose flesh is gleaming.

Fish Baked on a Bed of Broccoli, Corn and Red Pepper

Baking fish fillets on top of cut fresh vegetables creates an easy and nutritious one-dish dinner high in protein, vitamins, and minerals but low in fat and calories. You can change the vegetables depending on what is in season at the market or to suit your personal tastes.

PER SERVING

210 calories / 3% from fat

1 g saturated fat, 6 g total fat

56 mg cholesterol

340 mg sodium

16 g total carbohydrate

3 g dietary fiber

25 g protein

PREP TIME 15 min. | COOK TIME 50 min. | SERVES 4

- 4 sole or any firm white fillets (4–6 ounces each), fresh or frozen and thawed
- 2 tablespoons fat-free Italian dressing
- 1 tablespoon fine dry unseasoned bread crumbs
- 1 tablespoon grated Parmesan cheese
- ¼ teaspoon paprika
- 1 tablespoon olive oil
- 2 cups broccoli florets
- 1 cup fresh or frozen corn kernels, thawed
- 1 red bell pepper, seeded and cut into thin strips
- 1 small red onion, thinly sliced
- 2 tablespoons chopped parsley
- 1 tablespoon chopped fresh basil
- ⅛ teaspoon salt
- ⅛ teaspoon black pepper

1 Place fish in shallow baking dish and brush lightly with Italian dressing. Cover and refrigerate. In small bowl, combine bread crumbs with Parmesan cheese and paprika until blended.

2 Preheat oven to 425°F. Brush 4 individual or one 13 x 9 x 2-inch ovenproof dish with oil. In large bowl, combine broccoli, corn, red bell pepper, onion, parsley, basil, salt, and black pepper.

3 Divide vegetable mixture evenly among dishes. Cover with aluminum foil and bake until vegetables are just tender, about 35 to 40 minutes.

4 Uncover dishes and top vegetables with fish fillets. Cover again and bake until fish is barely cooked and still moist in thickest part, about 8 to 10 minutes. Uncover dishes, sprinkle with bread-crumb mixture, and continue to bake, uncovered, until topping is golden, about 2 to 3 minutes.

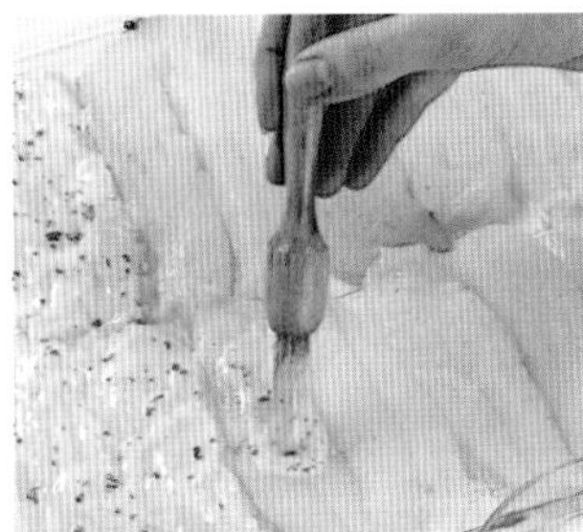

STEP 1 *Brush fish lightly with Italian dressing.*

STEP 3 *Divide vegetable mixture among dishes.*

STEP 4 *Cover again and bake for 8 to 10 minutes.*

HEALTH HINT

Firm white fish—sole, haddock, or cod, for example—is the ideal food for improving our diets and health. A rich source of protein, vitamins, and minerals, it has little unsaturated fat. Fish is also low in calories.

secret to success

Avoid broccoli with yellow flowers blossoming; this is a sign they're too mature. The stalks and stems should be firm but tender, and the leaves should have a vibrant color and not be wilted.

Cook's Clue

Fish is naturally tender and cooks quickly, so it is easy to overcook. Fish is ready when the flesh is white all through, flakes easily, or comes off the bone. (It should not be translucent.) Once done, remove the fish from heat immediately.

Sole en Papillote

A packet, a pocket, a papillote . . . an elegant envelope with supper inside! If you've never cooked fish this way, give it a try. Cooking en papillote *seals in the food's natural flavor and juices, so you can get away with adding little—if any—fat. The presentation is bound to impress!*

PER SERVING

204 calories / 18% from fat

1 g saturated fat, 4 g total fat

54 mg cholesterol

732 mg sodium

15 g total carbohydrate

5 g dietary fiber

24 g protein

PREP TIME 15 min. | **COOK TIME 15 min.** | **SERVES 4**

- 5 ounces fresh spinach, washed and trimmed
- 1 medium onion, chopped
- 4 sole fillets (4 to 6 ounces each)
- 1 teaspoon salt
- ½ teaspoon black pepper
- 2 medium tomatoes, chopped
- 4 medium carrots, cut into matchstick strips
- 4 scallions, sliced
- ½ cup dry white wine or chicken broth
- 2 teaspoons olive oil
- 8 thin lemon slices
- 4 sprigs fresh thyme

1 Preheat oven to 400°F. Cut four 15-inch squares of parchment paper and fold in half diagonally, forming triangles. Open and coat with nonstick cooking spray.

2 Divide spinach and onion among parchment pieces. Cut sole fillets in half crosswise and top each portion of vegetables with 2 fillet halves, overlapping them slightly. Sprinkle each with ¼ teaspoon salt and ⅛ teaspoon black pepper. Top evenly with tomatoes, carrots, and scallions. Drizzle each with 2 tablespoons wine and ½ teaspoon oil. Top each with 2 lemon slices and 1 thyme sprig.

3 Fold parchment over filling. Fold two open sides of triangle over to seal. Fold over points at ends of creased side, making a five-sided packet. Lightly coat packets with nonstick cooking spray and set on jelly-roll pan.

4 Bake until packets puff, about 15 minutes. Transfer to plates and cut open tops of packets (be careful of steam). Serve immediately.

Cook's Clue

"*En papillote*" refers to food baked inside a packet made of parchment paper. Cut the parchment large enough to fold over the edges several times, nice and tight. As steam builds inside them, the packets puff up. If the seals burst, the steam escapes, and the food won't cook evenly and thoroughly. You can use foil, though it doesn't puff up as high. (It also doesn't need to be coated with nonstick cooking spray.)

STEP 2 *Layer vegetables and sole on one side of parchment. Top with lemon slices and thyme sprig.*

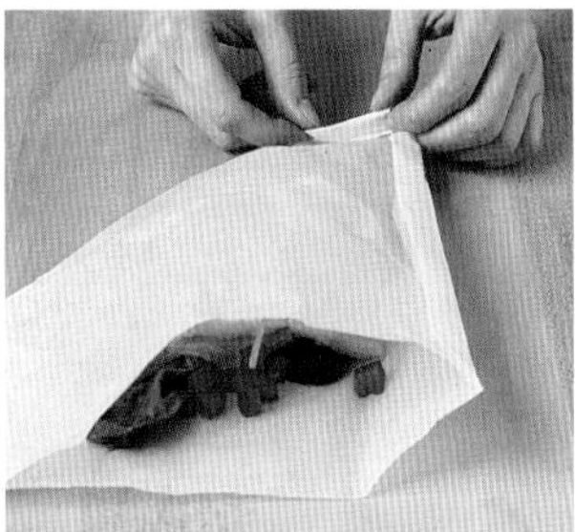

STEP 3 *Fold parchment edges over several times to form air-tight seal.*

STEP 4 *Using scissors, cut open packets carefully, avoiding steam.*

living smart
FOR A HEALTHY HEART

SPOTLIGHT ON MAGNESIUM

If you eat lots of tofu, legumes, seeds, nuts, whole grains, and green leafy vegetables, such as spinach, you are doing your heart a favor. Why? These foods supply helpful amounts of the cardioprotective mineral magnesium. This important mineral is required for regulation of heart rhythm, clotting of blood, energy production, formation of bones and teeth, and maintenance of nerves and muscles. Magnesium may also play a role in lowering blood pressure and maintaining cardiovascular health.

Lemon-Glazed Flounder Fillets

Floundering over what to make for supper? Here's a smart solution—grill fish fillets on top of fresh lemon slices. Top them with a light citrus sauce. Try this same recipe with any white flatfish fillets. It's a tasty and quick way to get the servings of fish you need each week. And best of all, it's ready in less than 25 minutes.

PER SERVING

167 calories / 27% from fat
1 g saturated fat, 5 g total fat
10 mg cholesterol
428 mg sodium
15 g total carbohydrate
2 g dietary fiber
23 g protein

PREP TIME 15 min. | **COOK TIME 8 min.** | **SERVES 4**

- 5 large lemons
- 6 large fresh basil leaves
- 1 tablespoon olive oil
- 1 garlic clove, minced
- 4 flounder fillets (4 ounces each)
- ½ teaspoon salt
- ¼ teaspoon black pepper
- ½ cup reduced-sodium chicken broth
- 1½ teaspoons cornstarch
- 2 teaspoons sugar

1 Roll 1 lemon on a counter surface to get juices flowing; grate zest from this lemon and squeeze juice. Cut 3 lemons into twelve ¼-inch slices. Slice remaining lemon into 8 wedges. Make basil chiffonade: Stack basil leaves and roll up tightly (to resemble a long cigar). Slice across the roll, making cuts about 1/16 inch apart. Set aside for garnish. Heat oil in small saucepan over medium heat. Add garlic and cook until golden, about 2 minutes. Whisk in lemon juice and remove from heat.

2 Coat grill rack or broiler pan rack with nonstick cooking spray. Preheat grill to medium or preheat broiler. Lightly brush both sides of fish with garlic mixture and sprinkle with salt and black pepper. Place 3 lemon slices on grill or broiler rack and put 1 flounder fillet on top. Repeat with remaining lemon slices and fish. Grill or broil fish, without turning, until just opaque throughout, about 6 minutes. Cook lemon wedges alongside until browned, about 2 minutes on each side.

3 Meanwhile, blend broth and cornstarch in cup until smooth. Whisk cornstarch mixture, sugar, and ¼ teaspoon lemon zest into remaining garlic mixture. Bring to a boil over medium-high heat and cook until sauce thickens, about 1 minute.

4 Transfer fish to plates, lemon slices down. Spoon sauce over fish and sprinkle with basil chiffonade and remaining lemon zest. Garnish with grilled lemon wedges.

STEP 1 *To make a basil chiffonade, slice across rolled leaves, about 1/16 inch apart.*

STEP 2 *On a preheated grill, place each fish fillet on top of 3 lemon slices.*

Cook's Clue

If flounder is not available, substitute fillets of any other white flatfish in this recipe. Halibut, sole, and turbot are good choices.

secret to success

Never overcook flounder. By whatever means you cook it, the flesh of the flounder will turn opaque when it's done, and should remain moist. You should be able to easily poke it with a fork.

HEALTH HINT

Most nutrition experts recommend eating at least 6 ounces of fish per week. Fish has more protein, fewer calories, and less fat per serving than most meats.

Grilled Salmon with Pepper-Corn Relish

The rich flavor of salmon is a clue to its bountiful supply of heart-healthy omega-3 fatty acids—and just about everybody loves the taste. To keep it a good-for-you dish, the spice-rubbed fish is served with a colorful confetti of diced vegetables instead of a heavy cream- or mayonnaise-based sauce.

PER SERVING

287 calories / 30% from fat
1.5 g saturated fat, 9.5 g total fat
81 mg cholesterol
359 mg sodium
20 g total carbohydrate
2 g dietary fiber
31 g protein

PREP TIME 10 min. | **COOK TIME 10 min.** | **SERVES 4**

- ¼ teaspoon plus 2 tablespoons sugar
- 1 teaspoon ground coriander
- ½ teaspoon salt
- ½ teaspoon cinnamon
- ¼ teaspoon cardamom
- ¼ teaspoon black pepper
- 4 salmon steaks (6 ounces each)
- ½ teaspoon yellow mustard seeds
- ⅓ cup distilled white vinegar
- 1 zucchini, cut into ¼-inch dice
- 1 orange or red bell pepper, seeded and cut into ¼-inch dice
- 1 cup corn kernels, fresh or thawed frozen

1 Spray grill rack with nonstick cooking spray. Preheat grill to medium. Combine ¼ teaspoon of sugar, coriander, salt, cinnamon, cardamom, and black pepper in small saucepan. Measure out 1¼ teaspoons of spice mixture and rub into one side of each salmon steak.

2 Add remaining 2 tablespoons sugar, mustard seeds, and vinegar to spice mixture in saucepan, and bring to a boil over medium heat. Add zucchini, bell pepper, and corn, and cook until bell pepper is crisp-tender, about 4 minutes.

3 Place salmon, spice-side down, on grill and cook, without turning, until just done, about 5 minutes. Serve salmon topped with relish.

Round Out the Meal

Serve with grilled new potatoes and arugula salad. For dessert, try fresh blueberries.

HEALTH HINT

Don't worry if you can't find fresh corn, you'll still get the same heart-healthy nutrients—such as fiber, folate, potassium, and vitamin C—in frozen corn. Yellow corn also provides the added nutritional benefit of carotenoids—important disease-fighting phytochemicals.

Cook's Clue

When grilling salmon, oil your grill well and baste frequently. Since salmon is leaner than most fish, it lacks self-basting fat. Frequent basting keeps it moist and full of flavor.

How to Cut Kernels from a Corncob

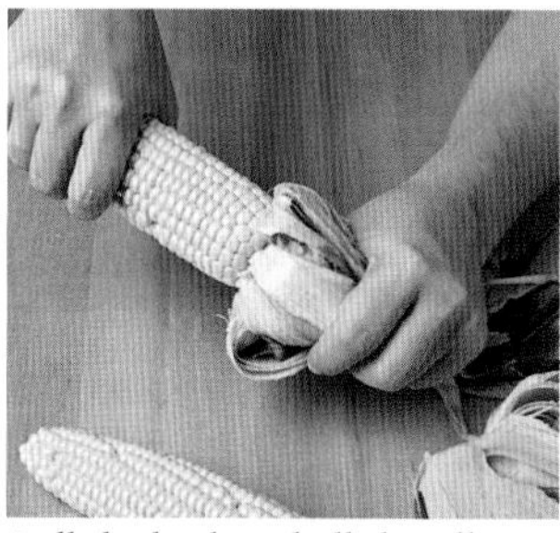

Pull the husk and all the silk from the corncobs.

Hold the cob upright in a large bowl, and use a paring knife to cut the kernels off the cob, letting them fall into the bowl.

To get as much corn as possible, run the dull side of a knife down the cob to press the remaining pieces of corn into the bowl.

Salmon Cakes with Creamy Tomato Sauce

If you want to give your heart a break, give those fatty beef burgers a rest and try these thick, juicy salmon "burgers" for a change. And while you're at it, leave the ketchup in the fridge, and slather the salmon patties with freshly made tomato-garlic sauce.

PER SERVING

263 calories / 34% from fat
2 g saturated fat, 10 g total fat
41 mg cholesterol
863 mg sodium
29 g total carbohydrate
2 g dietary fiber
17 g protein

PREP TIME 15 min.	COOK TIME 15 min.	SERVES 4

- ¼ cup sun-dried tomatoes (not oil packed)
- 4 garlic cloves, peeled
- ⅓ cup plain fat-free yogurt
- ½ teaspoon hot red pepper sauce
- 1 large baking potato (10 ounces), thinly sliced
- 1 can (14 ¾ ounces) pink salmon, drained
- 2 tablespoons plus ½ cup plain dried bread crumbs
- ½ cup minced fresh dill
- 1 tablespoon capers, rinsed and drained
- ½ teaspoon salt
- 1 tablespoon olive oil

1 Cook sun-dried tomatoes and 2 garlic cloves in small pot of boiling water for 3 minutes. Drain, reserving ⅓ cup cooking liquid. Transfer tomatoes and garlic to mini food processor. Add reserved cooking liquid, yogurt, and hot pepper sauce, and puree until smooth.

2 Meanwhile, cook potato and remaining 2 garlic cloves in medium pot of boiling water until tender, about 7 minutes. Drain and transfer to large bowl. With potato masher, mash potato and garlic.

3 Stir in salmon, 2 tablespoons bread crumbs, dill, capers, and salt. Shape salmon mixture into 8 cakes.

4 Heat oil in large nonstick skillet over medium heat. Dredge salmon cakes in remaining ½ cup bread crumbs. Add to skillet and sauté until golden brown and heated through, about 3 minutes per side. Serve with tomato sauce.

STEP 2 *Mash together potato and garlic.*

STEP 3 *Shape salmon mixture into medium-size patties.*

STEP 4 *Coat salmon cakes with bread crumbs, shaking off excess.*

Round Out the Meal

Serve with steamed green beans, and offer rice pudding with dried cherries for dessert.

HEALTH HINT

Why is canned salmon so healthy? For one thing, salmon in general is rich with omega-3 fatty acids—highly nutritious oils that help lower blood cholesterol levels. But canned salmon also contains a fair amount of calcium, which helps lower blood pressure. The calcium comes from the salmon bones, which are softened and made edible in the canning process.

living smart
FOR A HEALTHY HEART

FISH TALES

Eat fatty fish, recommends the American Heart Association. A study found that older adults who eat fatty fish such as tuna, salmon, and mackerel at least once a week greatly lower their risk of dying from heart attack. The average age of the people studied was 71, which suggests it's never too late to start eating better. As shown in previous studies of middle-age adults, eating fatty fish increases your blood levels of omega-3 fatty acids, known to protect against heart attack. Leaner fish, such as cod and flounder, although healthy, don't provide these same fatty acids.

Crispy Tuna Steaks in Citrus Sauce

Everyone knows fish is a good choice for heart-healthy eating—it's lower in saturated fat than meat and poultry. Their beefy texture makes tuna steaks a favorite with affirmed meat eaters. The seasoned cornmeal seals in its juicy flavor. Who could resist?

PER SERVING

338 calories / 16% from fat
1 g saturated fat, 6 g total fat
76 mg cholesterol
355 mg sodium
28 g total carbohydrate
3 g dietary fiber
41 g protein

PREP TIME 15 min.	COOK TIME 9 min.	SERVES 4

- 2 large oranges
- 1½ cups orange juice
- 2 tablespoons dry white wine (optional)
- 2 tablespoons cornstarch
- 2 tablespoons chopped fresh cilantro
- 2 tablespoons cornmeal
- ½ teaspoon salt
- ¼ teaspoon black pepper
- 4 tuna steaks (½ inch thick, 6 ounces each)
- 4 teaspoons olive oil

1 Peel oranges.

2 Section oranges. Whisk orange juice, wine (if using), and cornstarch in small saucepan until smooth. Bring to a boil over medium-high heat and cook, stirring, until sauce boils and thickens, about 2 minutes. Remove from heat and stir in orange sections. Keep warm.

3 Mix cilantro, cornmeal, salt, and black pepper in pie plate. Coat both sides of tuna steaks with cornmeal mixture, pressing firmly so mixture adheres.

4 Heat 2 teaspoons oil in large cast-iron skillet over medium-high heat until hot but not smoking. Sear tuna until done to taste, 2 to 3 minutes on each side for medium-rare. Add remaining oil just before turning fish. Serve with sauce.

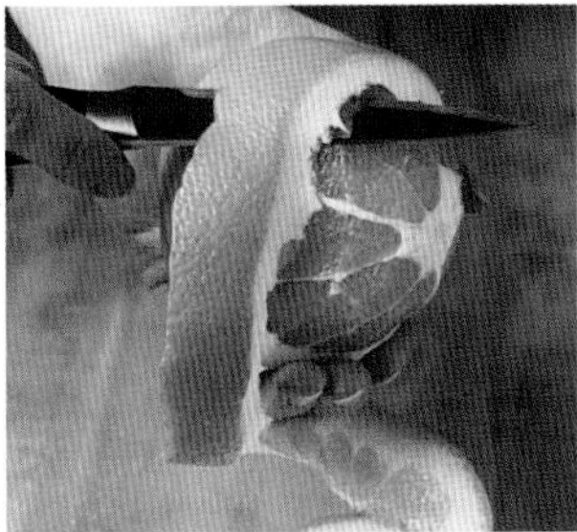

STEP 1 *Cut off peel and white pith with paring knife while turning orange.*

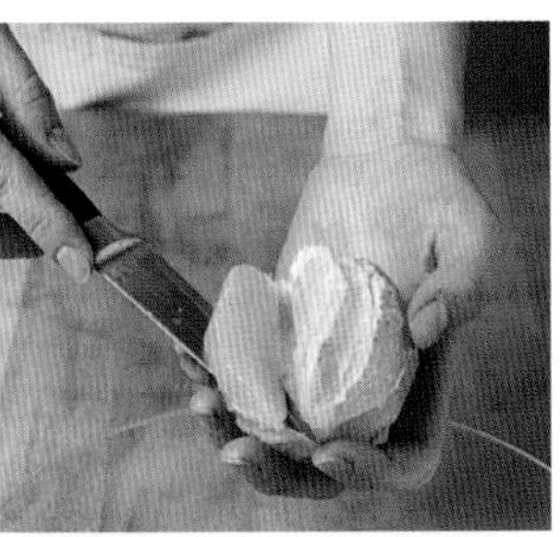

STEP 2 *Cut between membranes with paring knife, then lift out sections, one by one.*

STEP 3 *Press on crust firmly to help it adhere during cooking.*

secret to success

Be careful not to overcook tuna, as it dries out. Tuna is done once the flesh is opaque, and the inside is moist.

Cook's Clue

Of the many varieties of tuna, the most common sold fresh is yellowfin. It's a good choice for this recipe because it holds its shape and is flavorful enough to stand up to the seasonings in the crust and sauce. For variety, try this recipe with salmon, swordfish, or mahi mahi.

HEALTH HINT

Tuna is a member of the mackerel family. It is high in heart-protecting omega-3 fatty acids (canned albacore tuna has the highest levels). Omega-3s are special fats that help prevent artery disease. Like most fish, tuna is especially rich in B vitamins, including niacin, thiamin, and vitamin B_6.

Oven-Fried Catfish with Sweet Pepper Relish

PER SERVING

317 calories / 16% from fat

1.5 g saturated fat, 5.5 g total fat

103 mg cholesterol

560 mg sodium

35 g total carbohydrate

4 g dietary fiber

32 g protein

No longer just for Southerners, catfish has come into its own as the farm-raised variety has become widely available. We've lightened batter-fried catfish, a Southern favorite, by baking the fish in the oven. A tangy vegetable relish brightens the plate and adds some fiber to the meal.

PREP TIME 15 min. + marinating | COOK TIME 20 min. | SERVES 4

- 1/3 cup cider vinegar
- 2 tablespoons honey
- 3/4 teaspoon mustard seeds
- 3/4 teaspoon salt
- 1/4 teaspoon allspice
- 2 bell peppers, 1 red and 1 green, seeded and cut into 1/2-inch squares
- 2 celery stalks, cut into 1/2-inch pieces
- 1 small onion, coarsely chopped
- 1/2 cup buttermilk
- 4 skinless, boneless catfish fillets (5 ounces each)
- 1/2 cup flour
- 1/4 cup toasted wheat germ

1 Combine vinegar, honey, mustard seeds, 1/4 teaspoon salt, and allspice in large skillet. Bring to a boil over medium heat. Add bell peppers, celery, and onion and cook, stirring frequently, until vegetables are crisp-tender, about 7 minutes. Cool relish to room temperature, then refrigerate until serving time.

2 Pour buttermilk in shallow bowl. Add catfish and turn to coat. Marinate 30 minutes or up to overnight, turning catfish over midway.

3 Preheat oven to 425°F. Spray a baking sheet with nonstick cooking spray. Combine remaining 1/2 teaspoon salt, flour, and wheat germ in shallow bowl. Lift catfish from buttermilk and dredge in flour mixture, patting coating onto fish. Place fish on baking sheet and bake until crisp and cooked through, about 10 minutes. Serve fish with relish.

Round Out the Meal

Serve with stewed okra and low-fat red cabbage coleslaw. For dessert, offer frozen yogurt and crushed pineapple sundaes.

secret to success

Do not overcook catfish. Like most fish, regardless of cooking method, catfish is cooked once it becomes opaque and can be poked easily with a fork.

HEALTH HINT

Adding toasted wheat germ to the coating mixture for fish and poultry provides a crunchy texture along with plenty of heart-healthy benefits. Wheat germ is the germ or "heart" of the wheat kernel and supplies important nutrients such as vitamin E, B vitamins, fiber, and the minerals selenium, magnesium, and iron.

STEP 1 *Cook bell peppers, celery, and onion in vinegar mixture to make the relish.*

STEP 2 *Marinate catfish fillets in buttermilk, turning them to coat both sides.*

STEP 3 *Dredge the catfish fillets in seasoned flour mixture, patting coating onto the fish.*

Poultry and Game Birds

Tandoori Chicken

Spices are turning out to be surprising sources of disease-fighting phytochemicals—good reason to be generous with the seasoning in the marinade for this chicken. In the classic rendition of tandoori chicken, the spicy marinade protects the chicken from the fierce heat of the Indian clay oven called a tandoor. Although your broiler's not as hot, the marinade still works to keep the chicken juicy.

PER SERVING

262 calories / 22% from fat
1.5 g saturated fat, 6.5 g total fat
89 mg cholesterol
416 mg sodium
15 g total carbohydrate
3 g dietary fiber
36 g protein

PREP TIME 10 min. + marinating | **COOK TIME** 10 min. | **SERVES** 4

- ½ cup plain low-fat yogurt
- 1½ tablespoons chili powder
- 1 tablespoon coriander
- 2 teaspoons cumin
- ¾ teaspoon ground ginger
- ½ teaspoon salt
- ½ teaspoon black pepper
- ½ teaspoon cinnamon
- 3 garlic cloves, peeled
- 4 skinless, boneless chicken breast halves (5 ounces each)
- ¼ cup golden raisins
- 2 tablespoons slivered almonds, toasted

1 Combine yogurt, chili powder, coriander, cumin, ginger, salt, black pepper, cinnamon, and garlic in a blender and puree until smooth.

2 With a chef's knife, make several shallow slits on one side of each chicken breast half. Place in a shallow plastic container that will hold chicken in a single layer.

3 Pour yogurt mixture over chicken, turning to coat well. Cover and refrigerate at least 6 hours or up to overnight.

4 Preheat broiler. Spray broiler pan with nonstick cooking spray. Reserving marinade, remove chicken and place on broiler pan. Broil 4 inches from heat for 4 minutes. Turn chicken over, brush with reserved marinade, and broil until chicken is cooked through, about 4 minutes. Discard any remaining marinade.

5 Serve chicken with raisins and almonds sprinkled over top.

STEP 2 *Cut several shallow slits in top of chicken breasts.*

STEP 3 *Pour yogurt marinade over chicken breasts.*

STEP 4 *After chicken has broiled on one side, turn breasts over and brush with remaining marinade.*

Round Out the Meal

Serve with brown basmati rice and steamed cauliflower and peas. For dessert, try lime sherbet with mango cubes.

Cook's Clue

You can freeze the chicken right in its container of marinade for up to 2 weeks. The morning of the day you plan to serve it, put the container in the refrigerator to thaw, and the chicken will be ready to broil at dinner time.

HEALTH HINT

Low-fat yogurt is low in calories and rich in protein and the cardioprotective minerals calcium and potassium. Yogurt also contains a compound called conjugated linoleic acid, which may help reduce body fat, slow the growth of certain cancers, and reduce the risk of heart disease.

secret to success

Cutting slits in chicken breasts allows marinade to permeate chicken, making it more tender and flavorful.

Ginger-Lemon Chicken

Unlike the breaded and fried version served at many Chinese restaurants, this chicken is steamed in a light lemon sauce. Steaming is a favorite cooking technique among Asian chefs and heart-smart cooks everywhere—and it's no wonder. Besides being healthful, the food stays moist, and the flavor of the dish is absolutely pure.

PER SERVING

234 calories / 22% from fat

1 g saturated fat, 6 g total fat

99 mg cholesterol

382 mg sodium

3 g total carbohydrate

0 g dietary fiber

41 g protein

PREP TIME 10 min. | **COOK TIME 15 min.** | **SERVES 4**

- 2 tablespoons lower-sodium soy sauce
- ½ teaspoon grated lemon zest
- 2 teaspoons fresh lemon juice
- ½ teaspoon sugar
- 4 skinless, boneless chicken breast halves (about 1½ pounds)
- ¼ cup minced fresh ginger
- 1 tablespoon sesame oil
- 2 scallions, thinly sliced

1 Combine soy sauce, lemon zest, lemon juice, and sugar in small bowl. Place chicken on heatproof plate large enough to hold chicken in single layer, yet small enough to fit in skillet. Spoon soy mixture and ginger over chicken.

2 Place rack in large skillet, and pour water to come just below rack. Place plate on rack and bring water to a simmer. Cover and cook, turning chicken over midway, 15 minutes or until chicken is just cooked through.

3 Place chicken on dinner plates. Pour juices and ginger from plate into small bowl. Stir in sesame oil and scallions and spoon over chicken.

secret to success

There are many forms of ginger: crystallized (candied), dried, fresh, ground, pickled, powdered, or preserved. Its flavor is slightly sweet, slightly peppery, and it has a spicy scent. Fresh ginger, like other spices, loses flavor with cooking, and if burned, it will taste bitter. Ground ginger has a distinct flavor from the other forms and is often used in sweet desserts.

HEALTH HINT

Skinless chicken breasts contain half the fat and half the saturated fat of breasts eaten with their skin. Interestingly, cholesterol is the same in both. That's because cholesterol is found in the flesh of meat and poultry, not in the fat. However, human blood cholesterol levels are greatly affected by saturated fat in the diet, so it pays to remove poultry skin.

Cook's Clue

To steam chicken in a skillet, use a small wire cooling rack and a high, domed lid for the pan. If the lid isn't deep enough, you can invert a large, heatproof bowl over the skillet. Turn the heat off before carefully removing the bowl, using two potholders. Watch out for rising steam.

Halving a Whole Breast

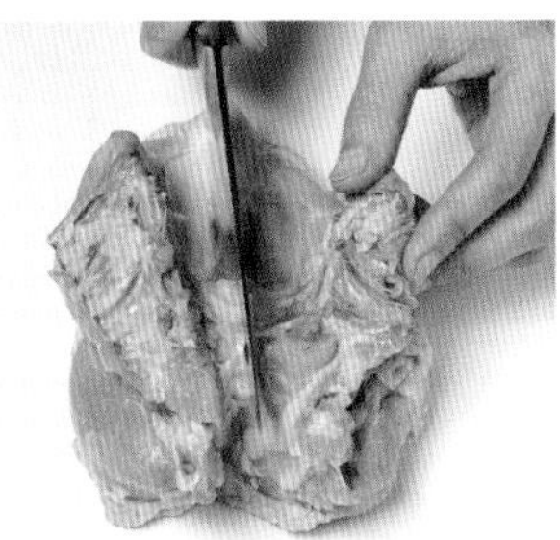

Cut down along both sides of the breastbone without cutting all the way through.

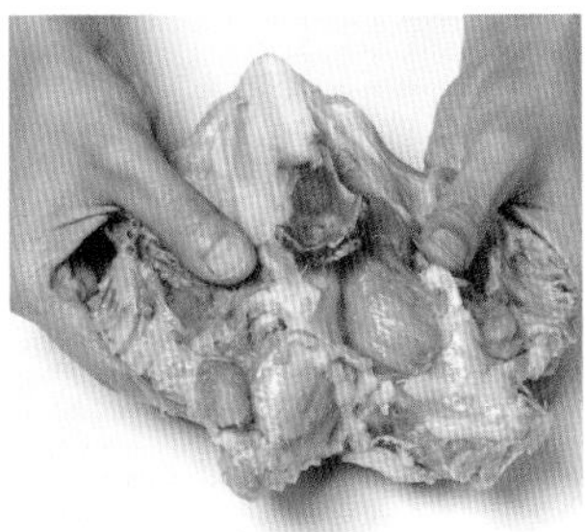

Bend the two sides back until the breastbone pops up.

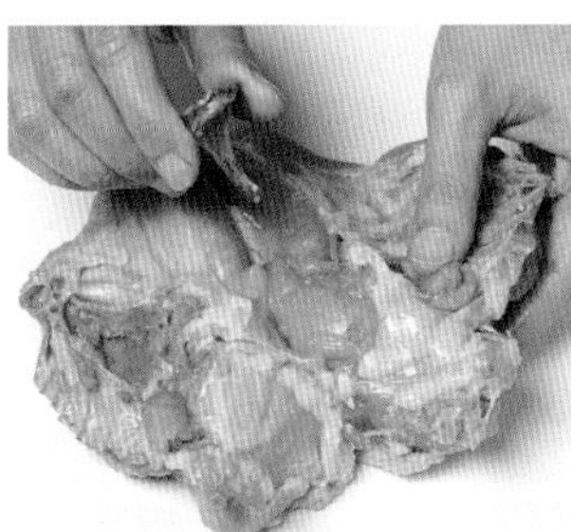

Pull out the breastbone.

Chicken Breasts with Roasted Garlic–Tomato Sauce

Looking for a new way to serve chicken? Here's a recipe that turns the ordinary into the extraordinary. Chicken simmered in a rich tomato sauce seasoned with roasted garlic is dinner for two that's high in vitamins A, C, B_6, and niacin and is low in fat, fabulous in flavor.

PER SERVING

562 calories / 5% from fat

1 g saturated fat, 3 g total fat

82 mg cholesterol

571 mg sodium

72 g total carbohydrate

6 g dietary fiber

48 g protein

PREP TIME 20 min.	COOK TIME 1 hr.	SERVES 2

- 2 heads garlic, papery skin removed
- 2 bone-in chicken breast halves (8 ounces each), skin removed
- ½ teaspoon black pepper
- 2 carrots, thinly sliced
- 1 large shallot, finely chopped
- 4 canned tomatoes, seeded and chopped
- ½ cup reduced-sodium chicken broth
- ½ cup dry white wine or additional chicken broth
- 1 teaspoon chopped fresh rosemary or ¼ teaspoon dried
- 1 tablespoon chopped flat-leaf parsley
- 2 cups cooked fettucine

1 Preheat oven to 350°F. Cut top off each head of garlic and wrap heads in foil. Bake until soft, about 1 hour.

2 Meanwhile, coat medium ovenproof skillet with lid with nonstick cooking spray and set over medium-high heat. Sprinkle chicken with black pepper and cook until golden brown, 4 to 5 minutes on each side. Transfer to plate.

3 Add carrots and shallot to skillet and sauté until shallot is soft, about 2 minutes. Return chicken, skinned-side down, to skillet. Add tomatoes, broth, wine, and rosemary. Bring to a simmer. Cover and transfer to oven. Bake chicken until juices run clear, 30 to 45 minutes.

4 Remove garlic cloves from their skins with tip of paring knife.

5 Mash garlic until smooth. Stir garlic into sauce and sprinkle with parsley. Serve over fettucine.

STEP 1 *Cut ½ inch off top of garlic head.*

STEP 4 *Push out roasted cloves, one by one.*

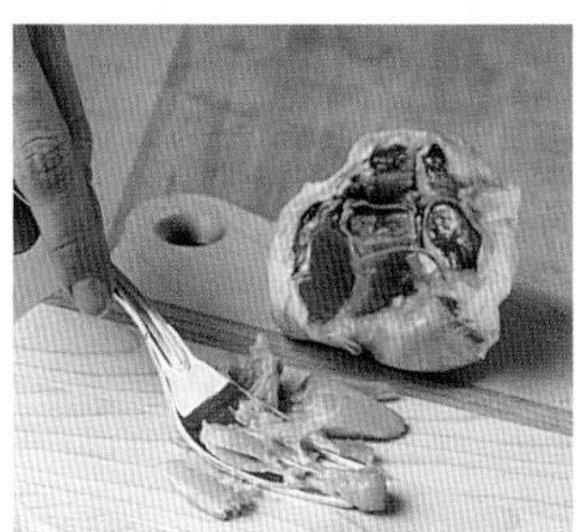

STEP 5 *Mash garlic with fork until smooth.*

Round Out the Meal

Get your greens with a romaine and endive salad, and serve biscotti with scoops of chocolate sorbet for dessert.

secret to success

Shallots caramelize similar to onions. Though available year-round, the best time to purchase shallots is from April to August. Shallot-savvy shoppers know that the vegetables should be firm and heavy. Avoid shallots with soft spots or those that are dry and light. The bigger the shallot, the more intense its smell and taste.

HEALTH HINT

Nutrition experts recommend 20 to 35 grams of fiber every day, but most of us consume less than half that amount. Much of the fiber in this dish comes from the tomatoes, which also provide healthy amounts of vitamins A and C.

Cook's Clue

Roasted garlic can also be stirred into soup, tossed in a salad, or spread on bread.

Coq au Vin

Have a look at a traditional French recipe for chicken with wine. Hmmm . . . a quarter-pound of bacon, 4 tablespoons of oil, and 3 tablespoons of butter, not to mention the fat from the chicken. That's no way to feed your heart! By using skinless chicken breasts, turkey bacon, and just 2 teaspoons of olive oil, we've recreated this classic dish with magnificent flavor and very little fat.

PER SERVING

362 calories / 15% from fat

1 g saturated fat, 6 g total fat

88 mg cholesterol

513 mg sodium

30 g total carbohydrate

3 g dietary fiber

37 g protein

PREP TIME 15 min.	COOK TIME 40 min.	SERVES 4

1 tablespoon sugar

2 tablespoons water

2 cups frozen pearl onions, thawed and well drained

8 ounces mushrooms, quartered

2 carrots, halved lengthwise and cut crosswise on the diagonal into thick slices

2 teaspoons olive oil

2 slices turkey bacon, cut into ½-inch-wide strips

4 boneless, skinless chicken breast halves (5 ounces each), halved crosswise

1 medium onion, finely chopped

3 garlic cloves, minced

1 cup dry red wine

½ teaspoon thyme

½ teaspoon salt

1½ teaspoons cornstarch blended with 1 tablespoon water

1 Combine sugar and water in large nonstick skillet over medium heat. Bring to a boil. Add pearl onions and cook until golden, about 5 minutes.

2 Add mushrooms and carrots, and cook, stirring often, until carrots are crisp-tender, about 5 minutes. Transfer mixture to medium bowl; set aside. Wipe skillet out.

3 Heat oil in skillet over medium heat. Add bacon and cook until crisp, about 4 minutes. Transfer bacon to paper towels.

4 Add chicken to skillet and cook until golden brown, about 2 minutes per side. Transfer chicken to plate.

5 Add chopped onion and garlic to skillet, and cook, stirring frequently, until onion is tender, about 5 minutes. Stir in wine, thyme, and salt, and bring to a boil. Return chicken to skillet. Reduce heat, cover, and simmer until chicken is cooked through, 12 to 15 minutes.

6 Remove chicken from skillet and place on a platter. Bring liquid in pan to a boil. Stir in cornstarch mixture and cook, stirring frequently, until sauce is slightly thickened, about 1 minute. Add pearl onion mixture and bacon to skillet, and cook until heated through, about 2 minutes. Spoon sauce and vegetables over chicken.

STEP 1 *Cook pearl onions in nonstick skillet until golden.*

STEP 5 *Return browned chicken to skillet with cooked onions.*

STEP 6 *Add crumbled bacon to sauce and vegetables in pan.*

Round Out the Meal

Serve with parslied noodles, mesclun salad, and poached pears for dessert.

HEALTH HINT

Moderate consumption of red wine appears to benefit cardiovascular health. It provides antioxidants and is the only dietary factor that shows an inverse correlation with coronary heart disease, creating a "French paradox." This term refers to the fact that though their diets contain high intakes of fat, the French have the lowest rate of heart disease.

Honey–Mustard Chicken and Winter Vegetables

This satisfying one-dish meal makes the most of tasty winter vegetables—turnips, parsnips, and butternut squash—that are not only filling but also packed with nutrients and phytochemicals that protect your heart. By using skinless chicken for this dish, you get the flavor without all the fat.

PER SERVING

349 calories / 18% from fat

1 g saturated fat, 7 g total fat

99 mg cholesterol

893 mg sodium

30 g total carbohydrate

5 g dietary fiber

43 g protein

PREP TIME 15 min. | **COOK TIME 50 min.** | **SERVES 4**

- 1 tablespoon olive oil
- 8 garlic cloves, unpeeled
- 10 ounces white turnips, peeled and cut into ½-inch wedges
- 8 ounces parsnips, peeled, quartered lengthwise, and cut into 2-inch lengths
- 8 ounces butternut squash, peeled and cut into ½-inch chunks
- ¼ cup soft sun-dried tomatoes (not oil-packed), coarsely chopped
- ½ teaspoon salt
- ¼ cup Dijon mustard
- 4 teaspoons honey
- 1 tablespoon fresh lemon juice
- 4 skinless, bone-in chicken breast halves (8 ounces each)

1 Preheat oven to 350°F. Combine oil and garlic in 9 x 13-inch metal baking pan. Roast until garlic is fragrant, about 5 minutes.

2 Add turnips, parsnips, butternut squash, and sun-dried tomatoes. Sprinkle with salt and stir to combine. Roast until vegetables start to color, about 15 minutes.

3 Meanwhile, combine mustard, honey, and lemon juice in small bowl.

4 Drizzle 2 tablespoons of mustard mixture over vegetables and toss to coat. Place chicken on vegetables and spoon remaining mustard mixture on chicken. Bake until chicken is almost done and vegetables are tender, about 25 minutes.

5 Preheat broiler. Broil until chicken is golden brown and cooked through, about 5 minutes. Serve chicken with vegetables, squeezing the garlic from its skin and discarding skin before eating.

STEP 2 *Sprinkle salt evenly over vegetables, then toss carefully.*

STEP 3 *Mix mustard, honey, and lemon juice to make a glaze for vegetables and chicken.*

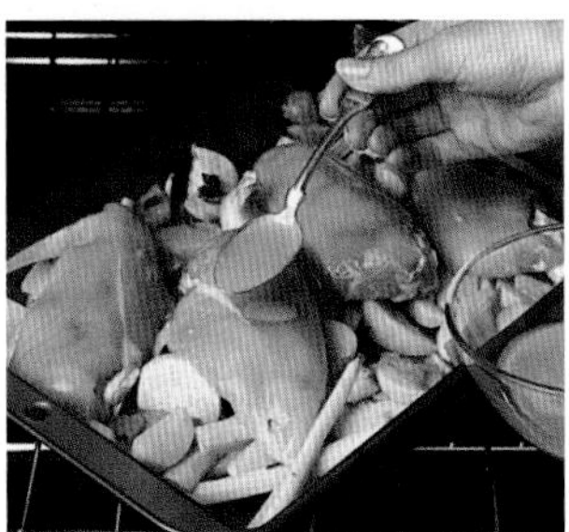

STEP 4 *Before baking chicken, drizzle with honey–mustard mixture.*

Round Out the Meal

Spread roasted garlic on whole-wheat baguette and serve with a frisée salad with lemon vinaigrette. For dessert, offer toasted angel food cake with sliced peaches.

Cook's Clue

Although this recipe is designed to serve four, it could easily be doubled for a larger group—or so that you have "planned-overs," which you can serve as is or use in a salad.

HEALTH HINT

A winter squash like butternut contains folate, which the body needs to break down homocysteine, a toxic amino acid that damages blood vessel walls. High levels are associated with increased risk for heart attack and stroke, therefore, experts recommend a high folate diet.

secret to success

If honey has crystallized, immerse the container in hot water for 15 minutes, but do not heat it in the microwave, or the taste will alter. Always use honey in liquid form to prevent sticking.

North Carolina Chicken Barbecue

This barbecued chicken is glazed with a luscious sweet-tart sauce that combines the traditional cider vinegar of a North Carolina barbecue sauce with lycopene-rich tomatoes. We also used skinless chicken breasts, the meat of choice for heart-smart BBQ chefs.

PER SERVING

535 calories / 15% from fat

2 g saturated fat, 9 g total fat

123 mg cholesterol

674 mg sodium

65 g total carbohydrate

6 g dietary fiber

51 g protein

PREP TIME 20 min. + marinating | **COOK TIME 50 min.** | **SERVES 8**

- ¾ cup cider vinegar
- 2 tablespoons plus ¼ cup packed brown sugar
- 1¼ teaspoons salt
- 2 teaspoons hot red pepper sauce
- 8 bone-in chicken breast halves (8 ounces each), skin removed
- 8 ears corn
- 3 pounds small red-skinned potatoes, cut into thick wedges
- 3 tablespoons light mayonnaise
- 2 tablespoons prepared mustard
- 6 scallions, thinly sliced
- ½ cup plain low-fat yogurt
- 1 can (15 ounces) no-salt-added tomato sauce

1 Combine ½ cup vinegar, 2 tablespoons brown sugar, ¾ teaspoon salt, and hot pepper sauce in large plastic zip-close bag. Add chicken to bag and seal. Refrigerate, turning bag several times, for 2 to 4 hours.

2 Preheat oven to 375°F. Prepare corn for grilling (*see photos, right*).

3 Lift chicken from marinade, transfer to baking pan, and bake 10 minutes. Meanwhile, preheat grill. Wrap potatoes together in large sheet of heavy-duty foil. Grill until cooked through, about 20 minutes. Unwrap and cool slightly.

4 Meanwhile, whisk together 3 tablespoons vinegar, remaining ½ teaspoon salt, mayonnaise, and mustard. Add warm potatoes and scallions and toss to combine. Add yogurt and toss again. Refrigerate until ready to serve.

5 Stir together remaining ¼ cup brown sugar, 1 tablespoon vinegar, and tomato sauce in medium bowl. Place chicken and corn on grill and cook 10 minutes. Brush chicken with tomato mixture and cook until chicken and corn are cooked through, about 10 minutes.

Cook's Clue

If you're lucky enough to have leftovers from this menu, use them to make a light chicken salad. Cut the corn from the cobs and shred the chicken. Toss these with a tangy low-fat vinaigrette made with 1 part cider vinegar and 1 part olive oil. Serve on a bed of greens.

HEALTH HINT

Chicken has less fat than other meats, contains high levels of vitamin B6, and reduces levels of the amino acid, homocysteine, which damages blood vessel walls and is detrimental for cardiovascular health.

secret to success

For the freshest ears, buy from a roadside stand or farmer's market. Eat corn the day you purchase or keep cool and eat the day after, while still sweet.

Preparing Corn on the Cob for Grilling

Pull the corn husks away from the cob, but leave them attached at the stem.

Pull the corn silk off the cob.

Close the husks back around the cobs, and place in a bowl of cold water to soak while you preheat the grill.

Chicken with Apples and Calvados

PER SERVING
300 calories / 15% from fat
2 g saturated fat, 5 g total fat
93 mg cholesterol
402 mg sodium
26 g total carbohydrate
2 g dietary fiber
35 g protein

Looking for a meal that can be on the table in 30 minutes yet is elegant enough to serve at a dinner party? This dish looks and tastes like it comes from a fine French bistro. Whether you're feeding family or feasting with friends, no one will ever guess it has been trimmed down for smart eating!

PREP TIME 10 min.	COOK TIME 20 min.	SERVES 4

- 2 medium shallots, finely chopped
- 2 tart apples, peeled and cut into ¼-inch slices
- 1 cup apple juice
- ¾ cup reduced-sodium chicken broth
- 1 tablespoon Calvados, applejack, or apple juice
- ¼ cup all-purpose flour
- ½ teaspoon salt
- ½ teaspoon freshly ground black pepper
- 4 boneless, skinless chicken breast halves (5 ounces each)
- 2 tablespoons heavy cream

1 Lightly coat large heavy nonstick skillet with nonstick cooking spray and set over medium-high heat. Slice shallots and sauté until soft, about 2 minutes. Add apples and sauté until lightly browned, about 3 minutes. Add apple juice, broth, and Calvados. Cook, stirring, until apples are tender, about 5 minutes. Transfer to medium bowl. Wipe skillet clean.

2 Meanwhile, combine flour, salt, and black pepper on sheet of waxed paper. Coat chicken breasts with seasoned flour, pressing with your hands so flour adheres and chicken is flattened evenly.

3 Lightly coat skillet again with cooking spray and set over medium-high heat. Cook chicken until browned and almost cooked through, about 3 minutes on each side. Return apple mixture and any juices to skillet and bring to a boil. Reduce heat and simmer 2 minutes. Stir in cream and remove from heat.

STEP 1 *Cut lengthwise and crosswise slits in shallot, then slice down, letting small pieces fall away.*

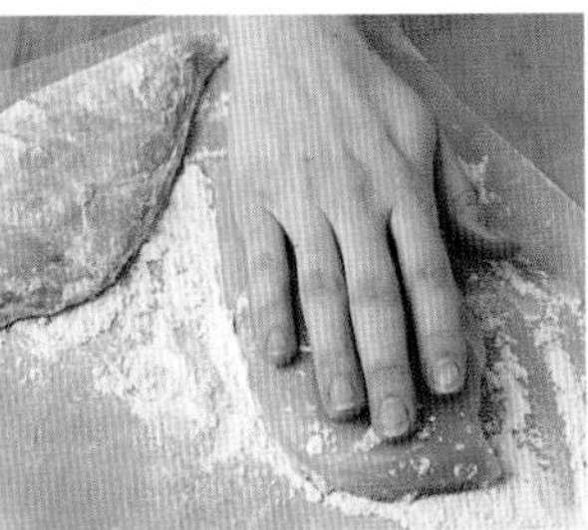

STEP 2 *Pat flour onto chicken, pressing gently to flatten.*

STEP 3 *To finish sauce, stir in cream, then remove from heat.*

secret to success

To give the sauce a lush, satiny smoothness, stir in a smidgen of heavy cream at the end. A small amount adds a satisfying richness to sauces without ruining your healthy eating goals.

way back when... Apples began their crucial role in history with the Bible story of Adam and Eve. Norse mythology dictated that a magic apple could keep people eternally young. In the 1800s, American John Chapman, better known as Johnny Appleseed, walked barefoot across the country and planted apple trees.

(Source: www.whfoods.com)

HEALTH HINT

An apple a day may not keep the doctor away, but several studies suggest a link between apple consumption and a reduced risk of cardiovascular disease. Apples contain ellagic acid, an antioxidant substance that protects against heart disease and cancer. They're also a good source of cholesterol-lowering soluble fiber.

Round Out the Meal

Serve with wild rice, sautéed green beans, and raspberry sorbet with diced mango for dessert.

Finger-Lickin' Fried Chicken

Low-fat fried chicken? Yes! With its crispy, golden crust and savory, juicy meat, you'll never guess this chicken dish is heart smart. Fry a batch for your family, or go all out with a triple batch for friends—either way, the pieces will fly from the platter! Drizzle it with a little honey for a real treat.

PER SERVING

399 calories / 29% from fat

2 g saturated fat, 13 g total fat

104 mg cholesterol

867 mg sodium

27 g total carbohydrate

1 g dietary fiber

43 g protein

PREP TIME 15 min. + soaking	COOK TIME 30 min.	SERVES 4

- 4 bone-in chicken breast halves (8 ounces each)
- 1 cup low-fat buttermilk
- 1 cup all-purpose flour
- 1 teaspoon salt
- 1 teaspoon paprika
- ½ teaspoon black pepper
- 2 tablespoons canola oil

1 Remove skin and any visible fat from chicken. Trim cartilage and rib bone tips. Put chicken in shallow baking dish and add buttermilk. Cover and refrigerate at least 1 hour or up to 8 hours, turning chicken occasionally.

2 Preheat oven to 400°F. Lightly coat 13 x 9-inch baking pan with nonstick cooking spray. Combine flour, salt, paprika, and black pepper in a paper or heavy plastic bag. Shake chicken, two pieces at a time, in seasoned flour.

3 Heat oil in very large nonstick skillet over medium-high heat until hot but not smoking. Brown chicken in skillet until golden brown, about 4 minutes on each side.

4 Put in baking pan and transfer to oven. Bake, uncovered, until chicken is crispy and juices run clear, about 10 minutes on each side.

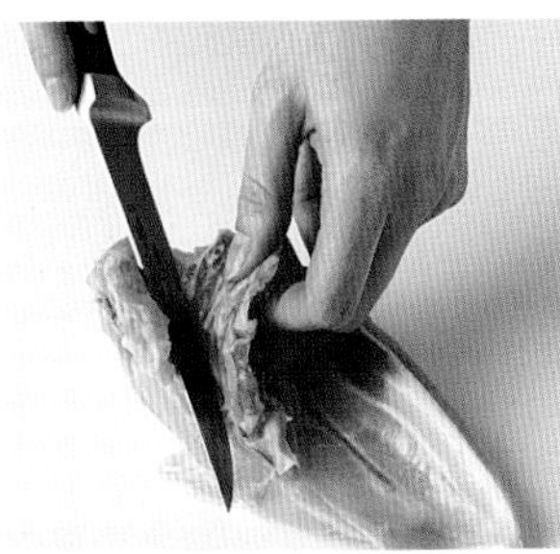

STEP 1 *Trim away white cartilage and 1 inch of rib bones.*

STEP 3 *Use tongs to turn chicken when golden brown.*

STEP 4 *Transfer chicken to oven to finish cooking.*

secret to success

This fried chicken is lower in fat than most because the skin is removed before cooking. In addition, it's fried in just a couple of tablespoons of oil, then baked in the oven till crisp, rather than being immersed in oil in a deep-fat fryer.

Round Out the Meal

Serve with lightly steamed sugar snap peas and roasted garlic mashed potatoes. Serve small amounts of mixed-berry cobbler for dessert.

HEALTH HINT

Chicken is an excellent source of high-quality protein with all of the essential amino acids. It also provides iron (essential to the blood's distribution of oxygen in the body), zinc (important in cell division and immune function), phosphorus (plays a role in energy production and cell formation), and potassium (regulates heart contractions).

Cook's Clue

Add paprika near the end of the cooking process since heat diminishes the color and lessens the flavor. Paprika is a less common ingredient, so experiment to find your desired amount. Try sweet or hot paprika, or combine them.

Country Captain Chicken

In the 19th century, when no place seemed more exotic to Americans than India, this "foreign" chicken dish offered a welcome change from plain old chicken stew. Country Captain is rich with tomatoes, an excellent source of the phytochemical lycopene, which may help fight heart disease. Lycopene is most available when the tomatoes are cooked with a little fat, as they are in this recipe.

PER SERVING

258 calories / 28% from fat
1 g saturated fat, 8 g total fat
82 mg cholesterol
431 mg sodium
12 g total carbohydrate
3 g dietary fiber
35 g protein

PREP TIME 10 min. | **COOK TIME** 35 min. | **SERVES** 4

- 2 teaspoons olive oil
- 4 boneless, skinless chicken breast halves (5 ounces each)
- 1 small onion, thinly sliced
- 3 garlic cloves, minced
- 1 tablespoon curry powder
- 1⅓ cups canned crushed tomatoes
- ¼ cup dried apricots, thinly sliced
- ½ teaspoon salt
- ½ teaspoon dried thyme
- ¼ teaspoon black pepper
- ¼ cup sliced almonds

1 Heat oil in large nonstick Dutch oven over medium heat. Add chicken and sauté until golden brown, about 3 minutes per side. With tongs or slotted spoon, transfer chicken to plate.

2 Add onion and garlic to pan and cook until onion is tender, about 5 minutes.

3 Stir in curry powder and cook for 1 minute. Add tomatoes, apricots, salt, thyme, and black pepper and bring to a boil.

4 Return chicken (and any accumulated juices) to Dutch oven. Reduce to a simmer, cover, and cook until chicken is cooked through, about 20 minutes. (Recipe can be made ahead to this point and refrigerated. Reheat in 325°F oven.) Serve sprinkled with almonds.

STEP 1 *Transfer sautéed chicken to a plate, and set aside while you cook remaining ingredients.*

STEP 3 *Add sliced apricots to tomato mixture in pan.*

STEP 4 *Return chicken to tomato–curry mixture in pan. Be sure to include any chicken juices that accumulated on the plate.*

Round Out the Meal

Serve with brown rice pilaf with red onions and low-fat peach ice cream with sliced fresh peaches for dessert.

HEALTH HINT

The fat in almonds is mostly monounsaturated, the type that helps lower LDL ("bad") cholesterol and preserves HDL ("good") cholesterol levels. Like all plant foods, almonds have no cholesterol.

way back when... This dish comes from an early 19th-century British sea captain stationed in Bengali, India, who shared the recipe with friends in the ports of Savannah, Georgia—one of that era's major crossroads for the spice trade. It was named after Indian officers, or "Country Captains." In Bengal, it denotes a dry form of curry and is served for breakfast.

(Source: www.whatscookingamerica.net)

Chicken with 40 Cloves of Garlic

If you're a garlic lover, you've already decided to serve this for dinner tonight. But if the thought of 40 cloves of garlic scares you, remember that slow cooking tames garlic's pungency, turning it into a mellow, low-fat "butter." Squeeze the cooked garlic cloves out of their skins onto bread or toast.

PER SERVING

355 calories / 23% from fat

2 g saturated fat, 9 g total fat

119 mg cholesterol

847 mg sodium

31 g total carbohydrate

3 g dietary fiber

32 g protein

PREP TIME 15 min.	COOK TIME 45 min.	SERVES 4

- 2 teaspoons olive oil
- 1 pound small white boiling potatoes, quartered if large
- 3 celery stalks, thickly sliced
- 2 carrots, halved lengthwise and cut crosswise into 1½-inch lengths
- 40 garlic cloves, unpeeled
- ¾ teaspoon tarragon
- ½ teaspoon rosemary, minced
- ¾ teaspoon salt
- 1 cup reduced-sodium, fat-free chicken broth
- ½ cup dry vermouth or chicken broth
- 4 boneless, skinless chicken thighs (5 ounces each)
- ¼ cup chopped parsley

1 Preheat oven to 350°F. Combine oil, potatoes, celery, carrots, garlic, tarragon, rosemary, and salt in Dutch oven or flameproof casserole. Toss to combine.

2 Add broth and vermouth to pan and bring to a boil over medium heat. Reduce to a simmer, cover, and cook 10 minutes.

3 Add chicken, cover, and place in oven. Bake until chicken is cooked through and potatoes and garlic are tender, about 30 minutes. (Recipe can be made ahead to this point and refrigerated. Reheat in 350°F oven before proceeding.) Stir in parsley just before serving.

Round Out the Meal

Serve with a tossed salad with a red wine vinaigrette, spread the cooked garlic on peasant bread, and offer raspberry sorbet for dessert.

way back when... James Beard is credited with introducing this dish in his book *How to Eat Better for Less Money*, first published in 1954. He reassured readers that the garlic would lose its sharpness when cooked, so it is "perfectly feasible to use . . . what would seem . . . like an inordinate amount of garlic."

Cook's Clue

Tarragon can be tricky. Because oils dissipate in dried tarragon, its flavor is more intense, and it should be used sparingly. To keep fresh flavor in tarragon, freeze sprigs in an airtight bag for three to five months, but use within a year. Heat dramatically intensifies the flavor.

HEALTH HINT

Studies show garlic's strong antioxidant qualities that contribute to cardiovascular health, and the seasoning can reduce LDL or "bad" cholesterol levels. It is also a blood-thinning agent that helps avoid blood clots that lead to heart attack or stroke.

STEP 1 *Toss vegetables to coat well with oil and seasonings.*

STEP 2 *Add vermouth and chicken broth to casserole.*

STEP 3 *After bringing ingredients to a boil, add chicken and transfer casserole to oven.*

Roast Chicken with Old-Fashioned Stuffing

PER SERVING

419 calories / 28% from fat

3.5 g saturated fat, 13 g total fat

145 mg cholesterol

862 mg sodium

22 g total carbohydrate

2 g dietary fiber

51 g protein

Always an impressive dish, a whole chicken provides plenty of protein, little saturated fat, and good amounts of B vitamins and zinc. A meal like this is perfect for noteworthy occasions—even for something as simple as the whole family being home for dinner.

PREP TIME 30 min.	COOK TIME 2 hrs. 15 min.	SERVES 6

- 2 tablespoons fresh thyme leaves, plus sprigs for stuffing
- 2 tablespoons chopped fresh sage
- ½ teaspoon salt
- ½ teaspoon freshly ground black pepper, or to taste
- 1 whole chicken (about 4 pounds), giblets removed
- 1 lemon, thinly sliced
- 3 medium onions, chopped
- 3 celery stalks, chopped
- 1 can (14½ ounces) low-fat chicken broth
- 4 cups dry herb bread stuffing

Round Out the Meal

Serve with steamed broccoli florets, honey-glazed carrots, and cranberry relish for a celebratory supper any day of the week.

1 Preheat oven to 425°F. Mix thyme, sage, salt, and black pepper in small bowl. Gently separate chicken skin from breast, and insert one-third of herb mixture and lemon slices under skin. Sprinkle another one-third of herb mixture in cavities and over chicken.

2 Lightly coat large nonstick skillet with nonstick cooking spray and set over medium-high heat. Sauté onions and celery until soft, 5 minutes. Stir in remaining herb mixture. Pour in 1 cup broth and 1 cup water. Bring to a boil. Add stuffing and toss until liquid is completely absorbed. Remove from heat.

3 Loosely stuff chicken cavities with stuffing, top stuffing with thyme sprigs, and tie legs together. Place chicken, breast-side down, on rack in roasting pan. Pour in remaining broth and 1 cup water. Roast 30 minutes. Turn chicken breast side up.

4 Reduce temperature to 350°F. Roast chicken, basting every 20 minutes with pan drippings, until thermometer inserted in thigh (not touching bone) reads 180°F and juices run clear, about 1½ hours longer. Transfer stuffing to bowl and discard thyme leaves. Let chicken stand 10 minutes before carving. Discard lemon slices and skin before serving.

HEALTH HINT

Lemons and limes contain vitamin C, an important antioxidant. It neutralizes free radicals that damage healthy cells in the body and cause inflammation and swelling. Vitamin C also helps prevent free radicals from damaging blood vessels and causing cholesterol to build up in artery walls.

STEP 1 *Gently insert fresh herbs under skin.*

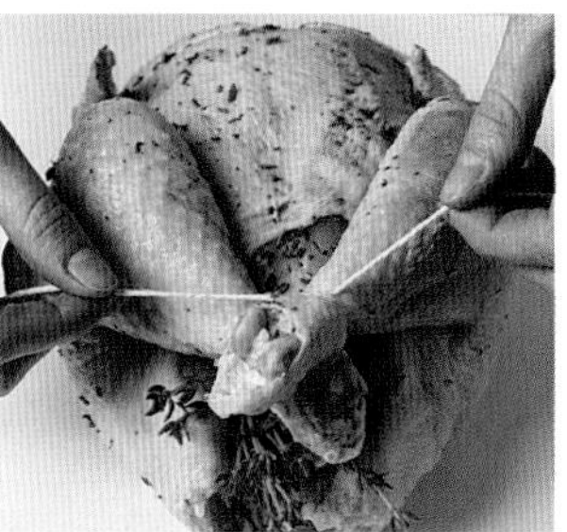

STEP 3 *Tie legs together with kitchen string.*

secret to success

To ensure a juicy bird, start roasting it breast-side down so the juices flow over the breast. Finish roasting it breast-side up, basting the bird frequently to add extra moisture. Cook with the skin on to seal in the juices, but be sure to discard it before eating, since most of the fat is found in the skin.

Orange-Glazed Cornish Hens

The best of the hardy White Rock chicken and England's flavorful Cornish hen—all in one small meaty, tender bird. And with this recipe, the hens are glazed as they roast with a delicious orange–tea marmalade. Plus, a wealth of heart-healthy vitamins and minerals come in each little hen.

PER SERVING

280 calories / 19% from fat
1.5 g saturated fat, 6 g total fat
136 mg cholesterol
262 mg sodium
31 g total carbohydrate
5 g dietary fiber
32 g protein

PREP TIME 20 min.	COOK TIME 1 hr. + standing	SERVES 4

- 1 tea bag, such as Earl Grey
- 2 medium oranges
- ½ cup no-sugar-added orange marmalade
- 4 Cornish hens (1 pound each), thawed if frozen
- ½ teaspoon black pepper
- ¼ teaspoon salt
- 2 medium onions, sliced
- 8 sprigs fresh rosemary
- 8 sprigs fresh thyme

1 Preheat oven to 375°F. Fit a roasting pan with rack. Steep tea bag in ¼ cup boiling water for 5 minutes in small saucepan. Discard tea bag. Squeeze juice from 1 orange into tea, and then stir in marmalade until melted. Keep warm. Cut remaining orange into quarters (do not peel).

2 Remove and discard giblets from hens. Wash hens and dry thoroughly, and then sprinkle cavities with black pepper and salt. Loosen breast skin slightly.

3 Stuff large cavity of each hen with 1 orange quarter, one-fourth of the onion slices, 1 rosemary sprig, and 1 thyme sprig. Tie legs together with kitchen string. Place hens, breast-side up, on rack in roasting pan. Brush hens over and under skin with about one-fourth of glaze.

4 Pour enough water into pan to cover bottom (water should not reach rack).

5 Roast hens on middle oven rack, basting over and under skin every 20 minutes with remaining glaze, until browned and juices run clear, about 1 hour. Let hens stand 10 minutes. Discard rosemary, thyme, onions, and orange from cavities of hens. Garnish with remaining rosemary and thyme sprigs. Discard skin before eating.

Round Out the Meal

Serve each hen on a bed of wild rice cooked with chopped onions and dried apricots. Add fresh green peas tossed with mint and a spoonful of cranberry sauce on the side. End the meal perfectly with a bowlful of raspberries topped with a little lemon ice.

STEP 2 *Wipe hens dry, inside and out, with paper towel.*

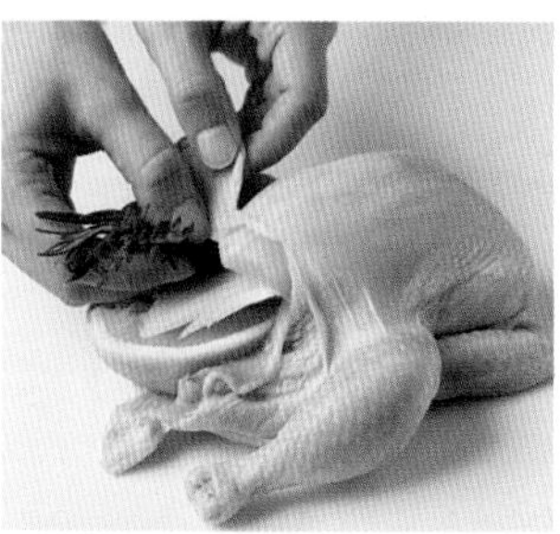

STEP 3 *Stuff cavity with onion, orange, and a sprig each of rosemary and thyme.*

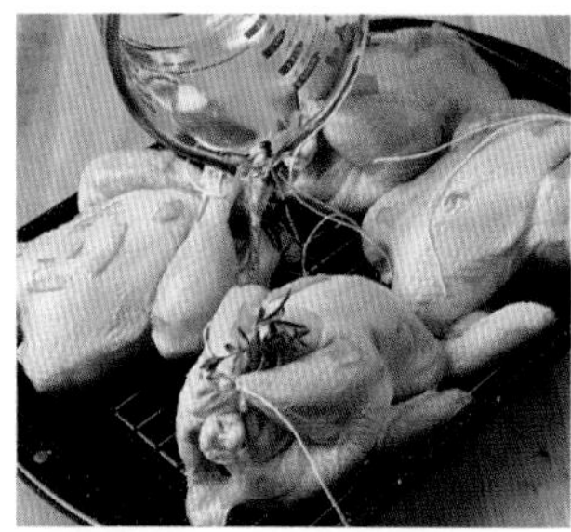

STEP 4 *Pour in enough water to just cover bottom of pan.*

Cook's Clue

Don't cry over cutting onions, follow these simple steps: Chill the onion an hour before cutting, use a sharp knife, and stand with eyes as far away as possible. If this doesn't work, try goggles.

secret to success

Buy fresh Cornish hens if you can find them. If not, frozen hens are fine. Thaw them in the refrigerator overnight, leaving them wrapped so they don't dry out. Or place hens in a large bowl of cool water until they are soft to the touch, about 4 hours, changing water every 30 minutes.

HEALTH HINT

Cornish hens with skins removed are relatively low in total fat, especially saturated fat.

Grilled Jamaican Jerk Chicken

PER SERVING
302 calories / 22% from fat
1.5 g saturated fat, 7.5 g total fat
82 mg cholesterol
558 mg sodium
25 g total carbohydrate
4 g dietary fiber
35 g protein

The saucy seasoning mixture that adds spark to Jamaican-style "jerk" meats and poultry is a uniquely Caribbean blend of spicy, sweet, and hot. For a healthfully varied meal, we've added bell peppers, pineapple, and scallions to the dish. To spare tender palates, we've substituted a pickled jalapeño for the more traditional and extremely hot Scotch Bonnet chiles.

PREP TIME 15 min. + marinating | **COOK TIME 15 min.** | **SERVES 4**

- 1 tablespoon ground allspice
- 4 garlic cloves, minced
- 1 tablespoon minced fresh ginger
- 1 large pickled jalapeño pepper, minced
- ¼ cup white wine vinegar
- 1½ tablespoons light brown sugar
- 1½ tablespoons olive oil
- 1¼ teaspoons black pepper
- ¾ teaspoon salt
- 4 boneless, skinless chicken breast halves (5 ounces each)
- 8 scallions
- 2 large red bell peppers, seeded and cut into 32 chunks
- 24 canned pineapple chunks (about 1½ cups)

Cook's Clue

To cut and seed peppers, use a paring knife to cut around the stem and remove it, then cut the pepper lengthwise in half, and clean out the core and seeds. With skin side down on the cutting board, cut desired size or shape.

1 Combine allspice, garlic, ginger, jalapeño, vinegar, brown sugar, oil, black pepper, and salt in large bowl. Measure out 2 tablespoons of mixture and set aside. Add chicken to mixture remaining in bowl and turn to coat on all sides. Refrigerate for 1 hour. (Don't leave chicken longer than 1 hour or ginger and vinegar will start to break down the fiber of chicken.)

2 Trim scallions, leaving just a small portion of tender green. Cut each scallion into 3 pieces.

3 Preheat grill to medium. On each of 8 long skewers, alternately thread 3 pieces of scallion, 4 pieces of bell pepper, and 3 pieces of pineapple.

4 Lift chicken from marinade and place chicken on grill. Brush reserved 2 tablespoons spice mixture over skewers and place on grill. Grill, turning chicken and skewers once, until chicken is cooked through and vegetables are crisp-tender, 5 to 10 minutes for the skewers, 10 to 15 minutes for the chicken.

Round Out the Meal

Serve with basmati and wild rice pilaf, and sliced mango for dessert.

HEALTH HINT

Learning to cook with spices is a heart-smart way of reducing the need for oil and salt in many recipes. Some spices, such as ginger and garlic, also contain cardioprotective antioxidants that provide additional health benefits.

STEP 1 *Turn chicken to coat with spicy jerk marinade.*

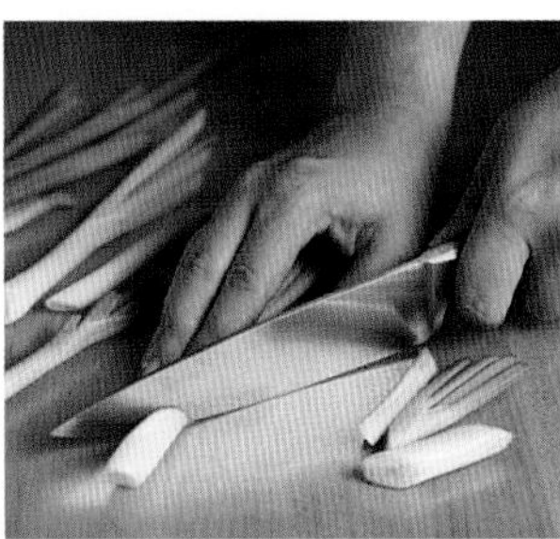

STEP 2 *After trimming dark green tops off, cut each scallion into 3 pieces.*

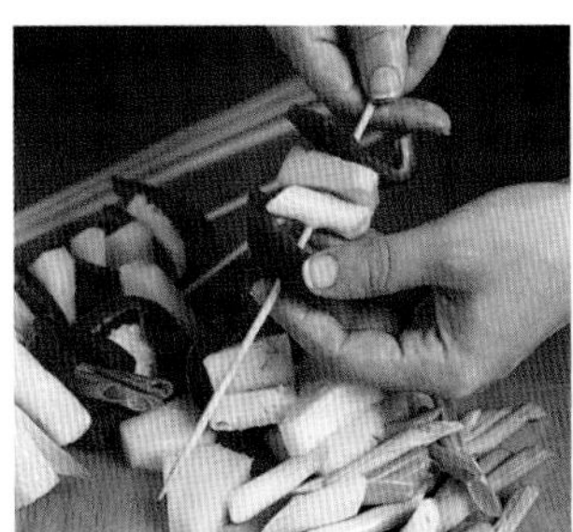

STEP 3 *Thread scallions, bell peppers, and pineapples onto skewers.*

One-Crust Chicken Potpies

PER SERVING
425 calories / 28% from fat
4 g saturated fat, 13 g total fat
72 mg cholesterol
580 mg sodium
42 g total carbohydrate
3 g dietary fiber
32 g protein

Satisfy your appetite for homey, honest fare like Mom used to make with chicken potpies—updated for the way you cook today. They're lower in fat (reduced-fat milk and just a little bit of margarine make sure of it) and faster to put together (frozen vegetables and refrigerated piecrusts do the trick). Yet they're still full of big helpings of old-fashioned flavor.

PREP TIME 20 min. | **COOK TIME 55 min.** | **SERVES 6**

- 1½ pounds boneless, skinless chicken breasts
- ½ teaspoon salt
- 1 refrigerated piecrust (1 crust from 15-ounce package)
- 1 egg white, lightly beaten with 1 teaspoon water
- 2 medium carrots, peeled and thinly sliced
- 1 cup frozen corn kernels
- 1 cup frozen green peas
- 1 cup frozen small white onions
- 1 cup nonfat half-and-half
- 6 tablespoons all-purpose flour
- 1 tablespoon margarine
- ¼ teaspoon black pepper

1 Bring chicken breasts, ¼ teaspoon salt, and enough water to cover to a simmer in large saucepan over medium-high heat. Reduce heat to low, and gently poach chicken until juices run clear, about 15 minutes. Transfer chicken to cutting board; cool and cut into bite-size pieces. Reserve 2 cups poaching liquid.

2 Preheat oven to 425°F. Lightly coat baking sheet and six 1-cup ovenproof dishes with nonstick cooking spray.

3 Dust work surface lightly with flour. Unfold piecrust on surface and roll out ⅛ inch thick. Cut out 6 squares to fit on top of pies.

4 Make 6 decorations and attach 1 cutout to each pastry square with egg white. Brush tops of decorated pastries with egg white. Transfer to baking sheet and bake until crisp and golden brown, about 12 minutes. Transfer to wire rack to cool.

5 Meanwhile, cook carrots in boiling water until tender, about 5 minutes; drain. Rinse frozen vegetables with hot water; drain. Whisk half-and-half and flour in small bowl until smooth. Melt margarine in medium saucepan over medium heat. Whisk in half-and-half mixture, then reserved poaching liquid. Cook until sauce thickens and boils, about 5 minutes. Stir in chicken, carrots, corn, peas, onions, black pepper, and remaining salt. Cook until heated through, about 3 minutes; divide among dishes and bake until pie is bubbling, about 15 minutes. Top each with a pastry square.

Cook's Clue

Tired of soggy pastry? Bake pastry squares separately on a baking sheet until crisp, as in our recipe. When pies are ready, pop the pastries on top.

STEP 3 *Using a pastry cutter, cut 6 pastry squares to fit baking dishes.*

STEP 4 *Make 6 decorations and attach.*

STEP 5 *Quick-thaw frozen vegetables with hot water.*

Round Out the Meal

Start off with a baby spinach salad mixed with avocado slices and dried cranberries. Drizzle lightly with a cranberry vinaigrette and top with fresh ground pepper.

Chicken Roulades with Spinach and Mushrooms

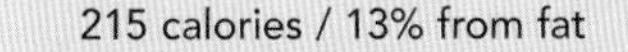

PER SERVING

215 calories / 13% from fat

1 g saturated fat, 3 g total fat

84 mg cholesterol

531 mg sodium

8 g total carbohydrate

4 g dietary fiber

38 g protein

Elegant and delicious—a winner of a dinner! Skinless, low-fat chicken breasts are rolled around a luscious spinach–portobello mixture, cooked to perfection, and then sliced to show off the swirls of filling inside. Pamper yourself with this classy dish, or let it star at your next dinner party.

PREP TIME 20 min. | **COOK TIME 23 min.** | **SERVES 4**

- 1 large portobello mushroom
- 4 scallions, sliced
- 1 package (10 ounces) fresh spinach, cleaned and coarsely chopped
- 2 tablespoons plain dry bread crumbs
- 2 tablespoons grated Parmesan cheese
- ½ teaspoon salt
- ½ teaspoon black pepper
- 4 boneless, skinless chicken breast halves (5 or 6 ounces each)
- ½ cup reduced-sodium chicken broth

1 Preheat oven to 350°F. Remove stem from mushroom; coarsely chop cap. Coat large nonstick ovenproof skillet with nonstick cooking spray and set over medium-high heat. Sauté mushroom and scallions until mushroom is tender, about 5 minutes. Stir in spinach and cook until wilted, about 2 minutes; transfer vegetables with slotted spoon to large bowl. Add bread crumbs, Parmesan, ¼ teaspoon salt, and ¼ teaspoon black pepper. Toss to coat.

2 Pound chicken breasts between two sheets of plastic wrap to ¼ inch thick. Sprinkle with remaining salt and black pepper. Spread 2 heaping tablespoons of spinach filling on each breast to about ½ inch from edges. Starting at one of the narrower ends, roll up. Secure roulades with toothpicks.

3 Coat skillet again with cooking spray; set over high heat. Add roulades, seam-side down, and cook until browned all over, about 6 minutes. Pour in broth. Cover skillet and transfer to oven. Bake chicken until juices run clear, about 8 minutes.

4 To serve, remove picks from roulades. Diagonally cut chicken into ½-inch slices. Serve, drizzled with pan drippings.

Round Out the Meal

Serve with spaghetti and broiled tomato halves topped with a sprinkling of seasoned bread crumbs. For dessert, offer poached peeled pears in cranberry juice.

HEALTH HINT

Spinach contains many heart-friendly nutrients and vitamins, such as vitamins A and C, folate, and magnesium. The beta-carotene (vitamin A) and antioxidant (vitamin C) synergize to prevent cholesterol from oxidizing, sticking, or building up in blood vessel walls, causing heart attack or stroke. The magnesium in spinach helps lower blood pressure and protects against heart disease.

STEP 1 *Toss bread crumbs, Parmesan, salt, and black pepper with sautéed vegetables.*

STEP 2 *Roll up flattened chicken breast from narrow end, enclosing filling.*

STEP 3 *Sauté roulades until golden brown.*

Cook's Clue

Placing roulades seam-side down in skillet to brown seals them closed and helps prevent unrolling.

Grilled Duck Breast Peking Style

If you started from scratch and made a classic Peking duck, you'd have to begin preparations several days ahead of time. For this version, we've pared the effort (and the fat) way down. Use a scallion brush to spread hoisin sauce on a tortilla, and top with duck, lettuce, oranges, and scallions.

PER SERVING

487 calories / 11% from fat
1 g saturated fat, 6 g total fat
163 mg cholesterol
979 mg sodium
68 g total carbohydrate
6 g dietary fiber
42 g protein

PREP TIME 15 min. | **COOK TIME 10 min.** | **SERVES 4**

- 2 teaspoons five-spice powder
- 1 teaspoon light brown sugar
- ½ teaspoon salt
- 4 skinless, boneless duck breasts (5 ounces each)
- 8 low-fat flour tortillas (8 inches)
- ¼ cup hoisin sauce
- 1 tablespoon rice vinegar
- 2 cups shredded lettuce
- 2 cups orange segments
- 8 scallions, cut into scallion brushes (*see photos, right*)

1 Combine five-spice powder, brown sugar, and salt in small bowl. Rub mixture into both sides of duck breasts. Spray a grill or stovetop grill pan with nonstick cooking spray. Preheat grill or place grill pan over medium heat.

2 Grill duck 4 inches from heat or in pan over medium heat until just cooked through, about 3 minutes per side. When cool enough to handle, but still warm, thinly slice duck across the grain.

3 Meanwhile, grill tortillas until golden, about 20 seconds on each side.

4 Whisk together hoisin sauce and vinegar in small bowl.

5 On each of 4 plates, arrange tortillas, lettuce, orange segments, sliced duck, and scallion brushes. To eat, spread hoisin sauce mixture on tortillas, top with remaining ingredients, and fold tortillas over.

Round Out the Meal

Serve with vegetarian hot and sour soup, and fortune cookies for dessert.

Cook's Clue

Hoisin sauce is sold in most supermarkets, but if you can't find it, substitute a mixture of ¼ cup plum jam and 2 teaspoons soy sauce. No five-spice powder? For a streamlined (four-spice) version that will taste as good, combine ½ teaspoon each of ground anise, cinnamon, cloves, and black pepper for a total of 2 teaspoons.

HEALTH HINT

Skinless duck breast is even leaner than skinless chicken breast. A 3-ounce serving of skinless cooked duck breast has only 2 grams of fat compared to 3 grams in an equal amount of chicken breast.

secret to success

For high juice content, choose oranges with smoothly textured skin that are firm and heavy for their size. Typically, smaller oranges are juicier than larger oranges.

Making Scallion Brushes

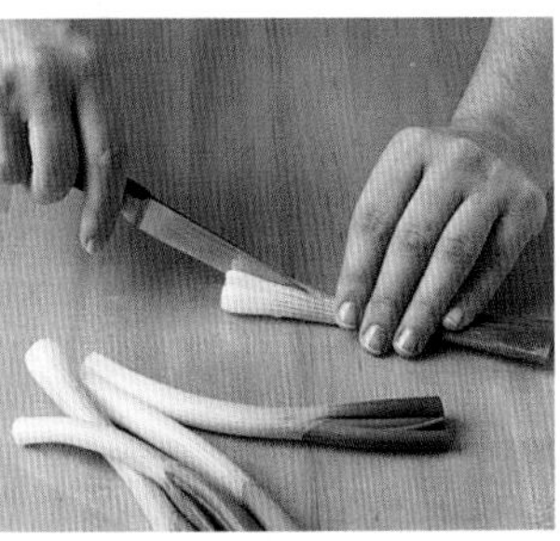

Trim both ends from the scallions. With a small paring knife, cut lengthwise through the white bulb.

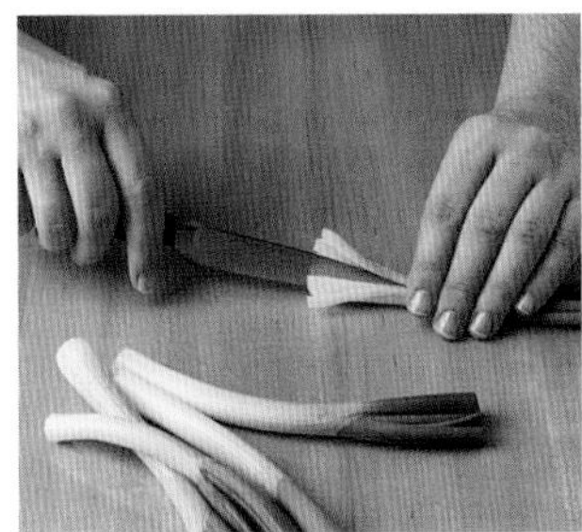

Give the scallion a quarter turn and cut the bulb again. Repeat several more times to make a "brush" end.

If desired, use the tip of a knife to feather the green end of the scallion as well. Place in a bowl of ice water to make the brushes open up.

Turkey and Black Bean Enchiladas

PER SERVING

369 calories / 17% from fat

3.5 g saturated fat, 7 g total fat

62 mg cholesterol

1,088 mg sodium

45 g total carbohydrate

9 g dietary fiber

34 g protein

Make way for the Mexican Express! Fifteen minutes in the oven, and these hearty, easy-to-fix enchiladas, packed with lean turkey, heart-healthy black beans, and melted reduced-fat cheese, are bubbling hot and ready to serve.

PREP TIME 15 min.	COOK TIME 15 min.	SERVES 4

- 2½ cups medium salsa
- ¼ cup chopped cilantro
- 1 teaspoon ground cumin
- 8 corn tortillas (6 inches)
- 8 ounces cooked turkey breast, shredded
- ¾ cup canned black beans, rinsed and drained
- 1 small red onion, finely chopped
- 1 cup shredded reduced-fat cheddar cheese (about 4 ounces)

1 Preheat oven to 350°F. Spray 7 x 11-inch baking dish with nonstick cooking spray, coating lightly but evenly.

2 Combine salsa, cilantro, and cumin in shallow bowl at least 6 inches in diameter.

3 Working with 1 at a time, dip tortilla in salsa mixture, coating it completely.

4 Place on plate or sheet of wax paper. Top each tortilla with 2 tablespoons salsa mixture. Top with ⅛ of turkey, beans, and red onion. Sprinkle with 1 tablespoon cheese. Roll tortilla up and place seam-side down in baking dish. Repeat filling and rolling with remaining tortillas.

5 Spoon remaining salsa mixture over enchiladas and sprinkle with remaining ½ cup cheese. Bake until bubbling, about 15 minutes.

Round Out the Meal

Serve with a fresh slaw of slivered green, red, and yellow bell peppers. Offer chilled mango cubes with lime wedges for dessert.

HEALTH HINT

All dried beans have good quantities of folate, but black beans are particularly rich in this important B vitamin, which lowers homocysteine levels in the blood—a known risk factor for heart disease. One cup of these nutritious beans gives you more than half of the day's requirement for folate.

secret to success

It took a while, but reduced-fat cheese has come into its own as a tasty, heart-smart ingredient. The sharper the cheese, the further the flavor goes, so use a sharp or extra-sharp cheddar for this recipe.

Cook's Clue

Presoak fresh beans to shorten cooking time and make them easier to digest. In a saucepan, add 2 to 3 cups of water for each cup of beans. Boil for 2 minutes, and let stand for 2 hours. Or soak beans for 8 hours with the pan in the refrigerator so the beans won't ferment. Before cooking, drain and rinse with clean water.

STEP 3 *Dip both sides of tortillas in salsa mixture to coat them completely.*

STEP 4 *Place bean–turkey filling down center of tortilla and roll up.*

STEP 5 *Arrange enchiladas seam-side down in baking dish and sprinkle evenly with cheddar.*

Apple-Stuffed Turkey Breast with Orange Marmalade Glaze

Feast on the best—while doing your heart good at the same time. This golden, glazed turkey breast, fragrant with fruit and herbs, is the perfect meat to roast any time of the year. It's a dish fit for a king . . . yet its fat intake is a humble 6 grams a serving!

PER SERVING

256 calories / 21% from fat
1.5 g saturated fat, 6 g total fat
43 mg cholesterol
636 mg sodium
32 g total carbohydrate
3 g dietary fiber
16 g protein

PREP TIME 15 min. | **COOK TIME** 1 hr. 15 min. + standing | **SERVES** 6

- 1 whole bone-in turkey breast (3 to 3½ pounds)
- 1½ teaspoons salt
- 1 teaspoon black pepper
- 2 celery stalks, cut into 1-inch pieces
- 2 large apples, peeled and thinly sliced
- 1 large onion, thinly sliced
- 5 sprigs fresh thyme plus 1 teaspoon chopped
- ½ cup low-sugar orange marmalade, warmed
- 2 cups apple juice
- ½ cup dry white wine or apple juice or cider

1 Preheat oven to 350°F. Rinse turkey, pat dry with paper towels, and rub skin all over with salt and black pepper.

2 Combine celery, half of apples, half of onion, and 3 thyme sprigs in roasting pan, and mound in center. Toss ¼ cup of the marmalade and the chopped thyme with remaining apples and onion in medium bowl. Stuff half of mixture under turkey skin; place remaining mixture in neck cavity.

3 Place turkey on top of vegetable mixture in roasting pan. Lightly coat turkey with nonstick cooking spray (preferably olive-oil flavored) and top with remaining thyme sprigs. Pour apple juice into pan. Roast 1 hour, discard thyme sprigs, and baste turkey with 2 tablespoons marmalade. Continue roasting until turkey is golden brown and instant-read thermometer inserted in thickest part of turkey (not touching bone) reaches 170°F, about 15 minutes longer, basting with remaining marmalade. Let stand 10 minutes to set juices.

4 Transfer turkey to platter. Stir wine into apples and vegetables in pan (do not strain). Bring to a boil over medium-high heat, and cook, scraping up browned bits from bottom of pan with wooden spoon, until pan liquid is reduced by half. Serve apple-vegetable sauce alongside turkey. Discard skin before eating.

Cook's Clue

Be careful handling raw turkey. Be sure it does not get close to other food, especially foods served uncooked. Thoroughly wash the cutting board, cooking utensils, and hands with hot soapy water after handling all meats and poultry.

HEALTH HINT

Skinless turkey breast has less fat and fewer calories than any other poultry: A 3-ounce serving of plain roasted turkey breast has only 135 calories and 3 grams of fat. So enjoy!

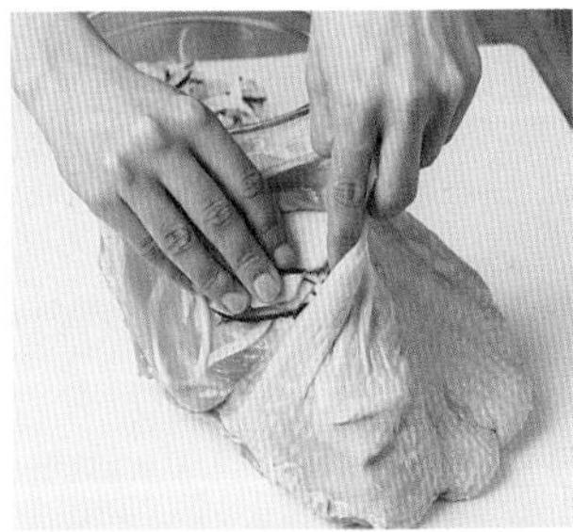

STEP 2 *Stuff apple–onion–thyme mixture under turkey skin.*

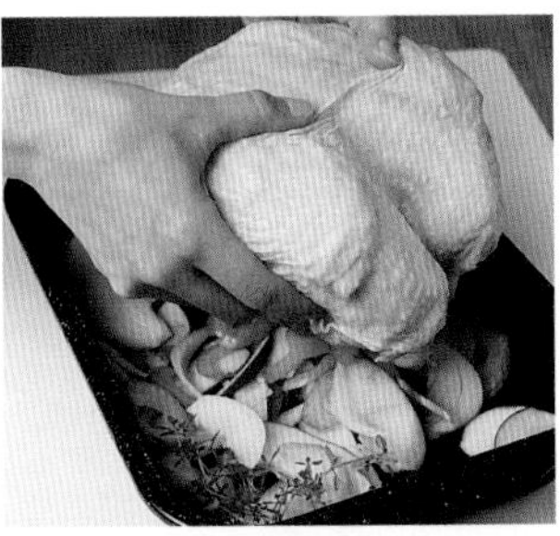

STEP 3 *Place turkey breast on mound of stuffing in pan.*

STEP 4 *Stir wine into apples and vegetables in pan and cook, scraping up browned bits.*

Round Out the Meal

Serve with sautéed baby red potatoes and a spinach–mushroom–red onion salad. End with a fruit tart.

Turkey Piccata

Company coming on a weeknight? Versatile turkey breast to the rescue! With today's widely available turkey breast cutlets, all kinds of luxurious, low-fat main dishes are always just minutes away. In this case, the turkey is cooked like veal cutlets, in a classic garlic–lemon sauce with capers. You'll have dinner ready in the time it takes to set a pretty table.

PER SERVING

187 calories / 19% from fat
1 g saturated fat, 4 g total fat
70 mg cholesterol
178 mg sodium
6 g total carbohydrate
0.5 g dietary fiber
30 g protein

PREP TIME 10 min.	COOK TIME 10 min.	SERVES 4

- 1 tablespoon olive oil
- 4 turkey cutlets (4 ounces each)
- 2 tablespoons flour
- 2 garlic cloves, minced
- 1 teaspoon grated lemon zest
- ¼ cup lemon juice
- 1 cup reduced-sodium, fat-free chicken broth
- 1 teaspoon cornstarch blended with 1 tablespoon water
- 1 tablespoon capers, rinsed and drained
- 2 tablespoons chopped parsley

1 Heat oil in large nonstick skillet over medium heat. Dredge turkey in flour, shaking off excess.

2 Sauté turkey until golden brown and cooked through, about 2 minutes per side. With tongs or slotted spoon, transfer turkey to plate; cover loosely with foil to keep warm.

3 Add garlic to pan and cook, stirring, until tender, about 1 minute. Add lemon zest, lemon juice, and chicken broth to pan and bring to a boil. Boil 1 minute.

4 Stir in cornstarch mixture and capers, and cook until slightly thickened, about 1 minute. Stir in parsley. Serve turkey with sauce spooned on top.

STEP 1 *Dredge turkey cutlets in flour and shake off excess.*

STEP 2 *After browning turkey on both sides, transfer to plate.*

STEP 4 *Stir cornstarch mixture and capers into pan juices, and cook to thicken sauce slightly.*

Round Out the Meal

Serve with brown rice with slivered almonds, steamed broccoli rabe, and poached plums with sweetened ricotta for dessert.

HEALTH HINT

Not only does lemon zest enhance flavor, but its potent phytochemicals may fend off the damaging free radicals that contribute to clogged arteries.

way back when... Not only does turkey remind us of family Thanksgiving dinners, but Benjamin Franklin wanted to declare turkey the national bird. Even astronauts Neil Armstrong and Buzz Aldrin ate roasted turkey for their first meal on the moon!

(Source: www.whfoods.com)

Cook's Clue

Dusting the turkey cutlets with a coating of flour helps lock in their juices so the turkey cooks up tender and juicy, with a tempting golden crust.

Italian Turkey Loaf

This memorable meatloaf is destined to become a family favorite, and because it's made from turkey breast—the leanest meat of all—it's especially kind to your heart. Moist and juicy, thanks to the addition of a bell pepper, parsley, and fat-free sour cream, the meatloaf is glazed with tomato paste.

PER SERVING

319 calories / 21% from fat

2.5 g saturated fat, 7.5 g total fat

109 mg cholesterol

805 mg sodium

16 g total carbohydrate

3 g dietary fiber

46 g protein

PREP TIME 15 min. | **COOK TIME 50 min.** | **SERVES 4**

- 1 tablespoon olive oil
- 1 large onion, finely chopped
- 5 garlic cloves, minced
- 1 tablespoon fennel seeds
- 1 large red bell pepper, seeded and finely chopped
- ⅓ cup parsley, finely chopped
- 1¼ pounds boneless, skinless turkey breast, cut into chunks
- 1 slice whole-grain bread, torn into pieces
- ¼ cup fat-free sour cream
- 2 large egg whites
- ¾ teaspoon salt
- ½ teaspoon black pepper
- ⅓ cup grated Parmesan cheese
- 2 tablespoons tomato paste

1 Preheat oven to 350°F. Spray an 8½ x 4½-inch loaf pan with nonstick cooking spray, coating lightly but evenly.

2 Heat oil in large nonstick skillet over medium heat. Add onion, garlic, and fennel seeds to the skillet and cook, stirring frequently, until onion is golden brown, about 7 minutes. Add red pepper and cook, stirring frequently, until pepper is tender, about 5 minutes. Transfer vegetables to large bowl and stir in parsley.

3 Place turkey in food processor, and pulse on and off until coarsely ground. Add bread pieces, sour cream, egg whites, salt, and black pepper, and pulse on and off until combined. Transfer to bowl with sautéed vegetables. Add Parmesan and stir to blend.

4 Spoon turkey mixture into loaf pan and smooth top. Bake 30 minutes. Increase oven temperature to 450°F.

5 Brush top of loaf with tomato paste and bake until top is glazed, about 5 minutes.

Round Out the Meal

Serve with semolina bread toasts, grilled red onions, and Italian green beans. Offer honey-glazed baked apples for dessert.

STEP 3 *Add bread pieces to food processor after grinding turkey breast.*

STEP 4 *Spoon turkey mixture into loaf pan and smooth top.*

STEP 5 *Brush top of loaf evenly with tomato paste.*

secret to success

Always store onions at room temperature, away from direct light in a well-ventilated area. Storage length depends on the type of onion. All onions should be kept away from potatoes, as potatoes absorb the moisture and ethylene gas of onions and cause them to spoil easier.

HEALTH HINT

To ensure that you're getting the leanest ground turkey (and thus the least amount of saturated fat), it's best to grind skinless turkey breast yourself whenever possible (as we've done in this recipe).

Beef, Pork, Veal and Lamb

Roasted Beef Tenderloin in Red Wine Sauce

PER SERVING
515 calories / 24% from fat
5 g saturated fat, 14 g total fat
139 mg cholesterol
590 mg sodium
48 g total carbohydrate
4 g dietary fiber
41 g protein

Cancel those dinner reservations! You can make the kind of show-off dinner you find in fine restaurants—and you don't have to be a chef to do it. The tenderloin almost cooks itself, and the vegetables that roast alongside it complement the meat perfectly.

PREP TIME 15 min. | **COOK TIME** 50 min. + 10 standing | **SERVES** 10

- 1 beef tenderloin roast (4 pounds), trimmed
- 2 teaspoons salt
- 1½ teaspoons coarsely ground black pepper
- 2 cups dry red wine (alcoholic or nonalcoholic)
- 2 pounds onions, chopped
- 3 garlic cloves, crushed
- 6 sprigs fresh thyme
- 10 ounces white mushrooms, trimmed
- 1 tablespoon sugar
- 12 ounces baby carrots (2 cups)
- 1 pint red or yellow cherry tomatoes
- 16 ounces wide egg noodles

secret to success

Never cook this cut beyond medium-rare. It loses tenderness and becomes dry the longer it's cooked. To test for doneness, don't cut into the meat because flavorful juices escape! Instead, use the touch method, pressing into the meat. If it is soft but springs back slightly, it is medium-rare. It is overdone if it feels firm.

1 Preheat oven to 450°F. Rub roast with salt and black pepper. Tuck ends under and tie with string. Mix wine with 1½ cups water.

2 Coat large heavy skillet with nonstick cooking spray and set over medium-high heat. Add tenderloin, one-third of onions, and garlic and sear meat until browned on all sides, about 10 minutes. Discard garlic and onion and transfer to roasting pan. Pour in half of wine mixture. Add 3 thyme sprigs and put pan in oven.

3 Meanwhile, set aside 5 mushrooms and slice remaining ones. Sauté sliced mushrooms, remaining onions, and sugar in skillet until brown, about 7 minutes. Cook carrots in boiling water in saucepan until crisp-tender, 5 to 7 minutes. Drain.

4 After meat roasts 20 minutes, add carrots and sautéed vegetables to pan. Pour in remaining wine mixture. Continue to roast until done to taste, about 25 minutes longer for medium. Transfer meat to cutting board and let stand 10 minutes. Add tomatoes to pan, cover, and let stand.

5 Meanwhile, cook noodles according to package directions. Drain. Trim reserved mushrooms and flute with paring knife. Coat small skillet with cooking spray and set over medium heat. Sauté mushrooms until golden, about 5 minutes. Arrange noodles and vegetables on platter. Slice beef and add to platter. Garnish with mushrooms and remaining thyme. Serve with pan juices.

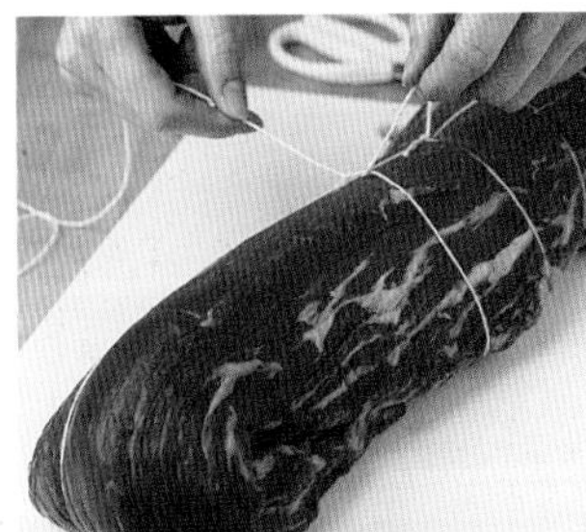

STEP 1 *Tuck end of tenderloin under to make even thickness and tie at 2-inch intervals.*

STEP 2 *Using tongs, turn meat frequently as it sears.*

STEP 5 *For an edible garnish, cut thin slivers out of mushroom caps, then sauté until golden.*

Italian Braised Beef with Garlic and Mushrooms

Sunday will never be the same when you serve up velvety slices of slow-cooked beef with a rich and subtle sauce—and a surprisingly low fat content. If you're busy on Sundays, braise the beef a day or two ahead of time; its flavors grow richer while it "waits" in the fridge.

PER SERVING

367 calories / 27% from fat

4 g saturated fat, 11 g total fat

65 mg cholesterol

641 mg sodium

27 g total carbohydrate

6 g dietary fiber

31 g protein

PREP TIME 20 min. | **COOK TIME 1 hr. 40 min.** | **SERVES 4**

- ½ cup dried porcini mushrooms (½ ounce)
- 1 cup hot water
- 1 cup canned crushed tomatoes
- 1 cup dry red wine or chicken broth
- 2 tablespoons tomato paste
- 3 carrots, cut into matchsticks
- 2 celery stalks, cut into matchsticks
- 4 garlic cloves, slivered
- 4 teaspoons brown sugar
- ¾ teaspoon oregano
- ¾ teaspoon salt
- ½ teaspoon black pepper
- 1 pound well-trimmed boneless beef eye round roast

1 Combine mushrooms and hot water in small bowl. Let stand 20 minutes until softened. With fingers, scoop mushrooms out of liquid. Strain mushroom soaking liquid through fine-meshed sieve and set aside. Coarsely chop mushrooms.

2 Preheat oven to 350°F. Combine mushrooms, mushroom soaking liquid, tomatoes, wine, tomato paste, carrots, celery, garlic, brown sugar, oregano, salt, and black pepper in Dutch oven or flame-proof casserole. Bring to a boil over medium heat.

3 Add meat to pan and return to a boil. Cover, place in oven, and bake until meat is tender, about 1½ hours.

4 Slice meat and serve with vegetables and sauce. (Recipe can be made ahead. Add sliced meat to pan of sauce and vegetables and refrigerate. Reheat in 250°F oven.)

Round Out the Meal

Serve with steamed broccoli rabe and pasta or mashed potatoes. For dessert, serve biscotti and espresso.

STEP 1 *After scooping mushrooms out, strain soaking liquid through fine-meshed strainer.*

STEP 2 *Add carrots, celery, and garlic to mushrooms, strained soaking liquid, and tomatoes.*

STEP 3 *Add meat to braising mixture. Tying roast with kitchen string helps keep its shape as it cooks.*

HEALTH HINT

Lean cuts of beef, such as eye round, are good sources of the mineral selenium, which protect the heart by reducing the stickiness of the blood and prevent clotting.

way back when... With origins in Central Asia over 6,000 years ago, garlic has served numerous purposes outside the kitchen. The Egyptians worshipped garlic and put clay models of bulbs in Pharaoh Tutankhamen's tomb. It was even used as currency! Legends state that it scares away vampires and protects against the "evil eye." It's also been used as an aphrodisiac. America has incorporated garlic into many dishes as a key ingredient, and over 250 million pounds are consumed each year.

(Source: http://homecooking.about.com)

Chili Steak with Texas Toasts

From the land of Beef (with a capital B) comes this classic combo of juicy sliced steak, confetti-bright corn relish, and a hefty hunk of grilled garlic toast, all presented in heart-friendly fashion, of course! Broil the steak and toasts in the oven, or light a fire and grill them outdoors.

PER SERVING

390 calories / 22% from fat

3.5 g saturated fat, 9.5 g total fat

44 mg cholesterol

963 mg sodium

52 g total carbohydrate

5 g dietary fiber

26 g protein

PREP TIME 25 min.	COOK TIME 10 min. + standing	SERVES 4

- 2 teaspoons ground cumin
- 1½ teaspoons chili powder
- ¾ teaspoon oregano
- ¾ teaspoon salt
- ½ teaspoon black pepper
- ⅔ cup spicy tomato-vegetable juice
- 3 tablespoons fresh lime juice
- 2 cups frozen corn, thawed
- 2 scallions, thinly sliced
- 1 small red bell pepper, seeded and diced
- 12 ounces well-trimmed flank steak
- 1 loaf (8 ounces) Italian bread, halved horizontally, then halved crosswise
- 1 garlic clove, peeled and halved

1 Stir together cumin, chili powder, oregano, salt, and black pepper in small bowl. Place tomato-vegetable juice and lime juice in measuring cup. Measure out 2½ teaspoons of spice mixture and stir into tomato-lime juice mixture.

2 Combine corn, scallions, red pepper, and ½ cup of tomato-lime juice mixture in medium bowl. Stir to combine. Refrigerate until serving time.

3 Preheat broiler. Rub remaining 1 tablespoon spice mixture onto both sides of steak. Broil flank steak 4 inches from heat until medium, about 4 minutes per side. Remove steak but leave broiler on. Let steak stand 10 minutes before thinly slicing across the grain, on the diagonal.

4 Meanwhile, broil bread, cut-side up, until lightly toasted, about 30 seconds. Rub bread on toasted side with cut garlic. Brush toasted side with remaining tomato-lime juice mixture and broil until lightly browned, about 1 minute. Serve steak with corn relish and toasts.

STEP 2 *Use some of spiced tomato-vegetable juice mixture as a dressing for corn relish.*

STEP 3 *Rub spice mixture onto both sides of flank steak before broiling.*

STEP 4 *After toasting bread and rubbing with cut garlic, brush with spicy tomato-lime mixture and stick under broiler again.*

secret to success

The garlic bread served in restaurants is soaked with butter, but these grilled Texas toasts are just fine without the fat because they're rubbed with garlic, then brushed with a pleasantly spicy tomato-lime mixture.

Round Out the Meal

Serve with a salad of baby greens and slices of chilled watermelon for dessert.

Cook's Clue

Poke the meat to judge its doneness! Compare the feeling of the meat to an area of your palm. The pad at the base of the thumb equals rare. The middle of the palm equals medium. The base below the pinky finger is well done. If you're still unsure, cut into the meat with a knife to check.

Steak and Onions

Onions and their cousins (garlic, leeks, shallots, scallions) are packed with antioxidant flavonoids that appear to reduce the risk of heart disease, so "an onion a day" is a good bet. In addition to their health benefits, these tangy, tender, caramelized onions make a sublime "sauce" for thin slices of lean, spice-rubbed steak.

PER SERVING
334 calories / 19% from fat
2 g saturated fat, 7 g total fat
71 mg cholesterol
502 mg sodium
37 g total carbohydrate
7 g dietary fiber
31 g protein

PREP TIME 15 min. | **COOK TIME 35 min.** | **SERVES 4**

- 2 teaspoons olive oil
- 5 large onions, halved and thinly sliced
- 1 tablespoon sugar
- 3 tablespoons balsamic vinegar
- 1 tablespoon slivered orange zest
- ¼ cup fresh orange juice
- ¾ teaspoon oregano
- ¾ teaspoon salt
- ½ teaspoon black pepper
- 1 pound well-trimmed boneless beef top round, cut about 2 inches thick
- 1 teaspoon garlic powder
- ¼ teaspoon cayenne pepper

1 Heat oil in large nonstick skillet over medium-high heat. Add onions and sugar, and cook, stirring occasionally, until onions begin to brown, about 20 minutes.

2 Add vinegar, orange zest, orange juice, ½ teaspoon of oregano, ½ teaspoon of salt, and black pepper. Cook until onions are wilted and glazed, about 5 minutes.

3 Meanwhile, preheat broiler. Rub beef with remaining ¼ teaspoon oregano, ¼ teaspoon salt, garlic powder, and cayenne pepper. Broil beef 4 inches from heat until medium, about 5 minutes per side. Allow to rest 5 minutes before cutting into thin slices.

Round Out the Meal

Serve with mashed potatoes, broccoli, and lemon angel food cake with fresh strawberries for dessert.

HEALTH HINT

Onions are champions of heart health. Sulfur compounds give onions their pungency, and flavonoids contribute flavor and color. They team up with soluble fiber to help lower cholesterol.

Cook's Clue

In most cases, garlic powder runs a distant second to fresh garlic, but when a dry spice rub is required, garlic powder is the ideal ingredient.

secret to success

With heat, balsamic vinegar becomes sweeter and loses its acidity. To mellow the flavor, simply don't heat it. Otherwise, add it just before serving. You may substitute sherry or red wine vinegar, but the flavor changes significantly.

STEP 1 *Cook onions until golden brown.*

STEP 2 *Add orange zest to browned onions.*

STEP 3 *Place beef on broiler pan, and rub both sides with garlic-herb mixture.*

Sizzling Beef Fajitas

This Mexican fiesta-on-a-plate consists of strips of marinated steak, bell peppers, and onions presented smoking-hot from the broiler, to be enfolded in tortillas with lettuce, cilantro, and fat-free sour cream. It's a treat for the family, but also ideal party fare, so plan to double or triple the recipe if you're entertaining a crowd.

PER SERVING

379 calories / 21% from fat
3 g saturated fat, 9 g total fat
63 mg cholesterol
319 mg sodium
45 g total carbohydrate
6 g dietary fiber
29 g protein

PREP TIME 10 min. | **COOK TIME 20 min.** | **SERVES 4**

- ¼ cup fresh lime juice
- 1 teaspoon chili powder
- ¾ teaspoon oregano
- ¾ teaspoon ground coriander
- ¼ teaspoon black pepper
- 12 ounces well-trimmed beef sirloin
- 2 large onions, thickly sliced
- 2 large red bell peppers, seeded and cut lengthwise into flat panels
- ¼ cup minced cilantro
- 4 flour tortillas (7 inches)
- 4 cups shredded romaine lettuce
- ¼ cup fat-free sour cream

HEALTH HINT

The vegetable mixture for these fajitas provides more than twice your daily requirement for vitamin C. This important vitamin works as an antioxidant to fight off a wide range of diseases.

1 Combine lime juice, chili powder, oregano, coriander, and black pepper in medium bowl.

2 Place beef in a shallow bowl and spoon 2 tablespoons of lime mixture on top; turn to coat both sides. Let stand while you broil the vegetables.

3 Preheat broiler. Spray broiler pan with nonstick cooking spray. Place onions and pepper pieces, skin-side up, on broiler pan. Broil 4 inches from heat until peppers are charred and onions are golden brown, about 10 minutes.

4 Remove, and when cool enough to handle, peel peppers and thickly slice. Add peppers and onions to lime juice mixture in bowl. Add cilantro and toss.

5 Broil beef until done to medium, about 8 minutes, turning it over midway. Let stand 5 minutes before thinly slicing. Broil tortillas until lightly browned, about 15 seconds per side.

6 Place beef, peppers, onions, lettuce, sour cream, and flour tortillas in serving containers. Let each person fill his or her own tortilla.

Round Out the Meal

Serve with low-fat chocolate pudding topped with crumbled cinnamon graham crackers for dessert.

Cook's Clue

Buy fresh cilantro with bright green leaves uniform in color. Avoid yellow or wilted cilantro. The stems and roots of cilantro can be eaten. Immerse them in a glass of water, cover with a plastic bag, and put in the refrigerator. Cut off leaves as you need them and always re-cover. Do not wash until you are ready to use cilantro because too much moisture makes the leaves slimy.

STEP 3 *Place onions and bell pepper pieces (skin-side up) on a broiler pan.*

STEP 4 *Once peppers are cool enough to handle, pull off charred skin.*

STEP 5 *Cut beef across the grain into thin slices.*

Blue Cheese–Stuffed Burger

WHAT?!? A cheeseburger on a healthy diet? Once in a while, you just gotta give in! For the sake of your heart, use extra-lean ground beef and a variety of cheese so strong you only need a little bit for lots of flavor. Keep the accompaniments low in fat, and you've got the makings of a surprisingly nutritious meal.

PER SERVING

416 calories / 24% from fat

4 g saturated fat, 11 g total fat

65 mg cholesterol

614 mg sodium

44 g total carbohydrate

4 g dietary fiber

35 g protein

PREP TIME 10 min. | **COOK TIME 15 min.** | **SERVES 4**

- ¾ pound extra-lean ground beef
- 1 cup quick-cooking oats (uncooked)
- 2 tablespoons ketchup
- 2 teaspoons Dijon mustard
- ¼ teaspoon black pepper
- ¼ cup crumbled blue cheese
- 4 hamburger rolls
- Romaine lettuce leaves
- 1 firm-ripe tomato, sliced
- 1 small red onion, sliced

1 Preheat broiler. Mix beef, oats, ketchup, mustard, and black pepper in large bowl until well blended. Divide into 8 equal pieces and flatten into thin patties.

2 Place 1 tablespoon of crumbled cheese in the center of each of 4 patties.

3 Top with remaining patties and pinch edges to seal completely.

4 Broil 4 inches from the heat until well done—4 to 6 minutes on each side. Serve burgers on rolls with lettuce, tomato, and red onion.

Round Out the Meal

Serve with homemade oven fries, a tossed salad with fat-free dressing, and a big slice of watermelon.

STEP 2 *Top a thin meat patty with crumbled blue cheese.*

STEP 3 *Place a second thin patty on top and pinch edges together to seal.*

HEALTH HINT

Ground beef is rich in iron, zinc, and B vitamins. If you can't find extra-lean ground beef in your supermarket, grind it yourself with a meat grinder or food processor. Use lean, well-trimmed cuts of meat from the neck, shoulder, or leg such as eye round or chuck.

way back when... During the Middle Ages in Russia, the Tartars shredded their meat, eating it raw, creating the idea of the hamburger. The term originated from the German city, Hamburg. The original Hamburg steak was pounded until tender, not chopped or ground. Near the 20th century, Dr. James Salisbury invented chopped beef patties to strengthen the Civil War soldiers' immune systems and advised eating beef three times a day.

(Source: http://homecooking.about.com)

secret to success

We extended the meat with quick-cooking oatmeal, which adds fiber and cuts back on the amount of saturated fat and cholesterol in every bite. You can also use bread crumbs, leftover rice, or soy protein processed to resemble meat.

Italian Meatballs in Tomato Sauce

Teamed with a bowl of hot pasta, this traditional dish will become a family classic after just one meal. Penne is shown here, but spaghetti, fusilli, or wagon wheels would also be good. This low-fat, vitamin-rich sauce is a tasty way to add more vegetables to your main dishes.

PER SERVING

281 calories / 10% from fat
3 g saturated fat, 10 g total fat
70 mg cholesterol
523 mg sodium
21 g total carbohydrate
4 g dietary fiber
29 g protein

PREP TIME 25 min. | **COOK TIME 50 min.** | **SERVES 4**

- 1½ teaspoons olive oil
- 2 garlic cloves, finely chopped
- 2 celery stalks, finely chopped
- 8 ounces lean ground beef
- 8 ounces lean ground pork
- ½ cup fresh bread crumbs
- 1 egg white
- ¼ teaspoon dried oregano
- ¼ teaspoon dried basil
- 1 can (28 ounces) crushed tomatoes
- 2 onions, finely chopped
- 2 tablespoons tomato paste
- ½ cup sliced ripe olives (optional)
- 2 tablespoons chopped parsley
- ⅛ teaspoon black pepper

1 Preheat oven to 350°F. In small skillet, heat oil over moderate heat. Add garlic and celery and sauté until softened and lightly browned, about 5 minutes. Remove from heat and let cool slightly.

2 In bowl, combine ground beef, ground pork, bread crumbs, egg white, oregano, and basil. Stir in celery mixture until just combined.

3 Using your hands, shape mixture into 16 meatballs about 1½ inches across.

4 Spray rack with vegetable oil cooking spray. Place meatballs on rack over baking tray, and bake until well browned on all sides, about 10 to 15 minutes, turning occasionally. Transfer to plate and reserve. Meanwhile, in large nonstick skillet over moderate heat, combine tomatoes, onions, and tomato paste and bring to boil. Cover and simmer mixture until slightly thickened, about 12 minutes.

5 Return meatballs to skillet with ripe olives, if using. Cover and cook until cooked through, about 20 minutes. Stir parsley into tomato sauce and season with black pepper.

HEALTH HINT

Research shows that heart disease occurrences are much lower in Mediterranean countries where olive oil is a key ingredient than in countries or areas where olive oil is consumed much less. Studies prove that olive oil increases good blood cholesterol. While a monounsaturated fat, it is still a fat and should be used in moderation.

Cook's Clue

To cut down on fat even further, substitute lean ground turkey for the pork in this recipe. The tomato sauce will compensate for any loss of pork flavor.

STEP 2 *Stir in celery mixture until just combined.*

STEP 3 *Wet your hands to make shaping easier.*

STEP 5 *Return meatballs to skillet to finish cooking.*

secret to success

Typically, meatballs are fried. To keep them low-fat, we browned them in the oven on a rack over a baking pan. The fat drips into the pan, where it can be discarded, and the meatballs turn a lovely dark brown.

Spinach–Stuffed Meat Loaf

PER SERVING
294 calories / 18% from fat
2 g saturated fat, 6 g total fat
71 mg cholesterol
405 mg sodium
28 g total carbohydrate
2 g dietary fiber
32 g protein

Meat loaf never looked or tasted this good—and was certainly never this good for you! High in protein and low in fat, this nutritious new take on an old favorite—bolstered with antioxident vitamins A and C, folate, and potassium from the spinach—will protect your arteries from bad cholesterol.

PREP TIME 30 min. | **COOK TIME 1½ hours** | **SERVES 6**

- 1 pound lean ground beef
- 8 ounces lean ground turkey
- 1 small onion, finely chopped
- ½ cup fresh bread crumbs
- ⅛ teaspoon garlic salt
- 1 tablespoon tomato paste
- 1 egg white
- ½ cup part-skim ricotta cheese
- 1 package (10 ounces) frozen chopped spinach, thawed and drained
- ⅛ teaspoon salt
- ⅛ teaspoon black pepper
- 2 large onions, thinly sliced
- 2 carrots, coarsely chopped
- 1 can (28 ounces) crushed tomatoes

1 In bowl, mix beef, turkey, chopped onion, bread crumbs, garlic salt, and tomato paste. In another bowl, mix egg white, ricotta, spinach, salt, and black pepper.

2 Preheat oven to 350°F. Turn out beef mixture onto large sheet of wax paper, and form into 9 x 10-inch rectangle.

3 Spoon spinach stuffing lengthwise down center of meat, leaving about 1 inch uncovered at each short end.

4 With wax paper, lift long edges of meat. Fold meat over stuffing to enclose it. Using your fingers, pinch edges of meat together. Place loaf seam side down in nonstick roasting pan. Add onions, carrots, and tomatoes to pan.

5 Bake until meat and vegetables are cooked, about 1½ hours. Transfer meat to platter. Purée vegetables in blender and serve as sauce with meat loaf.

STEP 2 *Form meat loaf into rectangle using your hands.*

STEP 3 *Spoon spinach stuffing down the center.*

STEP 4 *With your hands underneath the wax paper, fold meat over stuffing and pinch together.*

secret to success

Meat loaf almost demands a high-fat gravy. In this healthy low-fat recipe, make a gravylike sauce by roasting onions, carrots, and tomatoes with the meat loaf and then puréeing them in a blender or food processor.

Cook's Clue

Always defrost meats in a refrigerator or using a microwave on defrost setting—never at room temperature.

HEALTH HINT

The carotenoid lutein—a yellow pigment found in high levels in kale, spinach, and corn—has long been linked to the prevention of eye diseases such as macular degeneration and cataracts. But the health benefits of lutein may be even greater: Now laboratory studies suggest that it may also have a restorative effect on cardiovascular health by helping ward off dangerous clogging of carotid (neck) arteries.

Roast Beef Hash

The question of what to do with leftover roast beef has never been answered more deliciously or more healthfully: Pan-fry chunks of last night's juicy roast with golden corn kernels and nuggets of potato and carrot for a filling, family-pleasing supper. It's such a treat, you might find the family "holding back" when roast beef is on the menu so they can have this heart-friendly hash the next day.

PER SERVING

288 calories / 30% from fat
2 g saturated fat, 9.5 g total fat
33 mg cholesterol
583 mg sodium
36 g total carbohydrate
5 g dietary fiber
16 g protein

PREP TIME 10 min.	COOK TIME 30 min.	SERVES 4

- 1 pound small red-skinned potatoes, cut into ¼-inch dice
- 2 carrots, quartered lengthwise and thinly sliced
- 1 tablespoon plus 2 teaspoons olive oil
- 1 medium onion, finely chopped
- 2 garlic cloves, minced
- 1¼ cups frozen corn
- ¾ teaspoon salt
- ¼ teaspoon black pepper
- 6 ounces cooked roast beef, cut into ⅓-inch dice

1 Cook potatoes in medium saucepan of boiling water until almost tender, about 6 minutes. Add carrots and cook 2 minutes longer. Drain.

2 Spray a large nonstick skillet with nonstick cooking spray. Add 1 tablespoon oil and heat over medium-low heat. Add onion and garlic to skillet and cook, stirring frequently, until onion is golden brown, about 7 minutes.

3 Increase heat to medium-high. Add remaining 2 teaspoons oil. Add potatoes and carrots, corn, salt, and black pepper, and cook, stirring occasionally, until mixture starts to form a crust, about 10 minutes.

4 Stir in beef and press down on mixture to help form a crust. Cook until crusty on the bottom, about 5 minutes.

STEP 1 *After potatoes are almost cooked through, add carrots to cooking water.*

STEP 3 *Thoroughly combine vegetables and seasonings, and cook, stirring only occasionally.*

STEP 4 *Once beef is added to hash, press mixture down so bottom can get well browned.*

Round Out the Meal

Start with tomato soup with rye toasts, then serve the hash with a salad of mixed greens and red onion slivers. Offer vanilla pudding with fresh raspberries for dessert.

HEALTH HINT

Eating potatoes with their skin on is good for your heart. The skins supply notable heart-healthy nutrients, including potassium, B vitamins, and plenty of cholesterol-lowering fiber.

secret to success

Though corned beef hash may be more traditional, it is far fattier than roast beef hash, because corned beef is made from brisket, one of the fattiest cuts of beef. And because it's brined, corned beef is also high in sodium.

Cook's Clue

Never cook meat immediately after removing from the refrigerator, as the insides are too cold, and the final product will not be tender. Since beef requires only a little fat to keep its flavor, trim excess fat before cooking. Lightly salt when half cooked.

Asian BBQ Beef

In Southeast Asia, skewered strips of marinated, grilled meat or chicken are a beloved street snack. These skewers, called saté or satay, are often served with a sauce made with coconut milk, which is loaded with artery-clogging saturated fat. We've taken a different tack with a light citrus–sesame–soy marinade. The water chestnut salad and rice add a nice helping of heart-healthy fiber.

PER SERVING

370 calories / 23% from fat
3 g saturated fat, 9.5 g total fat
37 mg cholesterol
614 mg sodium
51 g total carbohydrate
4 g dietary fiber
20 g protein

PREP TIME 20 min.+ marinating | **COOK TIME** 45 min. | **SERVES** 4

- 10 ounces well-trimmed flank steak
- ½ cup orange juice
- 2 tablespoons reduced-sodium soy sauce
- 2 teaspoons dark sesame oil
- 1 tablespoon plus 1 teaspoon light brown sugar
- 1 teaspoon ground ginger
- ¼ teaspoon red pepper flakes
- 1 red bell pepper, seeded and slivered
- 2 scallions, thinly sliced
- 2 tablespoons chopped fresh mint
- ½ teaspoon salt
- 1 can (8 ounces) sliced water chestnuts, drained
- 1 cup brown rice

1 Thinly slice flank steak across the grain to make 8 thin slices.

2 Combine ¼ cup orange juice, soy sauce, sesame oil, 1 tablespoon brown sugar, ginger, and ⅛ teaspoon red pepper flakes in shallow bowl. Add beef slices, tossing to coat. Cover and refrigerate for 1 hour or up to overnight.

3 Meanwhile, combine bell pepper, scallions, mint, and salt with remaining ¼ cup orange juice, 1 teaspoon brown sugar, and ⅛ teaspoon red pepper flakes. Add water chestnuts, toss to combine, and refrigerate until serving time.

4 Cook brown rice according to package directions. Fluff with fork.

5 Meanwhile, preheat broiler. Lift meat from its marinade and thread onto eight 12-inch skewers. Place skewers on broiler pan and broil 4 inches from heat, brushing with marinade after 2 minutes. Turn skewers over and broil 2 minutes. Serve skewers on rice with water chestnut salad.

Round Out the Meal

Serve clementines and almonds in the shell for dessert.

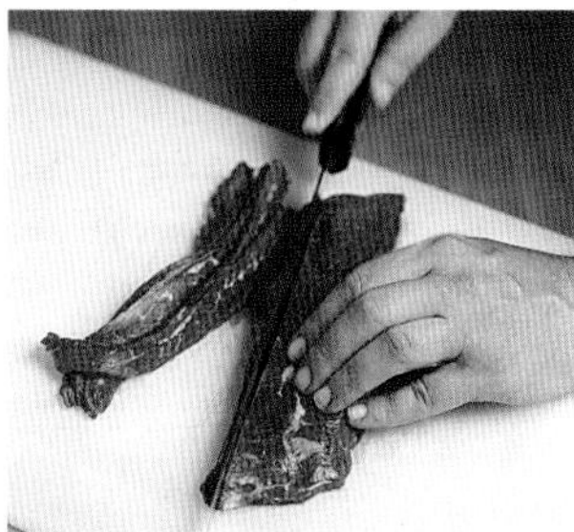

STEP 1 *Slice flank steak across grain to make beef more tender.*

STEP 2 *Marinate steak slices in orange juice-soy mixture for at least 1 hour or overnight.*

STEP 5 *Soak wooden skewers in water for 30 minutes. Thread ribbons of marinated beef onto skewers.*

Cook's Clue

For this recipe, trim off the thin, narrow tail end of your flank steak, and use the remaining thick center cut to slice long, even-sized ribbons of beef. You can use the leftover steak trimmings in a stir-fry, stew, or other recipe.

HEALTH HINT

Brown rice contains niacin, a B vitamin that acts to protect against heart problems and reduce total cholesterol. Vitamin B_6 in brown rice helps convert homocysteine into a helpful amino acid, reducing the risk of damaged blood vessel walls. Since high levels of homocysteine increase heart attack risk, vitamin B_6 should be added to your diet.

Pork Tenderloin with Honey–Mustard Sauce

For lots of good, healthy eating with relatively little fat and few calories, roast a pork tenderloin. This is the crème de la crème—tender, tasty, and terrific. And the sweet-spicy sauce turns it into a culinary masterpiece. Double the recipe, have a party, and enjoy the compliments. You'll deserve them!

PER SERVING

- 247 calories / 18% from fat
- **1 g saturated fat, 5 g total fat**
- 74 mg cholesterol
- 525 mg sodium
- 25 g total carbohydrate
- 1 g dietary fiber
- 25 g protein

PREP TIME 15 min. | **COOK TIME 30 min.** | **SERVES 4**

- 1 tablespoon chopped fresh rosemary or 1 teaspoon dried
- 2 garlic cloves, minced
- 1 teaspoon grated lemon zest
- ½ teaspoon salt
- 1 pork tenderloin (about 1 pound), trimmed
- ⅓ cup fresh lemon juice
- ¼ cup honey
- 3 tablespoons coarse Dijon mustard
- ½ cup nonfat half-and-half
- 1 tablespoon all-purpose flour

1 Preheat oven to 400°F. Line small roasting pan with foil. Combine rosemary, garlic, lemon zest, and salt in small bowl and rub evenly over pork tenderloin; transfer pork to pan. Mix lemon juice, honey, and mustard in small bowl. Transfer half to small saucepan and set aside.

2 Brush pork with 2 tablespoons honey–mustard sauce. Roast pork until glazed and golden brown or until instant-read thermometer reads 160°F, about 25 minutes, basting 2 or 3 times with remaining sauce.

3 Meanwhile, put half-and-half in small bowl and whisk in flour until smooth. Warm reserved honey–mustard sauce in small saucepan over low heat. Gradually whisk in half-and-half mixture and cook, whisking constantly, until sauce thickens, about 3 minutes. Serve with pork.

STEP 1 *Rub rosemary mixture into pork, covering entire surface.*

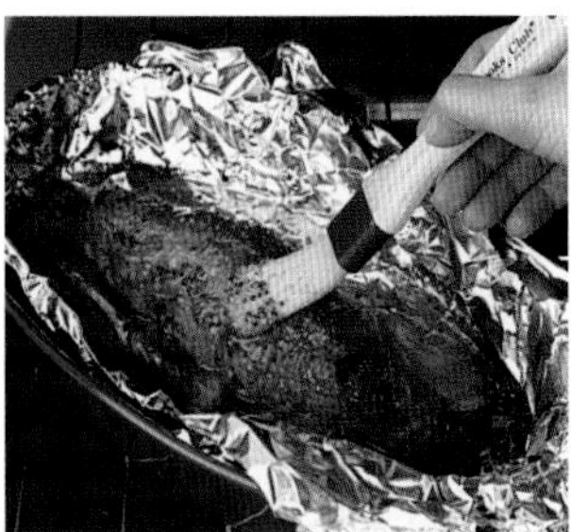

STEP 2 *Brush pork with honey–mustard basting sauce during roasting.*

STEP 3 *Gradually add half-and-half mixture to saucepan, whisking constantly.*

HEALTH HINT

Pork tenderloin is one of the leanest cuts of meat: A plain 3-ounce cooked portion has about 4 grams of fat and 140 calories. That's almost as low as a skinless, boneless chicken breast of the same size.

Round Out the Meal

Serve with a fresh spinach salad, cooked carrots sprinkled with fresh orange juice, and an apple–cherry crisp for dessert.

Cook's Clue

In most recipes, honey can be substituted for sugar. Not only is it a healthy replacement, but it requires less—almost half a cup of honey per cup of sugar. However, with cup substitution, reduce the amount of liquid in the recipe by 1/4 cup, and lower the temperature by 25°F, or the food will brown too easily.

Pesto-Coated Pork Chops

Pork chops on a heart-healthy menu? You bet! Pork is about 50 percent leaner than just a few years ago, which means it's lower in saturated fat as well. To keep these chops svelte but succulent, top them with a homemade pesto with a heady mix of basil and garlic. It uses just a smidgen of oil but seals in all the pork's juices at the same time.

PER SERVING

- 468 calories / 25% from fat
- **3.5 g saturated fat, 13 g total fat**
- 78 mg cholesterol
- 388 mg sodium
- 46 g total carbohydrate
- 2 g dietary fiber
- 39 g protein

PREP TIME 15 min.	COOK TIME 8 min.	SERVES 4

- 6 ounces eggless noodles
- 2 cups fresh basil leaves
- 3 garlic cloves, peeled
- ½ teaspoon salt
- ½ teaspoon freshly ground black pepper
- 2 tablespoons plain dry bread crumbs
- 2 tablespoons extra-virgin olive oil
- 4 center-cut pork loin chops (½ inch thick, about 4 ounces each)

1 Prepare noodles according to package directions. Drain and keep hot. Meanwhile, preheat broiler.

2 Put basil, garlic, and a pinch each of salt and black pepper in food processor. Pulse until roughly chopped. Add bread crumbs and process 30 seconds until incorporated.

3 With motor running, slowly add oil through feed tube until pureed. Set aside.

4 Coat large heavy ovenproof skillet and broiler rack with nonstick cooking spray. Set skillet over high heat until very hot but not smoking. Sprinkle both sides of chops with remaining salt and black pepper. Sauté chops until browned, about 1 minute on each side. Remove from heat. Spread chops on both sides with pesto and transfer to broiler pan.

5 Broil chops until pesto is slightly darker and juices run clear, about 2 minutes on each side. Divide noodles evenly among 4 plates and top with a pork chop.

STEP 2 *Place fresh basil leaves into food processor bowl, and then pulse to roughly chop.*

STEP 3 *While motor is running, pour oil slowly through the feed tube.*

Cook's Clue

How can you tell when a pork chop is done? Near the end of the suggested cooking time, make a slit with a small knife in the center of the chop. It's ready to eat when the juices run clear, the meat shows just a hint of pink (about 160°F), and the chop is still juicy and tender. Thanks to new sanitary breeding methods, pork is perfectly safe to eat at this stage.

Round Out the Meal

Finish the meal with a scoop of Italian gelato, available at Italian specialty stores, in many different flavors. It tastes as good as ice cream with less sugar and 1/3 the fat!

HEALTH HINT

Some cuts of pork are much kinder to the heart than others. Loin chops rank among the lowest in total fat, saturated fat, and cholesterol. Pork is a top source of thiamine, the B vitamin that helps metabolize carbohydrates and regulate the nervous system. It also supplies high-quality body-building protein—as well as iron, which is essential in carrying oxygen through the body.

secret to success

Typically, pesto sauce is whirled up from basil, olive oil, pine nuts, and Parmesan cheese—which adds up to a high percentage of fat. To slash the fat but save the flavor, substitute bread crumbs for the nuts and cheese. Blend everything with just enough olive oil to hold it together.

Sweet-and-Sour Glazed Pork with Pineapple

You'd do well to steer clear of traditional-style sweet-and-sour pork: The meat is battered and fried before it's simmered and sauced. However, your heart will thank you if you opt for this version, in which lean pork tenderloin is cooked with no added fat and basted with pineapple–mustard sauce.

PER SERVING

312 calories / 14% from fat
1.5 g saturated fat, 5 g total fat
67 mg cholesterol
750 mg sodium
42 g total carbohydrate
2 g dietary fiber
25 g protein

PREP TIME 5 min.	COOK TIME 35 min. + standing	SERVES 4

- 1 can (20 ounces) juice-packed pineapple wedges or rings
- ½ cup red currant jelly
- 2 tablespoons plus 2 teaspoons Dijon mustard
- ¾ teaspoon salt
- 1 pound well-trimmed pork tenderloin
- 1 tablespoon lemon juice

1 Preheat oven to 400°F. Drain pineapple, reserving juice. Dice pineapple.

2 Combine pineapple juice, currant jelly, 2 tablespoons of mustard, and ¼ teaspoon of salt in small saucepan. Cook over medium heat, stirring frequently, until jelly has melted and mixture is slightly syrupy and reduced to ⅔ cup, about 5 minutes. Cool to room temperature. Measure out ½ cup of mixture and set aside to be used as a sauce. Reserve mixture remaining in saucepan for a baste.

3 Place pork in 7 x 11-inch baking dish. Sprinkle with lemon juice and remaining ½ teaspoon salt. Brush pork with basting mixture. Roast pork, basting every 10 minutes with pan juices, until cooked through, about 30 minutes.

4 Meanwhile, combine diced pineapple with remaining 2 teaspoons mustard in small bowl. Let cooked pork stand 10 minutes before slicing. Serve sliced pork with reserved sauce and pineapple–mustard mixture in the side.

STEP 2 *Cook pineapple–mustard basting sauce until syrupy.*

STEP 3 *Brush pork tenderloin with basting sauce.*

STEP 4 *Stir mustard into diced pineapple to serve as relish.*

HEALTH HINT

Even condiments can contribute to good health. Mustard contains antioxidants that protect artery walls and enhance the immune system. Mustard has no cholesterol and is a good source of protein. Leaf mustard contains heart-healthy nutrients such as calcium, phosphorus, magnesium, and vitamin B.

Round Out the Meal

Serve with steamed baby squash, wild rice pilaf, and frozen yogurt topped with crumbled gingersnaps for dessert.

Cook's Clue

To double the recipe: Prepare two tenderloins (often packed that way) and double the sauce and pineapple–mustard mixture.

secret to success

To easily cut a fresh pineapple, start by removing the crown and base with a sharp knife. Point the base downward and slice off the skin. Use the tip of the knife to carve out any bits that remain. Then cut the pineapple into quarters, and if you wish, remove the core. Always slice from the fresh toward the rind. Once all rind is removed, the pineapple is ready to cut into the desired shape or size that the recipe requires.

Barbecued Pork Tenderloin "Ribs"

Barbecued pork "ribs" worthy of a blue ribbon, but with only one-fourth the fat of regular ribs. How? Make them from lean pork tenderloin instead of fat-laden baby back or spareribs. The tenderloin "ribs" taste just as delicious as the real McCoy and are more healthful, too.

PER SERVING

284 calories / 14% from fat
1.5 g saturated fat, 4.5 g total fat
74 mg cholesterol
454 mg sodium
36 g total carbohydrate
2 g dietary fiber
26 g protein

PREP TIME 30 min. | **COOK TIME 45 min.** | **SERVES 6**

- 2 pork tenderloins (about 12 ounces each), trimmed
- 1 medium red onion, chopped
- 1 medium red bell pepper, seeded and chopped
- 3 garlic cloves, minced
- 1 cup low-sodium ketchup
- ½ cup chili sauce
- ¼ cup unsulfured molasses
- 3 tablespoons Worcestershire sauce
- 2 tablespoons light brown sugar
- 2 teaspoons chili powder
- 2 teaspoons dry mustard
- Hot red pepper sauce, to taste

1 Soak four 12 to 15-inch wooden skewers in water 30 minutes. Butterfly pork tenderloins, then cut into "ribs" and thread on skewers (*see photos, right*). Cover and refrigerate.

2 Place oven rack in upper third of oven and preheat to 450°F. Lightly coat jelly-roll pan with nonstick cooking spray. Spread onion, red pepper, and garlic in pan and lightly coat with nonstick cooking spray. Roast vegetables, tossing frequently, until browned and tender, about 15 minutes.

3 Transfer vegetables to food processor. Add ketchup, chili sauce, molasses, Worcestershire, sugar, chili powder, mustard, and hot pepper sauce. Puree, then pour into medium saucepan. Cover and cook over medium-low heat, stirring occasionally, until bubbly and richly flavored, about 15 minutes. Remove 1 cup sauce for basting and keep remaining sauce hot.

4 Coat grill rack or broiler pan generously with nonstick cooking spray and preheat grill or broiler. Baste both sides of "ribs" generously with sauce. Grill or broil until cooked through, about 15 minutes, turning and basting every 4 minutes. Serve with remaining sauce on the side.

Cook's Clue

Because pork tenderloin is a lean cut of meat, it will toughen if overcooked, so watch carefully while grilling. Juicy and tender meat will need cooking for 8-10 minutes on each side, but use a thermometer to determine doneness. It should be 160°F for slightly pink meat.

Round Out the Meal

Serve these ribs with "confetti slaw"—thinly sliced carrots, cabbage, and a red bell pepper—made with low-fat mayonnaise. Don't forget to stir up a pitcher of fresh lemonade, too.

How to Cut the Tenderloin

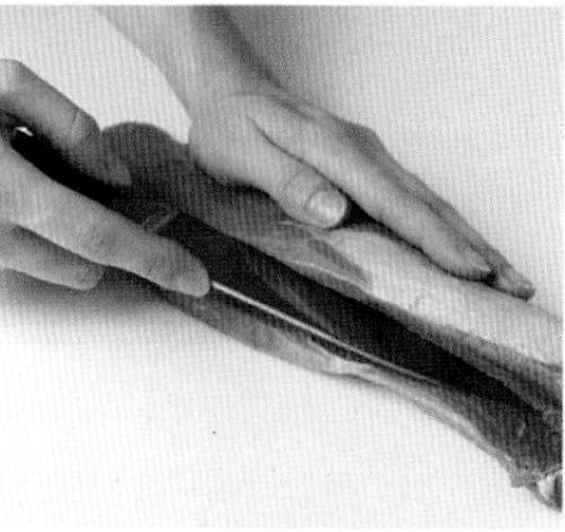

Slit tenderloin lengthwise three-fourths of the way through, then open it flat.

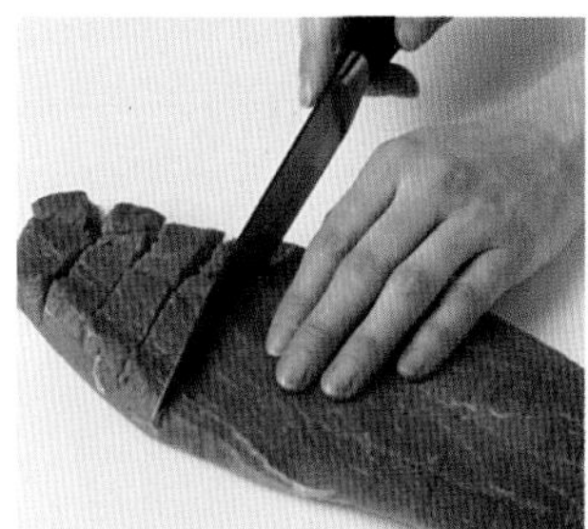

Cut into "ribs," three-fourths of the way across, about 1½ inches apart.

Thread long skewers through the "rack of ribs," from side to side, right at the point that vertical cuts end.

Bourbon Baked Ham

Ham on a heart-healthy diet? Absolutely. Thanks to vitamins and protein, ham can be a smart choice in moderation—just be sure to trim off the fat and serve it with low-in-salt side dishes. The combination of the sweet Southern-style glaze and slightly smoky ham will excite everyone's taste buds.

PER SERVING

262 calories / 21% from fat
2 g saturated fat, 6 g total fat
60 mg cholesterol
1,387 mg sodium
21 g total carbohydrate
0 g dietary fiber
24 g protein

PREP TIME 15 min. | **COOK TIME 2½ hr.** | **SERVES 18**

- 1 fully cooked smoked bone-in ham (8 to 10 pounds)
- 2 tablespoons whole cloves
- 2 cups apple cider or juice
- ½ cup bourbon or apple cider
- 1⅓ cups packed light brown sugar
- 1 tablespoon maple syrup
- 2 tablespoons all-purpose flour
- 1 tablespoon coarse Dijon mustard
- 1 teaspoon ground cinnamon

1 Preheat oven to 325°F. Trim fat from ham, leaving a ¼-inch layer. Place ham, fat-side up, on rack in roasting pan.

2 Score fat and stud with cloves. Pour 1 inch hot tap water into pan. Combine cider and ⅓ cup bourbon and pour about ¾ cup over ham.

3 Bake about 2 hours for 8-pound ham or 2½ hours for 10-pound ham, basting every 15 minutes with remaining cider mixture and adding more water to pan if necessary.

4 Mix sugar, syrup, remaining bourbon, flour, mustard, and cinnamon in small bowl to make thick but spreadable glaze. Thin with extra bourbon or cider if too thick. Remove ham from oven. Carefully remove cloves and discard. Gently spread glaze over ham. Return to oven, and bake about 30 minutes longer, until instant-read thermometer inserted into thickest part of ham (not touching bone) reaches 140°F.

STEP 1 *Trim fat from ham, leaving a thin layer.*

STEP 2 *Score fat to form diamonds, being careful not to cut into meat. Stud ham with cloves.*

secret to success

Bourbon is becoming an increasingly popular addition to well-known recipes. Because its flavor is similar to brandy, the two can be substituted for each other. While bourbon is typically used for dessertlike recipes, try mixing it with barbecue sauces or in main dishes to increase flavor.

Round Out the Meal

A spectacular entrée warrants simple accompaniments. Serve with thin wedges of baked acorn squash. End the meal with a dessert of fresh, sweet berries.

HEALTH HINT

Ham is high in thiamine, the B vitamin used to turn carbohydrates, fats, and proteins into energy. Thiamine performs many important functions in the body: It promotes normal nerve function, muscle tone, appetite, and digestion. Ham is high in sodium due to its curing process, but reduced-sodium hams are available. Whichever you choose, keep the serving size to about 3 ounces.

Cook's Clue

Whole hams usually weigh between 8 and 22 pounds and serve from 14 to 35 people. For a smaller group, consider half a ham. The shank makes a prettier presentation and is easier to slice. The butt end is meatier, but it is harder to carve because of the bone.

Leg of Lamb with Double Mint Sauce

Whether it's spring or not, treat yourself to lamb! A small leg serves six, plus it's extra lean and surprisingly low in fat. It deserves the crowning jewel of a fresh mint sauce that simmers up in seconds, yet tastes as if it took much more time. Celebrate—your heart will be glad you did!

PER SERVING

330 calories / 19% from fat

3 g saturated fat, 7 g total fat

109 mg cholesterol

313 mg sodium

28 g total carbohydrate

2 g dietary fiber

36 g protein

PREP TIME 20 min. | **COOK TIME 55 min. + standing** | **SERVES 6**

- ⅔ cup mint jelly
- 2 tablespoons fresh lemon juice
- ¼ cup chopped fresh mint
- 1 boneless leg of lamb, well trimmed (about 2¼ pounds)
- 2 garlic cloves, chopped
- 1 tablespoon chopped fresh rosemary
- ½ teaspoon salt
- ½ teaspoon black pepper
- 1 large lemon, halved
- ⅔ cup dry white wine or reduced-sodium chicken broth

HEALTH HINT

The lamb in this dish serves up excellent amounts of vitamin B_{12}, which is needed to make red blood cells and build nerve fibers. It's also an excellent source of the B vitamin niacin, which promotes normal growth.

1 Preheat oven to 400°F. Lightly coat roasting pan with nonstick cooking spray. Combine mint jelly, lemon juice, and fresh mint in small saucepan. Stir constantly over medium heat until jelly melts, about 5 minutes. Remove from heat and set aside.

2 Meanwhile, cut lamb horizontally three-quarters through with sharp knife. Open and spread flat like a book. Put meat between two pieces of plastic wrap and pound with meat mallet or rolling pin to about 1 inch thick.

3 Brush about 2 tablespoons sauce on lamb, and then sprinkle with garlic, rosemary, salt, and black pepper. Squeeze juice from one lemon half over lamb. Roll up lamb from one wide side.

4 Tie with kitchen string, in both directions. Transfer to pan, seam-side down. Squeeze remaining lemon half over lamb and pour on wine.

5 Roast until done to taste or an instant-read thermometer inserted in center reaches 140°F (medium), about 50 minutes. Let stand 10 minutes before slicing. Reheat remaining sauce. Remove strings from lamb and cut lamb into ½-inch slices. Serve with mint sauce.

Round Out the Meal

Serve with steamed asparagus spears and roasted red potatoes sprinkled with chopped chives. End the meal with frozen vanilla yogurt layered with fresh strawberries in tall goblets.

STEP 1 *Whisk mint sauce until it glistens and bubbles.*

STEP 3 *Starting at wide end, roll up seasoned lamb, jelly-roll style.*

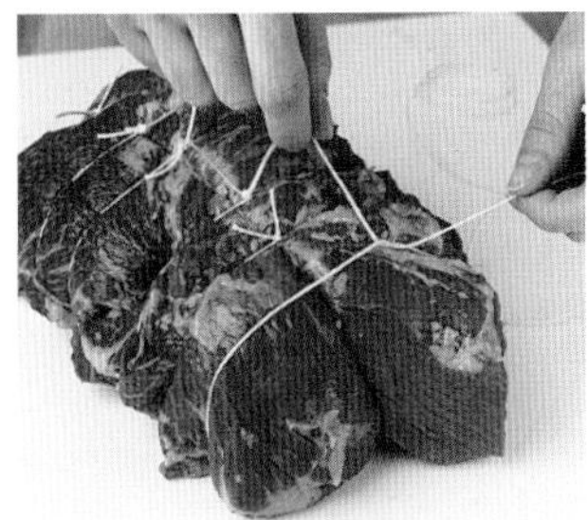

STEP 4 *Secure with kitchen string, making several crosswise ties and one lengthwise.*

Lamb Chops Teriyaki

Yes, you really can have lamb chops on a heart-healthy diet, provided you trim away the fat and cook them right. These are juicy, bursting with flavor, and brightened with Asian accents. Pair them with warm noodle and fresh vegetable salad for a special Saturday supper at home.

PER SERVING

390 calories / 18% from fat
3 g saturated fat, 8 g total fat
90 mg cholesterol
615 mg sodium
52 g total carbohydrate
6 g dietary fiber
27 g protein

PREP TIME 15 min.+marinating | **COOK TIME** 20 min. | **SERVES** 4

- 6 scallions
- 2 tablespoons sesame seeds
- ¼ cup low-sodium soy sauce
- 2 tablespoons cider vinegar
- 2 tablespoons honey
- 1 small garlic clove, minced
- ¾ teaspoon ground ginger
- 8 bone-in loin lamb chops (4 ounces each), well trimmed
- 8 ounces cellophane noodles
- 4 medium carrots
- 1 red bell pepper, seeded
- 1 cup drained whole baby corn
- 1½ teaspoons cornstarch

1 Cut 2 scallions into thin slices and cut remaining scallions into 2-inch pieces. Toast sesame seeds in small nonstick skillet over medium-high heat, stirring constantly, about 3 minutes. Remove from heat. Stir in soy sauce, vinegar, honey, garlic, ginger, and thinly sliced scallions.

2 Roll narrow tail end of lamb chops into medallions and secure with toothpicks. Put chops in baking dish and pour in soy mixture. Cover and refrigerate 1 to 2 hours, turning occasionally.

3 Cook noodles according to package directions. Drain. Cut carrots and peppers into 2½-inch lengths.

4 Stack carrot slices and cut into matchsticks. Blanch carrots and pepper in water to cover, 3 minutes. Add remaining scallions and corn. Blanch until vegetables are crisp-tender, about 2 minutes longer. Drain and toss with noodles.

5 Preheat broiler. Remove chops from marinade; pour marinade into small saucepan. Broil chops 6 inches from heat until done to taste, 4 minutes on each side for medium. Transfer to platter, remove toothpicks, and keep warm.

6 Bring marinade to a boil over medium-high heat. Cook, stirring, about 2 minutes. Dissolve cornstarch in ⅓ cup cold water and whisk into marinade. Boil over medium-high heat, whisking, until sauce thickens, about 2 minutes. Toss half of sauce with noodle mixture and drizzle remaining half over chops.

STEP 1 *Cut scallions on the diagonal into 2-inch pieces.*

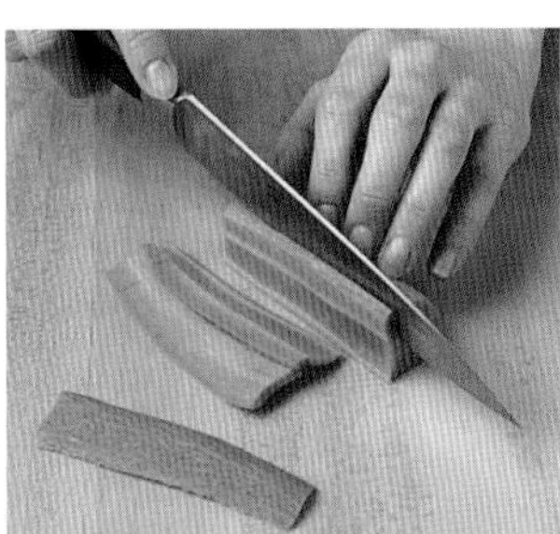

STEP 3 *Cut carrots into 2½-inch lengths. Thinly slice lengthwise.*

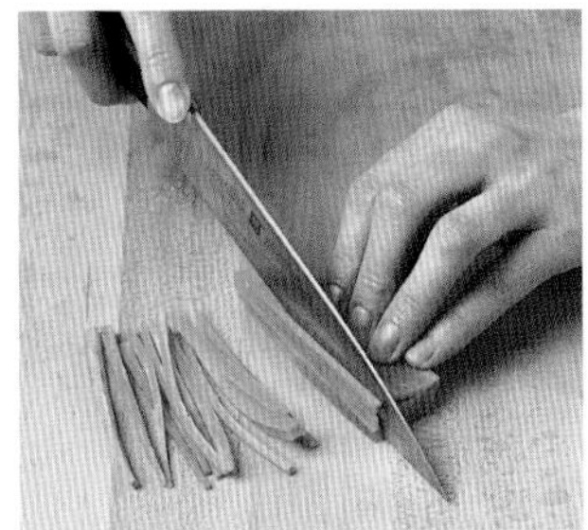

STEP 4 *Stack carrot slices and cut to make matchstick strips.*

Round Out the Meal

For dessert, indulge in low-fat green tea ice cream drizzled with a light raspberry coulee. Substitute heavy cream with low-fat or vanilla soy milk.

Greek Lamb Casserole

This scrumptious one-dish dinner is a lighter interpretation of pastitsio, a Greek pasta casserole. The original is topped with a heavy cream sauce, while this version bakes under a heart-healthy mixture of yogurt, egg whites, and flour. Lean lamb shoulder, and eggplant that's cooked with a minimal amount of oil, help to subtract more fat from the dish.

PER SERVING

425 calories / 17% from fat
2.5 g saturated fat, 8 g total fat
38 mg cholesterol
543 mg sodium
65 g total carbohydrate
6 g dietary fiber
25 g protein

PREP TIME 20 min. | **COOK TIME 1 hr. 5 min.** | **SERVES 6**

- 2 teaspoons olive oil
- 1 onion, finely chopped
- 3 garlic cloves, minced
- 8 ounces eggplant, peeled and cut into ½-inch chunks
- ¾ cup water
- 10 ounces well-trimmed lamb shoulder, diced
- 1 can (28 ounces) crushed tomatoes
- ¾ cup chopped fresh mint
- ¾ cup chopped fresh dill
- ¾ teaspoon salt
- 12 ounces orzo
- 1 cup plain low-fat yogurt
- ¼ cup all-purpose flour
- 2 large egg whites

1 Heat oil in large nonstick skillet over medium heat. Add onion and garlic, and cook, stirring frequently, until onion is soft, about 5 minutes. Add eggplant and water, and cook, stirring frequently, until eggplant is tender, about 5 minutes. Add lamb and cook until no longer pink, about 3 minutes.

2 Stir in tomatoes, ½ cup of mint, ½ cup of dill, and salt, and bring to a boil. Reduce to a simmer, cover, and cook 20 minutes, or until lamb is tender.

3 Meanwhile, cook orzo according to package directions. Drain.

4 Preheat oven to 350°F. Combine yogurt, flour, and egg whites in small bowl.

5 Stir drained orzo into lamb mixture. Spoon mixture into 11 x 7-inch baking dish. Cover and bake 10 minutes. Uncover dish and spoon yogurt mixture over top. Bake until pasta is piping hot, about 20 minutes. Sprinkle remaining ¼ cup mint and ¼ cup dill on top and serve.

STEP 1 *Cook eggplant until tender.*

STEP 2 *Add chopped dill to eggplant–lamb mixture in skillet.*

STEP 5 *Spoon yogurt mixture on top of partially baked casserole and return to oven.*

HEALTH HINT

Eggplant juice is thought to significantly lower blood cholesterol and cholesterol in artery walls and the aorta. Eggplant also relaxes the blood vessel walls, which improves blood flow.

Round Out the Meal

Serve with a green bean and red onion salad. For dessert, low-fat vanilla pudding with toasted almonds on top.

Cook's Clue

To make this dish ahead, bake it, let it come to room temperature, cover, and refrigerate. To reheat, spray foil with cooking spray, cover, and reheat in a 300°F oven until heated through, about 30 minutes.

Tuscan Veal Chops

Simple, elegant, and flavored to perfection—this creation is exactly what the cooking of Tuscany is famous for. Here are veal chops, grilled to your liking and served on top of a healthy mélange of fresh vegetables, all with the scintillating scent of fresh rosemary. They're the perfect ingredients for an elegant supper—just for two.

PER SERVING

- 219 calories / 25% from fat
- **2 g saturated fat, 6 g total fat**
- 110 mg cholesterol
- 501 mg sodium
- 16 g total carbohydrate
- 5 g dietary fiber
- 24 g protein

PREP TIME 15 min. | **COOK TIME 20 min.** | **SERVES 2**

- 2 bone-in rib or loin veal chops (¾ inch thick, about 5 ounces each)
- ¼ teaspoon black pepper
- 1 large carrot, cut into matchsticks
- 1 medium tomato, cut into 8 wedges
- 4 ounces green beans
- 1 small red onion, thinly sliced
- ¼ cup nonfat Italian dressing
- 2 tablespoons dry white wine
- 1 teaspoon chopped rosemary

1 Season chops on both sides with black pepper. Put in shallow dish with carrot, tomato, green beans, and onion. Shake dressing and wine in jar until mixed, drizzle over chops and vegetables, and toss to coat. Let stand at room temperature 5 minutes.

2 Coat nonstick ridged grill pan or grill rack with nonstick cooking spray. Set grill pan over medium heat or preheat grill to medium. Cook or grill chops until golden brown but still slightly pink in center, about 7 minutes on each side for medium.

3 Meanwhile, coat large nonstick skillet with cooking spray. Transfer vegetables and any liquid remaining in dish to skillet, and then sprinkle with rosemary. Sauté just until vegetables are tender, about 6 minutes. To serve, divide vegetables evenly between 2 plates and top with veal chop.

STEP 1 *Marinate chops and vegetables 5 minutes.*

STEP 2 *Grill chops until golden brown and juices run slightly pink in center.*

STEP 3 *Sauté vegetables just until tender.*

secret to success

Use tongs to flip the veal instead of a fork; you don't want to risk losing flavored juices by opening the meat. To determine doneness, make a tiny slit near the bone; the color should be slightly pink for medium-done meat. Cook to 160°F for well-done, if you have a meat thermometer available.

Round Out the Meal

Serve with curly leaf lettuce, orange, and scallion salad and a multigrain roll. End with a slice of fresh berry tart.

Cook's Clue

When buying veal, look for white meat with just a tinge of pink. If the chop is more red than pink, it often indicates that the veal is old and probably tough. Avoid overcooking veal. Because it is very lean, it can dry out and become tough easily if cooked too fast or too long. Marinating veal first, as in this recipe, ensures a moist and tender veal.

HEALTH HINT

Veal chops are lower in fat and calories than pork, lamb chops, or beef steaks but slightly higher in cholesterol.

Veal Cutlets with Lemon–Garlic Sauce

There's a whole head of garlic in this recipe, but after slow-roasting it comes out of the oven tasting mild and sweet. The mashed roast garlic adds a sublime but subtle perfume to the sauce. There's a lot to love about garlic, especially the fact that it can help keep your heart in good health.

PER SERVING

169 calories / 16% from fat

1 g saturated fat, 3 g total fat

96 mg cholesterol

384 mg sodium

6 g total carbohydrate

0 g dietary fiber

28 g protein

PREP TIME 5 min.	COOK TIME 50 min.	SERVES 4

- 1 head garlic
- 4 veal cutlets (4 ounces each)
- ½ teaspoon salt
- 1 tablespoon Dijon mustard
- 1 lemon, very thinly sliced
- ⅔ cup reduced-sodium, fat-free chicken broth
- ¼ cup fresh lemon juice
- 2 teaspoons cornstarch

1 Preheat oven to 375°F. Wrap garlic in foil and bake until tender (package will feel soft when pressed), about 45 minutes. When cool enough to handle, cut off top of bulb, squeeze out garlic pulp into small bowl, and mash until smooth.

2 Preheat broiler. Sprinkle cutlets with ¼ teaspoon salt and brush with mustard. Top each cutlet with 3 lemon slices. Broil cutlets 4 inches from heat until cooked through, about 2 minutes. Transfer cutlets to platter and cover loosely with foil to keep warm.

3 In small saucepan, whisk broth and lemon juice into cornstarch. Whisk in remaining ¼ teaspoon salt and roasted garlic. Bring to a boil over medium heat and boil until sauce is lightly thickened, about 1 minute. Spoon sauce over veal on platter.

Round Out the Meal

Start with sliced tomatoes drizzled with extra-virgin olive oil. Serve veal with steamed asparagus and boiled new potatoes sprinkled with chopped parsley. For dessert, offer pears and whole toasted walnuts.

HEALTH HINT

The pungent sulfur compounds responsible for garlic's distinctive odor may protect blood vessels against accumulation of fatty plaque that can lead to heart disease and stroke. In addition, phytochemicals in garlic are thought to encourage the formation of "good" HDL cholesterol.

Cook's Clue

Thin-skinned lemons have more flesh and more juice than thicker-skinned lemons. To determine thickness of the skin, find lemons heavy for their size, with peels that feel grained. Choose completely yellow lemons since green tinges indicate a higher amount of acidity. Avoid wrinkled, soft or hard patches, or dull colors on your lemons.

How to Squeeze Fresh Lemon Juice

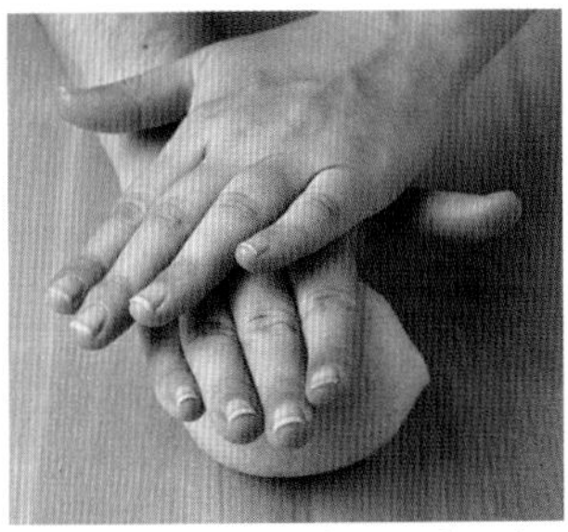

Pressing down with your hands, roll lemon on work surface to break down pulp inside, making it easier to juice.

With sharp knife, cut lemon in half crosswise.

Squeeze lemon on citrus reamer. The most efficient type of reamer strains out seeds and at the same time catches juice underneath.

Breads and Pizzas

Banana–Walnut Quick Bread

Over the past few years, quick breads have morphed into sticky-sweet loaf cakes. Gobs of butter, tons of sugar, chocolate chips, icing—what happened to the homey, simple quick breads of old? Well, they're back. This one, just sweet enough, is made with whole grains, fruit, and nuts that add up to a nutritious breakfast or snacking bread.

PER SLICE

194 calories / 23% from fat

0.5 g saturated fat, 5 g total fat

0 mg cholesterol

288 mg sodium

34 g total carbohydrate

2 g dietary fiber

4 g protein

PREP TIME 10 min.	COOK TIME 1 hr.	12 SLICES

- ½ cup old-fashioned rolled oats
- ⅓ cup walnuts, coarsely chopped
- 1¼ cups all-purpose flour
- ½ cup whole-wheat flour
- 2 teaspoons baking powder
- ¾ teaspoon baking soda
- ¾ teaspoon salt
- 1¼ cups mashed banana (from 3 bananas, about 1 pound)
- ⅔ cup packed dark brown sugar
- ½ cup buttermilk
- 2 large egg whites
- 2½ tablespoons walnut oil or extra-light olive oil

1 Preheat oven to 375°F. Spray an 8½ x 4½-inch loaf pan with nonstick cooking spray.

2 Toast oats and walnuts in oven on jelly-roll pan until oats are golden brown and walnuts are crisp, about 7 minutes. Set aside.

3 Stir together all-purpose flour, whole-wheat flour, baking powder, baking soda, and salt on a sheet of wax paper until well combined.

4 Combine mashed bananas, brown sugar, buttermilk, egg whites, and oil in large bowl. Stir to mix well.

5 Fold in flour mixture, oats, and nuts. Spoon batter into loaf pan.

6 Bake 50 to 55 minutes, or until a toothpick inserted in center of loaf comes out clean. Cool in pan for 10 minutes, then turn out of pan onto wire rack to cool completely.

STEP 2 *Spread oats and chopped walnuts on jelly-roll pan and toast in oven.*

STEP 4 *Stir egg whites into banana–buttermilk mixture in bowl.*

STEP 5 *Use a spatula to fold toasted nuts and oats into batter.*

secret to success

The modest amount of chopped walnuts in this bread is complemented with toasted rolled oats, which contribute their own nutlike flavor and coarse texture.

Round Out the Meal

For breakfast or a snack, serve with a smear of Neufchâtel cream cheese, a topping of apple or prune butter, and a mug of tea.

HEALTH HINT

Bananas are an important source of potassium, which helps maintain blood pressure levels and heart function. Bananas average 467 mg of potassium—no wonder they help prevent high blood pressure and reduce the risk of atherosclerosis. The fiber in this fruit also helps prevent heart disease.

Old-Fashioned Glazed Gingerbread

This is not your mother's—or your grandma's—gingerbread! Sure, it has that same memorable flavor and moistness that turned gingerbread into a well-loved, comforting snack. But in this heart-smart makeover, applesauce stands in for some of the fat, without sacrificing taste.

PER SERVING

191 calories / 20% from fat

1 g saturated fat, 4 g total fat

18 mg cholesterol

232 mg sodium

37 g total carbohydrate

1 g dietary fiber

2 g protein

PREP TIME 30 min. | COOK TIME 45 min. | SERVES 12

- 1⅓ cups all-purpose flour
- 1½ teaspoons pumpkin pie spice
- ¾ teaspoon baking soda
- ½ teaspoon salt
- ½ cup unsweetened applesauce
- ¼ cup light molasses
- 1 large egg, lightly beaten
- 4 tablespoons margarine
- ½ cup packed dark brown sugar
- 2 teaspoons grated, peeled fresh ginger
- 3 tablespoons crystallized ginger, finely chopped
- ¾ cup sifted confectioners' sugar

1 Preheat oven to 350°F. Generously coat 8-inch square cake pan with nonstick cooking spray. Place cooling rack on wax paper. Whisk flour, pumpkin pie spice, baking soda, and salt in medium bowl. Blend applesauce, molasses, and egg in separate bowl.

2 Cream margarine and brown sugar in medium bowl with electric mixer at high speed until light, 3 to 4 minutes. Reduce speed to low and beat in applesauce mixture. Stir in flour mixture with wooden spoon just until combined. Blend in fresh ginger.

3 Scrape batter into cake pan. Bake until cake tester inserted in center comes out with moist crumbs clinging, about 45 minutes. Cool in pan on wire rack 10 minutes. Remove from pan and set right-side up on rack. Cool completely.

4 Scatter crystallized ginger on top of gingerbread. Blend confectioners' sugar with enough water (about 1½ tablespoons) to make spreadable glaze. Drizzle glaze over crystallized ginger with fork, letting some glaze drizzle down sides.

STEP 2 *Blend applesauce–molasses mixture into butter–sugar mixture at low speed.*

STEP 3 *Gingerbread is done when cake tester comes out with moist crumbs clinging to it.*

STEP 4 *Drizzle glaze over top of gingerbread with fork.*

secret to success

Choose fresh ginger root that feels firm, looks smooth, and is mold-free. The best ginger smells spicy. It is found in two versions: young or mature. Young ginger is not always available and does not require peeling; mature ginger, the more popular, must be peeled. Look for it in your grocery's produce section. Avoid ginger with wrinkled flesh, as that is a sign of overmaturity.

way back when... Sweetening breads and cakes with honey or molasses date back to ancient times. In England, gingerbread was made with treacle (molasses) and flour, then frequently baked in wooden molds, shaped as little pigs or men, and sold at fairs. In the 17th century, white gingerbread resembling a spiced marzipan became popular. In America, gingerbread is usually a higher, lighter version of the British molasses–ginger recipe.

(Source: *The Oxford Companion to Food*, by Alan Davidson, Oxford University Press, NY, 1999)

Cook's Clue

Three types of ginger punch up the flavor in this bread: ground (in pumpkin pie spice), fresh, and crystallized.

Cinnamon Pull-Apart Bread

PER SERVING
177 calories / 27% from fat
1.5 g saturated fat, 5 g total fat
10 mg cholesterol
203 mg sodium
27 g total carbohydrate
1 g dietary fiber
4 g protein

A scrumptious showstopper! Dozens of homemade cinnamon rolls are piled high and ready to be pulled apart to enjoy. Towering and tasty. Easy to make. Spectacular to serve. A great old-fashioned bread guaranteed to impress at a brunch buffet or in a gift basket!

PREP TIME 25 min. + rising | COOK TIME 35 min. | SERVES 24

- 5 to 5¼ cups all-purpose flour
- ½ cup granulated sugar
- 2 packets (¼-ounce each) rapid-rise yeast
- 1½ teaspoons salt
- 1¾ cups milk
- 10 tablespoons margarine
- 1 large egg, at room temperature
- ¼ cup firmly packed light brown sugar
- 1 teaspoon cinnamon

secret to success

Traditional recipes for pull-apart bread call for each dough ball to be dipped in melted butter before it's placed in the pan. Drizzling each layer of dough, instead of each ball, with margarine, keeps the saturated fat to a minimum. The result? Each serving has 5 grams of fat compared to the 14 grams found in traditional recipes.

1 Mix 1¼ cups flour, ¼ cup granulated sugar, yeast, and salt with wooden spoon in large bowl. Heat milk and 4 tablespoons margarine in small saucepan over medium heat until very warm (120°F to 130°F). Stir into flour mixture. Stir in egg. Add enough remaining flour (at least 3½ cups) to form soft dough.

2 Dust work surface lightly with flour. Turn dough onto lightly floured surface, and knead until smooth and elastic, about 10 minutes, adding remaining flour to keep dough from sticking.

3 Melt remaining margarine. Coat 10-inch tube pan with nonstick cooking spray. Combine brown and remaining granulated sugars and cinnamon in small bowl. Pull off golf-ball-size pieces of dough and arrange in single layer in pan. Brush dough with half of melted margarine and sprinkle with half of sugar mixture.

4 Repeat to make second layer. Cover with damp kitchen towel. Let rise in a warm place until doubled, about 30 minutes.

5 Meanwhile, preheat oven to 375°F. Bake bread until browned on top, about 35 minutes. Cool in pan on wire rack 10 minutes. Unmold and serve warm.

HEALTH HINT

Cinnamon contains a high dietary fiber content, as well as the minerals iron, manganese, and calcium. Calcium and fiber combined help prevent colon cancer, atherosclerosis, and heart disease. This combination damages bile salts that, once removed by fiber, the body breaks down, helping lower cholesterol levels.

STEP 3 *Top sugar mixture with additional balls of dough.*

STEP 4 *Dough should double in bulk before baking.*

Cook's Clue

Rapid-rise yeast has two big advantages over regular yeast: It withstands hot water better (temperatures up to 130°F instead of 115°F). In addition, when rapid-rise yeast is mixed with water, it starts growing instantly, rising in half the time as regular yeast.

Butternut Squash Skillet Bread

Old-time cooks say nothing can match a cast-iron skillet for beautifully browned, crackling-crisp food, whether it's chicken, fried green tomatoes, or quick bread. But this crusty cornbread has more going for it than good looks and great taste. It's packed with heart-healthy ingredients like olive oil, egg whites, low-fat yogurt, and vitamin-rich winter squash.

PER WEDGE

138 calories / 26% from fat
0.5 g saturated fat, 4 g total fat
1 mg cholesterol
405 mg sodium
22 g total carbohydrate
2 g dietary fiber
4 g protein

PREP TIME 15 min.	COOK TIME 1 hr.	8 WEDGES

- 1 butternut squash (about 1¾ pounds), peeled, seeded, and cut into large chunks
- ½ cup flour
- ½ cup yellow cornmeal
- 2 tablespoons sugar
- 2½ teaspoons baking powder
- 1½ teaspoons chili powder
- ¾ teaspoon salt
- ½ teaspoon baking soda
- 4 scallions, thinly sliced
- ½ cup plain low-fat yogurt
- ¼ cup fat-free milk
- 2 tablespoons extra-light olive oil
- 2 large egg whites

1 Preheat oven to 400°F. Place butternut squash on a baking pan, cover, and roast until flesh is tender, 20 to 30 minutes. Leave oven on. Transfer to large bowl and mash with a potato masher. Measure out 1¼ cups mashed squash (reserve any extra for another use). Let cool slightly.

2 Combine flour, cornmeal, sugar, baking powder, chili powder, salt, and baking soda in medium bowl. Stir in scallions. Spray a heavy, 10-inch ovenproof skillet, preferably cast-iron, with nonstick cooking spray and place in oven to preheat.

3 Add yogurt, milk, oil, and egg whites to bowl with squash, stirring to combine.

4 Fold flour mixture into squash. Remove hot pan from oven and spoon batter into it.

5 Return to oven and bake until a toothpick inserted in center comes out clean, about 30 minutes. Cool in pan on rack for 5 minutes before cutting into 8 wedges.

STEP 1 *Place chunks of butternut squash in jelly-roll pan or shallow baking pan.*

STEP 3 *Add yogurt and olive oil to mashed squash.*

STEP 4 *With a rubber spatula, fold flour-cornmeal mixture into squash mixture.*

Round Out the Meal

Serve with a bowl of vegetable soup, and offer frozen coffee yogurt for dessert.

Cook's Clue

Butternut, a winter squash, easily decays, so handpick your squash carefully. Choose firm squash, heavy in size, and glossy with hard rinds. Soft rinds signal that the squash could lack flavor. As with all produce, avoid any signs of decay, soft spots, or mold.

HEALTH HINT

It'll do your heart good to know that olive oil can be used for more than salad dressings and sautéing. For example, extra-light olive oil, with its subtle, delicate flavor, and heart-healthy monounsaturated fats, can be used instead of melted butter or margarine in baking.

Anadama Bread

Anadama bread, a traditional New England loaf bread made with cornmeal and molasses, is already a more healthful choice than plain white bread. But we've improved on the original by adding whole-wheat flour and soy flour. For another heart-healthy twist, we made this delicious whole-grain bread with olive oil instead of butter.

PER SLICE

155 calories / 17% from fat

0.5 g saturated fat, 3 g total fat

13 mg cholesterol

235 mg sodium

27 g total carbohydrate

2 g dietary fiber

5 g protein

PREP TIME 15 min. + rising | **COOK TIME** 30 min. | **16 SLICES**

- 2 cups all-purpose flour
- 1 cup whole-wheat flour
- ¾ cup yellow cornmeal
- ½ cup soy flour
- ¼ cup fat-free dry milk
- 1 packet (¼ ounce) rapid-rise yeast
- 1 tablespoon sugar
- 1½ teaspoons salt
- 2 tablespoons extra-light olive oil
- 2 tablespoons unsulfured molasses
- 1 large egg
- 1¼ cups very warm (120°F to 130°F) water

1 Combine 1½ cups all-purpose flour, whole-wheat flour, cornmeal, soy flour, dry milk, yeast, sugar, and salt in large bowl.

2 Combine oil, molasses, egg, and warm water in medium bowl. Make a well in center of dry ingredients. Stir molasses mixture into flour mixture. Add remaining ½ cup all-purpose flour, stirring until combined.

3 Transfer dough to floured work surface and knead until smooth, about 5 minutes. Spray large bowl with nonstick cooking spray. Add dough, turning to coat. Cover and let rise in warm place until doubled in bulk, about 45 minutes.

4 Spray two 8½ x 4½-inch loaf pans with nonstick cooking spray. Punch dough down. Divide in half, shape each piece into a loaf, and place in pans. Cover loaves with dampened kitchen towel, and let rise in warm place until dough almost reaches top of pans, about 45 minutes.

5 Preheat oven to 350°F. Bake until loaves are golden brown, about 30 minutes. To check for doneness, remove loaves from pans and tap bottom of loaf; they should sound hollow when tapped. (Once cooled, loaves can be wrapped individually in foil and frozen. Reheat foil-wrapped frozen bread in 350°F oven.)

STEP 2 *Add molasses mixture to well in center of flour mixture and stir to combine.*

STEP 3 *Add ball of kneaded dough to bowl sprayed with nonstick cooking spray. Turn dough over so all sides of dough are coated.*

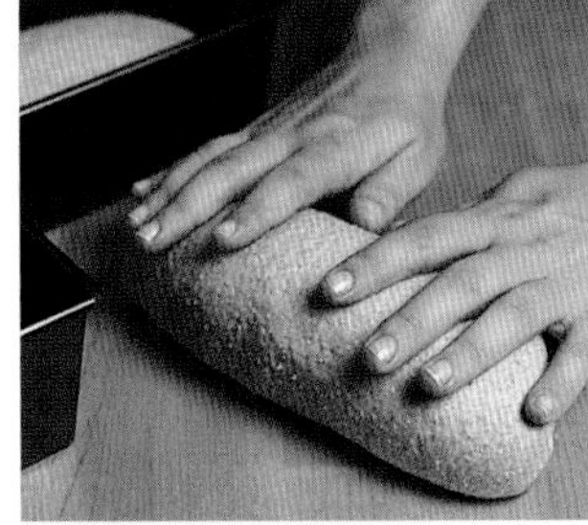

STEP 4 *After dividing dough in half, roll each piece into a log about the length of the loaf pan.*

Cook's Clue

Watched dough doesn't rise! To speed the process, follow these simple suggestions: Substitute fast-acting yeast for regular active dry yeast. Add ingredients at room temperature to dough with yeast, and allow dough to rise in warm place. Cover dough with damp towel to retain its natural moisture. The dough should double in size. To test dough, poke two fingers into it (about ½ inch). If your indents remain, it is ready.

HEALTH HINT

A rich source of protein, soy flour is made from ground soybeans. Soy protein helps reduce LDL ("bad") cholesterol levels in the blood without adversely affecting levels of HDL ("good") cholesterol.

Multigrain Soft Pretzels

Mmmmmm, soft pretzels—Philadelphia is famous for them, and you can be, too; they're never better than when freshly made and still warm from the oven. Pretzel baking makes a fun family project that will encourage everyone to cook and eat heart-healthy foods. Serve these chewy twists with a pot of mustard or a dip made of mustard and plain yogurt.

PER PRETZEL

146 calories / 6% from fat
0 g saturated fat, 1 g total fat
0 mg cholesterol
857 mg sodium
29 g total carbohydrate
3 g dietary fiber
6 g protein

PREP TIME 30 min. + rising | **COOK TIME 25 min.** | **12 PRETZELS**

- ¾ cup old-fashioned rolled oats
- 1¾ cups all-purpose flour
- 1 cup whole-wheat flour
- ½ cup toasted wheat germ
- 1 packet (¼-ounce) rapid-rise yeast
- 5 teaspoons sugar
- 1½ teaspoons table salt
- 1½ cups very warm water (120°F to 130°F)
- 3 tablespoons baking soda
- 1 tablespoon coarse or kosher salt

Cook's Clue

Always buy wheat germ packaged in sealed containers, preferably vacuum packaged. This protects from oxidization and rancidity, which occur due to its high oil content. Always seal it in glass jars in the refrigerator.

1 Toast oats in small skillet over low heat, stirring frequently, until golden brown, about 5 minutes. Transfer to large bowl.

2 To large bowl, add all-purpose flour, whole-wheat flour, wheat germ, yeast, 3 teaspoons of sugar, and the table salt. Stir in warm water. Transfer to floured work surface and knead until smooth, about 5 minutes. Transfer dough to ungreased bowl. Cover, let rise in warm spot until doubled, about 45 minutes.

3 Line 2 large baking sheets with parchment paper. Punch dough down and cut into 12 equal portions. With your hands, roll each portion into 16- to 18-inch rope.

4 Wrap each rope into pretzel shape (*see photos, right*). Place on baking sheets, cover, and let rise until almost doubled, about 20 minutes.

5 Preheat oven to 425°F. Bring large skillet of water to simmer and add remaining 2 teaspoons sugar and baking soda. Slide pretzels into simmering water, 3 at a time. Cook 15 seconds, turn pretzels over and cook another 15 seconds. Blot dry on paper towels.

6 Transfer to baking sheets. Sprinkle kosher salt over pretzel tops and bake 18 to 20 minutes, or until crisp and golden. Cool on wire rack. Serve pretzels warm or at room temperature.

HEALTH HINT

Whole-wheat flour and old-fashioned rolled oats give these pretzels a fiber boost that's hard to find in commercially prepared pretzels.

STEP 3 *After rolling dough into 16- to 18-inch rope, twist ends over one another 2 times.*

STEP 4 *Flip top loop of pretzel over twisted ends, and press ends into dough to seal.*

STEP 5 *Briefly cook pretzels in skillet of simmering water and baking soda to help them brown in the oven.*

Dutch Apple Muffins

We bet the Muffin Man never offered such healthful fare! Applesauce replaces some of the fat, and fresh apples and oatmeal add nutritious fiber. But they're still as delicious as any homemade muffin you can remember. The batter mixes up and bakes in a jiffy, so you can have a batch coming out of the oven in no time flat.

PER SERVING

221 calories / 29% from fat

1 g saturated fat, 7 g total fat

0 mg cholesterol

215 mg sodium

37 g total carbohydrate

2 g dietary fiber

3 g protein

PREP TIME 10 min. | COOK TIME 20 min. | SERVES 12

- 1⅔ cups all-purpose flour
- ¾ cup firmly packed brown sugar
- 2 packets (about 1.5 ounces each) apple-cinnamon instant oatmeal
- 2 tablespoons margarine
- 1 teaspoon baking soda
- ½ teaspoon apple pie spice
- ¼ teaspoon salt
- 1¼ cups unsweetened applesauce
- ¼ cup vegetable oil
- ½ cup fat-free egg substitute
- 1 large apple, chopped

1 Preheat oven to 375°F. Line 12-cup muffin tin with paper liners. Combine ⅓ cup flour, ¼ cup brown sugar, 1 packet oatmeal, and margarine in small bowl. Stir together with fingertips until margarine is incorporated into dry ingredients (mixture will be crumbly). Set aside.

2 Mix remaining flour, remaining oatmeal, baking soda, apple pie spice, and salt in medium bowl and make well in center of mixture.

3 Stir together applesauce, oil, remaining brown sugar, and egg substitute in another medium bowl until brown sugar dissolves. Pour all at once into well.

4 Stir just until combined (do not overmix; batter should be lumpy). Stir in apple.

5 Spoon batter into muffin cups. Sprinkle with reserved crumb topping. Bake until toothpick inserted in center comes out clean, about 20 minutes.

STEP 3 *Pour applesauce mixture into center of flour well.*

STEP 4 *Gently stir chopped apple into batter.*

STEP 5 *Fill paper-lined muffin cups three-fourths full.*

secret to success

By replacing most of the fat with applesauce, you'll have muffins that are more moist than the traditional ones, with a slightly fruity taste. The best part: They're kinder to your heart—and to your waistline, too!

Round Out the Meal

New butter substitutes such as Benecol *and* Smart Balance *not only make a delicious heart-smart spread, but reduce bad cholesterol as well.*

HEALTH HINT

Apples and oats both supply soluble fiber, the kind that withdraws the artery-clogging "bad" cholesterol from the blood. This action lowers your chances of developing heart disease.

Cook's Clue

Can't find apple pie spice at your market? Mix your own: Combine ¼ teaspoon ground cinnamon and ⅛ teaspoon each of ground cloves, mace, and nutmeg.

Dried Cranberry Scones with Orange Glaze

Enjoy that fine English tradition of taking tea, with a fresh batch of these scones and a pot of freshly brewed tea. These scones taste like they came from an exquisite British tea house; no one will guess they take mere minutes to make. Have more than one—they're low on the fat and cholesterol scales.

PER SERVING

167 calories / 22% from fat

1 g saturated fat, 4 g total fat

12 mg cholesterol

325 mg sodium

29 g total carbohydrate

1 g dietary fiber

4 g protein

PREP TIME 15 min. | COOK TIME 15 min. | SERVES 18

- 3 cups self-rising flour
- ¼ cup sugar
- 1¼ cups nonfat sour cream
- 6 tablespoons margarine, melted
- 1 large egg, lightly beaten
- 1 cup sweetened dried cranberries
- ½ cup sifted confectioners' sugar
- 1 teaspoon freshly grated orange zest
- 1 tablespoon fresh orange juice

1 Preheat oven to 400°F. Line 2 baking sheets with parchment paper. Stir flour and sugar in large bowl and make a well. Mix sour cream, margarine, and egg in small bowl and pour into well. Stir with fork until moistened, and stir in cranberries. Flour hands and gently knead dough in bowl just until it comes together.

2 Lightly sprinkle work surface with flour. Turn out dough and pat into 9-inch square, about 1 inch thick. Cut into nine 3-inch squares with a pizza wheel or small knife. Cut each square into 2 triangles, making 18. Place scones 1 inch apart on lined baking sheets. Bake until golden, about 15 minutes.

3 Meanwhile, set wire rack on piece of wax paper, parchment, or foil. Stir confectioners' sugar, orange zest, and juice in small bowl. Transfer scones to wire rack with spatula, and drizzle glaze over scones with a small spoon.

STEP 1 *Knead dough in bowl, just until it comes together.*

STEP 2 *Cut each square into 2 triangles, making 18 scones.*

STEP 3 *Drizzle orange glaze over scones with small spoon.*

living smart
FOR A HEALTHY HEART

FOODS LOWER BLOOD PRESSURE

A government program called Dietary Approaches to Stop Hypertension (DASH) showed that a diet high in fruits and vegetables and low in total fat may work like medication to lower blood pressure. In addition to a daily diet of 7–8 servings of grain foods, 2–3 servings of low-fat dairy foods, up to 6 ounces of lean meat/poultry/fish, and 4–5 weekly servings of legumes, nuts, and seeds, the DASH program recommends a whopping 8–10 servings of fruits and vegetables every day.

HEALTH HINT

Cranberries contain antioxidants that help protect LDL cholesterol from oxidizing, and research proves that cranberries decrease levels of total cholesterol. Regular consumption of cranberries or cranberry juice can reduce the risk of heart disease, as it raises plasma antioxidant capacity, which is associated with lowered risk.

Cook's Clue

If dried cranberries are not available, use dried cherries or traditional currants, and substitute lemon zest for orange. If you don't have self-rising flour, replace with 3 cups all-purpose flour, 1½ tablespoons baking powder, and ½ teaspoon salt.

Heavenly Angel Biscuits

Triple light, super high, with double helpings of delicious down-home taste. Straight from southern kitchens, angel biscuits bake up extra tall and flaky. The secret? Three leavening agents: yeast, baking powder, and baking soda. Mix up a batch of these low-fat delights tonight, or bake a double batch and give some to friends.

PER SERVING

160 calories / 28% from fat
1 g saturated fat, 5 g total fat
1 mg cholesterol
270 mg sodium
24 g total carbohydrate
2 g dietary fiber
4 g protein

PREP TIME 25 min. + resting	COOK TIME 15 min.	SERVES 12

- 1 packet (¼-ounce) active dry yeast
- 2 tablespoons sugar
- ⅓ cup lukewarm water (105°F to 115°F)
- 2½ cups all-purpose flour
- 1 tablespoon baking powder
- ¾ teaspoon salt
- ½ teaspoon baking soda
- 5 tablespoons cold margarine, cut into pieces
- ¾ cup low-fat buttermilk

1 Preheat oven to 400°F. Sprinkle yeast and 1 teaspoon sugar over water. Stir until dissolved, then let stand about 5 minutes.

2 Whisk flour, remaining sugar, baking powder, salt, and baking soda in large bowl. Cut in margarine with pastry blender or two forks until mixture resembles coarse crumbs. Add yeast mixture and buttermilk. Stir with fork just until soft dough forms. Do not overmix. Cover with plastic wrap and let rest 30 minutes.

3 Dust work surface lightly with flour. Turn out dough and gently knead for 30 seconds. Pat into a round about ¾ inch thick. Let rest 5 minutes. Cut out as many biscuits as possible with floured 2½-inch biscuit cutter. Gently knead dough scraps together and let rest 5 minutes before patting out again. Cut a total of 12 biscuits.

4 Place biscuits 1 inch apart on baking sheet. Let rest 15 minutes. Bake until golden, about 15 minutes. Serve warm.

Round Out the Meal

Biscuits drizzled with honey are a tasty complement to vegetable stew. Offer poached pears for dessert.

Cook's Clue

There are several tricks to making tender, flaky biscuits. First, be sure the buttermilk and margarine are very cold. Second, before you knead the dough, cool your hands under cold water, then knead with a light touch. To get biscuits that rise high and evenly, push the biscuit cutter straight down into the dough, and lift it straight up without turning it.

secret to success

Handle the dough as little as possible. While some recipes suggest hand kneading or using an electric mixer, use your hands, because an electric mixer tends to overmix the dough, causing it to become heavy and dense. Using parchment paper on the baking pan makes it easier to wash but also prevents the biscuits from turning brown or burning on the bottom. To give the biscuits a shiny, crisp top, glaze with a mix of egg and milk.

STEP 2 *Cut in margarine until coarse crumbs form.*

STEP 3 *Lift cutter straight out of dough (no twisting, please!).*

STEP 4 *Transfer biscuits to baking sheet with a spatula. Do not touch biscuits with fingers.*

Herb and Cheddar Drop Biscuits

Revive the tradition of homemade bread in your house with these fast and easy fresh-baked biscuits. There's no rolling or cutting required, so they go from flour bin to oven in just 15 minutes. And they smell and taste so delicious, you won't believe they've been lightened up.

PER SERVING

71 calories / 29% from fat

0.5 g saturated fat, 2.3 g total fat

1 mg cholesterol

227 mg sodium

10 g total carbohydrate

0 g dietary fiber

3 g protein

PREP TIME 15 min.	COOK TIME 12 min.	SERVES 18

1¾ cups self-rising flour

1 tablespoon snipped fresh chives

1 teaspoon chopped fresh thyme

¼ teaspoon baking soda

3 tablespoons margarine, cut into pieces

½ cup shredded reduced-fat cheddar cheese

¾ cup low-fat buttermilk

1 egg white, lightly beaten

secret to success

Old-fashioned cheese biscuits made with butter, cream, and full-fat cheddar are delicious—but they're off the charts in terms of cholesterol, fat, and calories. Trim them down with this recipe by using buttermilk made from low-fat milk, reduced-fat cheese, and just an egg white for glazing the tops of the biscuits.

1 Preheat oven to 450°F. Line baking sheet with parchment paper or coat with nonstick cooking spray. Mix flour, chives, thyme, and baking soda in large bowl.

2 Cut in margarine with pastry blender or two knives until mixture resembles coarse crumbs. Stir in ¼ cup cheddar. Make a well in center and pour in buttermilk. Mix with fork until a soft, sticky dough forms.

3 Drop heaping tablespoons of dough onto baking sheet, making 18 biscuits.

4 Brush biscuits with egg white.

5 Sprinkle with remaining cheddar. Bake until puffy and golden, about 12 minutes.

Cook's Clue

Do you prefer the more perfect look of rolled biscuits? Make dough, using 2 cups self-rising flour. Pat out dough on lightly floured surface to 1 inch thick. Using a 2½-inch cutter, make 18 biscuits. Glaze, top with cheese, and bake as directed.

way back when... A biscuit is not just a biscuit. In England, the word refers to a cracker or a cookie. And as early as 1828, Noah Webster defined the biscuit in America as "a composition of flour and butter, made and baked in private families." For centuries, Americans have baked biscuits: unleavened beaten biscuits in the Deep South, funeral biscuits decorated with ornate symbols, even super-high, extra-light angel biscuits made with both baking powder and yeast.

(Source: The Encyclopedia of American Food and Drink, *by John F. Mariani, Lebhar-Friedman Books, NY, 1999)*

STEP 2 *Mix just until a soft, sticky dough forms (overmixing makes biscuits tough!).*

STEP 4 *Brush biscuits lightly and evenly with egg white.*

STEP 5 *For golden biscuits with a more cheesy flavor, sprinkle tops with cheese.*

Double Corn Sticks

Baked in cast-iron pans with corncob-shaped indentations, these cute little quickbreads turn a bowl of tomato soup or a spinach salad into a tempting meal. They're also great for breakfast or snacks, spread with jam or fruit butter. Heart-friendly olive oil and low-fat yogurt replace the melted butter traditionally used to make corn sticks, thereby reducing the saturated fat.

PER CORN STICK

162 calories / 28% from fat
1 g saturated fat, 5 g total fat
5 mg cholesterol
285 mg sodium
24 g total carbohydrate
2 g dietary fiber
5 g protein

PREP TIME 10 min.	COOK TIME 17 min.	MAKES 12

- 3 tablespoons olive oil
- 3 strips turkey bacon, thinly sliced crosswise
- 1½ cups plain low-fat yogurt
- 2 egg whites
- 1 cup yellow cornmeal
- 1 cup flour
- 2 tablespoons sugar
- 2½ teaspoons baking powder
- ½ teaspoon baking soda
- ½ teaspoon salt
- ½ teaspoon cayenne pepper
- 1 cup frozen corn kernels, thawed
- 3 scallions, thinly sliced

1 Preheat oven to 400°F. Spray 12 corn stick molds with nonstick cooking spray. Heat 1 tablespoon oil in small skillet over medium heat. Add bacon and cook until crisp, about 5 minutes. Transfer to medium bowl along with remaining 2 tablespoons oil. Whisk in yogurt and egg whites and set aside.

2 Combine cornmeal, flour, sugar, baking powder, baking soda, salt, and cayenne pepper in large bowl. Make well in center of dry ingredients.

3 Pour in yogurt mixture. Stir until evenly moistened. Fold in corn kernels and scallions.

4 Spoon batter into corn stick molds and bake until a cake tester inserted in center of a corn stick comes out just clean, about 12 minutes. Invert onto wire rack. Serve warm or at room temperature.

STEP 2 *Make a well in the center of the cornmeal-flour mixture.*

STEP 3 *Pour the yogurt mixture into well.*

STEP 4 *Spoon the batter into a cast-iron corn stick mold.*

secret to success

Low-fat yogurt in place of melted butter not only cuts the saturated fat, but also gives the breads a slight tang and a tender texture.

HEALTH HINT

Skeptics of turkey bacon, give it a try. Regular bacon consists of nothing but fat with no nutritional value. Because turkey bacon is made from turkey meat and not pork, it has a significantly lower fat content—usually 97 percent fat-free. While the nutritional value is still low, it is low in fat and has some protein.

Cook's Clue

Corn stick pans are available in most kitchenware shops, but you can also use regular muffin pans. Line 12 muffin-tin cups with paper liners. Fill three-quarters full with batter, and bake at 400°F for 15 to 17 minutes, or until a cake tester inserted in the center of a muffin comes out clean.

Guilt-Free Pepperoni Pizza

Here's proof—you can enjoy a slice of pepperoni pizza and do your heart good. A few heart-smart substitutions and lots of vegetables make this pie much more healthful than a pizzeria's, and you get to savor the aroma as the pie bakes. Dig in with gusto—each slice is low in fat and calories.

PER SERVING

222 calories / 24% from fat

2.5 g saturated fat, 6 g total fat

17 mg cholesterol

704 mg sodium

31 g total carbohydrate

2 g dietary fiber

12 g protein

PREP TIME 10 min. | COOK TIME 17 min. | SERVES 6

- 5 ounces white mushrooms, trimmed and sliced
- 1 large onion, cut into thin wedges
- 2 garlic cloves, minced
- 2 teaspoons fresh oregano or 1 teaspoon dried
- ¼ teaspoon salt
- 4 plum tomatoes, sliced
- 2 teaspoons balsamic vinegar
- 1 package (10 ounces) refrigerated pizza dough
- ¾ cup pizza sauce
- 1 ounce turkey pepperoni (about 16 slices)
- 1 cup shredded part-skim mozzarella cheese
- 3 tablespoons chopped parsley

1 Place oven rack in center of oven. Preheat oven to 425°F. Line a 12-inch pizza pan or 15 x 12-inch baking sheet with parchment paper.

2 Lightly coat large nonstick skillet with nonstick cooking spray and set over medium-high heat. Sauté mushrooms, onion, garlic, oregano, and salt until mushrooms are golden brown, about 7 minutes. Stir in tomatoes, sprinkle with vinegar, and cover. Remove from heat and let stand 3 minutes.

3 Meanwhile, shape crust on parchment paper according to package instructions. Spread on pizza sauce. Top with vegetables, pepperoni, mozzarella, and parsley.

4 Bake until crust is golden brown and crisp and cheese is melted and bubbly, about 10 minutes.

HEALTH HINT

With its abundance of vegetables, this pizza provides a range of nutrients—especially vitamin C from the tomatoes—which promote the absorption of iron in your body. The ample amount of thinly sliced, lower-fat turkey pepperoni goes a long way to boost flavor without adding too much fat. An ounce of turkey pepperoni has 65% less saturated fat than regular pork-and-beef pepperoni. The part-skim mozzarella supplies 15% of the Daily Value of calcium and helps prevent osteoporosis.

Cook's Clue

Use fresh oregano as often as possible because it has a richer flavor. The leaves on fresh oregano should appear bright green; stems should be firm. Look for leaves with no discoloration, dark spots, or yellowing. Keep fresh oregano in the refrigerator wrapped in a damp towel. Keep dry oregano in a cool, dark place and store for around six months.

Making Pizza on a Peel

You can also make pizza on a pizza peel: Line a peel with parchment paper and press dough into a 12-inch circle, working from the center out.

Add toppings.

Transfer pizza on parchment to a preheated pizza stone, if you have one, or directly onto oven rack.

Quick Tortilla Pizzas

PER SERVING

215 calories / 20% from fat
2 g saturated fat, 7 g total fat
0 mg cholesterol
371 mg sodium
34 g total carbohydrate
2 g dietary fiber
9 g protein

It's easy to enjoy homemade pizza without spending a lot of time cooking. The trick is to use already-prepared breads like tortillas or pita rounds for the crust, instead of pizza dough. You can serve these quick Mexican-style tortilla pizzas as a substantial snack or a light meal. For meatier pizzas, sprinkle with chopped ham or leftover chicken.

PREP TIME 20 min. | COOK TIME 20 min. | SERVES 4

- 8 flour tortillas (6" diameter)
- ½ cup reduced-sodium tomato sauce
- 1 can (3 ounces) jalapeño or green chili peppers, drained and coarsely chopped
- 2 garlic cloves, finely chopped
- 2 tablespoons chopped parsley or cilantro
- ⅛ teaspoon black pepper
- ½ cup shredded low-fat cheddar cheese

1 Preheat oven to 300°F. Wrap tortillas together in foil and warm in oven for 10 minutes. Increase oven temperature to 375°F.

2 Unwrap tortillas and arrange in single layer on two nonstick baking sheets. Spread thin layer of the tomato sauce over each tortilla.

3 Sprinkle jalapeños, garlic, parsley, and black pepper over sauce. Sprinkle cheese on top. Bake 10 minutes or until cheese is melted and pizzas heated through.

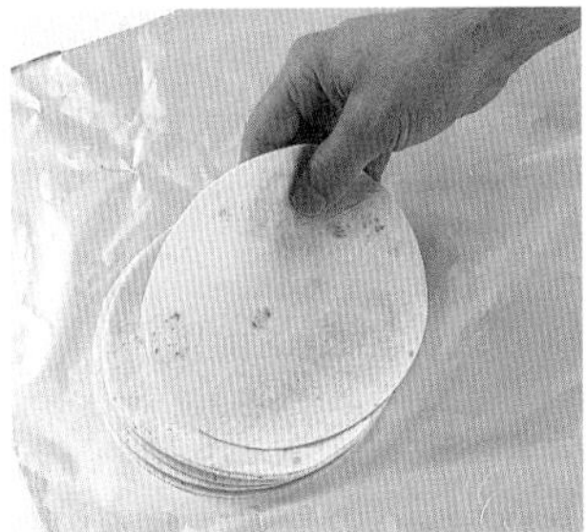

STEP 1 *Wrap tortillas in foil and warm in the oven for 10 minutes.*

STEP 2 *Spread tomato sauce over each tortilla.*

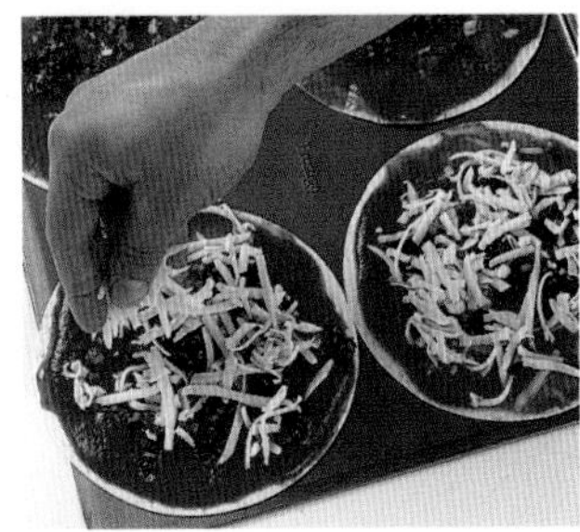

STEP 3 *Sprinkle jalapeños, garlic, parsley, black pepper, and cheese on top.*

HEALTH HINT

Hot peppers, garlic, and other seasonings add a strong flavor "kick" to food and contain powerful phytochemicals that may help fight heart disease and cancer.

secret to success

When buying jalapeños, make sure your peppers are firm, with smooth, glossy skin and uniform green coloring. Dry lines are signs of the pepper's maturity and indicate how hot it is. Avoid soft, bruised, or wrinkly peppers. Refrigerate for up to five days in a plastic bag.

way back when... Cheese was discovered about 10,000 years ago by accident. Legend has it that an Arabian traveling across the desert put milk in a canteen made from a sheep's stomach. Hours later, he realized the milk had transformed into cheese curds, thanks to the combination of the heat from the sun and a coagulating enzyme present inside the sheep. Cheese gained popularity, and in Rome, they had rooms designated for cheese making. (No wonder the Romans came up with cheese masterpieces like Parmesan!)

(Source: www.whfoods.com)

Cook's Clue

To boost fiber, look for whole-wheat tortillas. To lower fat even further, try fat-free tortillas. To double or triple the recipe, simply double or triple the amount of ingredients.

Salad Pizza

If you usually order a side salad with your pizza, you'll love this two-in-one idea: It offers the cool contrast of a vinaigrette-dressed salad atop a crisp, cheesy crust. You'll want to tuck into this pie with a knife and fork—with all this topping, it's not easy to pick up a slice. Pizza dough is sold at many pizza parlors and in the refrigerator case at the supermarket.

PER SERVING

320 calories / 13% from fat
1 g saturated fat, 4.5 g total fat
7 mg cholesterol
963 mg sodium
47 g total carbohydrate
3 g dietary fiber
21 g protein

PREP TIME 20 min. | **COOK TIME 20 min.** | **SERVES 6**

- 1 pound pizza or bread dough, thawed if frozen
- 2 tablespoons yellow cornmeal
- ¼ cup grated Parmesan cheese
- 2 tablespoons balsamic vinegar
- 1 tablespoon Dijon mustard
- 1 teaspoon light brown sugar
- ¼ teaspoon salt
- 12 ounces plum tomatoes, cut into ½-inch wedges
- 1 red onion, halved and thinly sliced
- 2 cups shredded fat-free mozzarella (8 ounces)
- 6 cups mixed salad greens, torn into bite-size pieces

1 Preheat oven to 425°F. Roll dough out to 12-inch square on unfloured work surface. Sprinkle large baking sheet with cornmeal and place dough on top. Sprinkle Parmesan over dough. Bake until Parmesan starts to brown and pizza begins to puff, about 15 minutes.

2 Meanwhile, whisk together vinegar, mustard, brown sugar, and salt in large mixing bowl. Add tomatoes and onion and toss to combine. Set aside.

3 Top pizza with mozzarella and return to oven. Bake until cheese has melted and pizza bottom is crisp, about 5 minutes.

4 Add salad greens to tomato mixture and toss to coat. Scatter salad over hot pizza and serve.

Round Out the Meal

Start with minestrone soup, and serve low-fat chocolate pudding for dessert.

HEALTH HINT

The list of important nutrients in mozzarella is long—calcium, phosphorus, protein, B vitamins, and riboflavin, to name a few! B vitamins are crucial for the body's energy production. B_{12}, in particular, helps prevent the molecule homocysteine from damaging blood vessel walls. If the number of homocysteine becomes too high, cardiovascular disease becomes a major threat. Low-fat mozzarella is a tasty way to put protein into your diet.

Cook's Clue

Don't be tempted to flour the work surface when you're rolling out the dough; pizza dough isn't sticky, and it will be easier to work with on an unfloured surface.

STEP 1 *Sprinkle grated Parmesan over rolled-out dough.*

STEP 3 *Top hot pizza with shredded mozzarella cheese.*

STEP 4 *Toss salad greens with tomato-onion mixture.*

Grilled Chicken and Red Pepper Pizzas

Rounds of Middle Eastern "pocket bread," or pita, make a perfect base for mini-pizzas topped with grilled chicken, feta cheese, red onions, and bell peppers. Because feta is so flavorful, you only need a small amount, and that helps keep the fat levels low.

PER SERVING

316 calories / 16% from fat

2.5 g saturated fat, 5.5 g total fat

49 mg cholesterol

515 mg sodium

44 g total carbohydrate

4 g dietary fiber

22 g protein

PREP TIME 20 min.	COOK TIME 25 min.	SERVES 4

- 8 ounces boneless, skinless chicken breast
- ½ teaspoon salt
- ¼ teaspoon black pepper
- 2 medium red onions, cut into thick rings
- 2 red bell peppers, seeded and cut lengthwise into flat panels
- 4 whole-wheat pita breads (6 inches)
- 2 ounces feta cheese, crumbled (scant ½ cup)
- 3 tablespoons chopped fresh mint

1 Spray a grill rack with nonstick cooking spray. Preheat grill to medium. Sprinkle chicken with salt and black pepper. Grill until just cooked through, about 4 minutes per side. When chicken is cool enough to handle, pull into shreds.

2 Place onions and bell pepper pieces skin-side down on grill. Cook until onions are tender and peppers are charred, about 10 minutes. When cool enough to handle, peel peppers and thickly slice.

3 Top pitas with onion rings, peppers, shredded chicken, and feta. Grill until pita is crisp, about 4 minutes. Sprinkle mint over tops.

STEP 1 *After grilling chicken breasts, pull meat into bite-size shreds.*

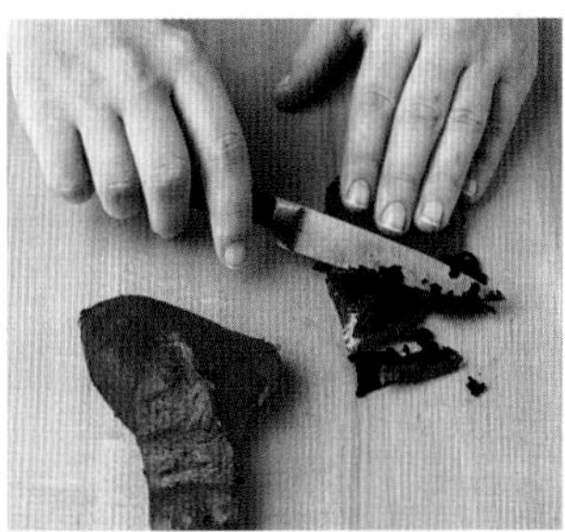

STEP 2 *Use paring knife or fingers to peel off charred skin on bell peppers.*

STEP 3 *Top pitas with crumbled feta cheese.*

way back when... In 1889, King Umberto I and Queen Margherita of Italy invited famous *pizzaioli* chef, Raffaele Esposito, to cook for them. To show his patriotic fervor, Raffaele chose to top flat bread with food that would represent the colors of Italy: red tomato, white mozzarella cheese, and green basil. It became a hot item and was sold on Naples streets for breakfast, lunch, and dinner. Various toppings were introduced to the pizza over the years. Pizza arrived in America toward the end of the 19th century, as a peddler walked the streets of Chicago carrying a washtub of pizzas on top of his head, in the traditional way it's sold in Naples.

(Source: http://aboutpizza.com)

Cook's Clue

If it's not a day for outdoor grilling, you can cook the chicken, onions, and peppers under the broiler. Be sure to place the peppers skin-side up on the broiler pan (as opposed to skin-side down when grilling).

HEALTH HINT

Whole-wheat bread brings the nutritional benefits of the whole grain's bran and germ. When shopping for whole-wheat bread, look for the word "whole" before "wheat flour" on the ingredient list on the label. If it just says "wheat flour," it is not whole wheat.

Round Out the Meal

Start with gazpacho, and serve sliced peaches for dessert.

Cakes, Pies and Sweets

Marble Cheesecake

Here's a dream "makeover" of a dessert that most people would die for. Just to get an idea of the nutritional difference between our version and a classic cheesecake, check the ingredients in a traditional recipe: a pound or two of cream cheese, a stick of butter, and three or more eggs. Now read the ingredients and the "numbers" on this chocolate-swirled beauty, and get baking!

PER SERVING

225 calories / 20% from fat

1 g saturated fat, 5 g total fat

21 mg cholesterol

245 mg sodium

35 g total carbohydrate

1 g dietary fiber

11 g protein

PREP TIME 15 min.	COOK TIME 55 min. + chilling	SERVES 12

- 3 ounces low-fat honey graham crackers (6 whole crackers)
- ½ cup toasted wheat germ
- 1 tablespoon plus 1 cup sugar
- 2 tablespoons extra-light olive oil
- 1 container (19 ounces) silken tofu, well drained
- 1 pound fat-free cream cheese
- 3 tablespoons flour
- 1 large egg plus 2 large egg whites
- 1 teaspoon vanilla
- ¼ cup chocolate syrup

1 Preheat oven to 350°F. Combine graham crackers, wheat germ, and 1 tablespoon sugar in food processor and process to fine crumbs. Add oil and process until moistened. Place mixture in 9-inch springform pan, and press into bottom and partway up sides. Bake until set, about 10 minutes.

2 Add drained tofu, remaining 1 cup sugar, cream cheese, flour, whole egg, egg whites, and vanilla to food processor (no need to clean bowl), and process until smooth and well blended.

3 Measure out 1 cup tofu mixture, place in small bowl, and stir in chocolate syrup. Pour remaining plain tofu mixture into crust in springform pan.

4 Pour chocolate mixture in a ring on top of batter and swirl in with a knife (*see photo, right*). Bake 45 minutes. Turn off oven and leave in oven 45 minutes undisturbed. Cool to room temperature before chilling overnight.

STEP 1 *Press crumb mixture into bottom and partway up sides of springform pan.*

STEP 3 *Stir chocolate syrup into 1 cup of tofu mixture.*

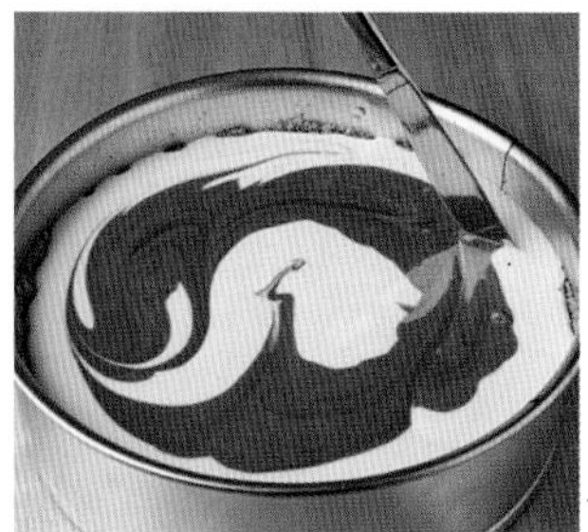

STEP 4 *Pull knife through both chocolate and plain mixtures to "marbleize" it.*

secret to success

One health secret to this delicious cheesecake is that it uses olive oil instead of melted butter in the graham cracker crumb crust. Use an olive oil labeled "light" or "mild-flavored" so there will be no pronounced olive flavor.

way back when... Tofu originated in China, most likely during the Han dynasty in the 2nd century B.C. A Chinese legend claims that tofu was invented when a cook experimented mixing cooked soybeans with the compound nagari. This resulted in bean curd. Nagari is still used in tofu production, and its production is similar to cheese. A coagulant curdles soymilk, then the curds are pressed into a block.

(Source: http://chinesefood.about.com)

HEALTH HINT

Tofu is rich in soy protein, a high-quality protein with heart-healthy properties; consuming at least 25 grams of soy protein each day can significantly improve cholesterol levels. Soy isoflavones (estrogen-like substances found in soy foods) are thought to team with soy protein to lower total and LDL ("bad") cholesterol.

Lemon–Poppy Seed Cupcakes

Of course you can bake tender, tasty cupcakes without loads of butter! And you'll enjoy them even more knowing they're a heart-smart treat for everyone. For an attractive presentation, nest each baked cupcake inside a second, decorative cupcake liner.

PER CUPCAKE

126 calories / 29% from fat
0.5 g saturated fat, 4 g total fat
18 mg cholesterol
179 mg sodium
20 g total carbohydrate
0.5 g dietary fiber
3 g protein

PREP TIME 15 min. | COOK TIME 22 min. + cooling | 12 CUPCAKES

- 1 cup flour
- 1 teaspoon baking powder
- ½ teaspoon salt
- ¼ teaspoon baking soda
- 2 tablespoons tub margarine
- 1 tablespoon extra-light olive oil
- ½ cup granulated sugar
- 1 large egg plus 1 large egg white
- 2 teaspoons grated lemon zest
- ½ cup buttermilk
- 2 tablespoons poppy seeds
- ⅓ cup confectioners' sugar
- 2 teaspoons fresh lemon juice

1 Preheat oven to 350°F. Line twelve 2½-inch muffin cups with paper liners.

2 Stir together flour, baking powder, salt, and baking soda in large bowl until well combined.

3 Beat margarine and oil together in large bowl until combined. Beat in granulated sugar until light and creamy. Add whole egg and then egg white, beating well after each addition. Beat in lemon zest.

4 Alternately fold flour mixture and buttermilk into egg mixture, beginning and ending with flour mixture. Stir in poppy seeds.

5 Spoon batter into muffin cups. Bake until golden brown and toothpick inserted in center of a cupcake comes out clean, 20 to 22 minutes. Remove from pans to cool on wire rack. (Once cooled, cupcakes can be wrapped and frozen. Thaw before proceeding.)

6 Combine confectioners' sugar and lemon juice in small bowl, stirring until smooth. Drizzle or spread lemon glaze over cooled cupcakes.

STEP 3 *Add grated lemon zest to margarine-sugar mixture.*

STEP 4 *Add poppy seeds to batter and stir in.*

STEP 6 *Use a spoon to drizzle lemon glaze over cooled cupcakes.*

secret to success

Confectioners' sugar is often sifted before measuring because it adds volume to the final product. Therefore, it is better weighed than measured in a cup. Because of today's milling process, it is finer and rarely has lumps to remove. Level the top of the cup with the edge of a spatula, and if you'd like to measure it, one cup weighs around 4 ounces.

Cook's Clue

Whenever a recipe requires fruit zest, as in this recipe, use organically grown. Most conventionally grown fruits have traces of pesticide on their skin. Use a zester, paring knife, or vegetable peeler to remove the zest, but don't remove too much: The white pith is bitter!

HEALTH HINT

The soft (tub) margarine used in these cupcakes is healthier than hard (stick) margarine because soft margarine has smaller amounts of trans fatty acids, which raise harmful blood cholesterol levels.

Cappuccino Chiffon Cake

When chiffon cakes first appeared in the 1940s, the focus was on how easy they were to mix; but today, we also value the fact that they can be made lower in fat and cholesterol. To make this lovely, light-textured cake even healthier for your heart, serve it topped with fresh fruit, such as sliced nectarines or peaches, raspberries, or strawberries.

PER SLICE

223 calories / 32% from fat
1 g saturated fat, 8 g total fat
27 mg cholesterol
138 mg sodium
36 g total carbohydrate
1 g dietary fiber
3 g protein

PREP TIME 15 min. | COOK TIME 45 min. | 16 SLICES

- 2¼ cups cake flour
- 1½ cups granulated sugar
- 1 tablespoon baking powder
- ¾ teaspoon cinnamon
- ½ teaspoon salt
- ½ cup walnut oil or extra-light olive oil
- 2 large eggs, separated, plus 4 large egg whites
- ¾ cup brewed espresso or other dark-roast coffee, at room temperature
- 2 tablespoons unsweetened cocoa powder
- 1 teaspoon vanilla
- ½ teaspoon cream of tartar
- 2 tablespoons confectioners' sugar

1 Preheat oven to 325°F. Stir together cake flour, granulated sugar, baking powder, cinnamon, and salt in medium bowl. Whisk walnut oil, egg yolks, espresso, cocoa powder, and vanilla together in large bowl until smooth. Fold flour mixture into egg mixture until well combined.

2 Beat 6 egg whites until frothy in separate bowl. Beat in cream of tartar, and continue beating until stiff peaks form. Gently fold egg whites into batter.

3 Pour batter into ungreased 10-inch tube pan. Bake until cake tester inserted in center comes out clean, about 45 minutes.

4 Invert pan to cool. Once cooled, run a metal spatula around the inner and outer edges of the cake and invert onto a serving plate. Dust cake with confectioners' sugar.

STEP 2 *Use rubber spatula to fold beaten egg whites into batter.*

STEP 3 *Pour batter into ungreased 10-inch tube pan.*

STEP 4 *To cool cake, invert pan (this keeps cake from sinking and becoming too dense). If you don't have a pan with legs (as above), hang tube pan over the neck of a bottle.*

HEALTH HINT

Walnut oil is a rich source of heart-friendly monounsaturated and polyunsaturated fats and the antioxidant vitamin E. It may help lower the risk of heart disease by increasing high-density lipoprotein (HDL) or "good" cholesterol.

secret to success

Whenever recipes call for instant coffee, substituting espresso powder adds an extra boost. If you're feeling experimental, brew flavored coffee, such as hazelnut, French vanilla, or raspberry chocolate, to add new flavor to the cake or recipe.

Cook's Clue

If you don't have cake flour (it can be hard to find in some areas), use 2 cups all-purpose flour plus ¼ cup cornstarch, stirred together.

Ginger–Pear Upside-Down Cake

Greet the first chilly day of fall with a tender yellow cake topped with caramelized pears. (Brown sugar in the bottom of the pan does the caramelizing all by itself.) Although very little fat goes into the batter—just 3 tablespoons of heart-smart light olive oil—the cake has a warm, spicy richness.

PER SERVING

196 calories / 23% from fat

1 g saturated fat, 5 g total fat

22 mg cholesterol

140 mg sodium

36 g total carbohydrate

1 g dietary fiber

3 g protein

PREP TIME 15 min. | COOK TIME 35 min. + cooling | SERVES 10

- 2 tablespoons dark brown sugar
- 3 firm-ripe Bartlett pears
- 1¼ cups cake flour
- 1 teaspoon ground ginger
- ¾ teaspoon baking powder
- ¼ teaspoon baking soda
- ¼ teaspoon salt
- 3 tablespoons extra-light olive oil
- ¾ cup granulated sugar
- 1½ teaspoons grated lime zest
- 1 teaspoon coconut extract
- 1 large egg plus 1 large egg white
- ¾ cup fat-free buttermilk

1 Preheat oven to 350°F. Spray bottom of 9-inch round nonstick cake pan with nonstick cooking spray. Sprinkle brown sugar over bottom, shaking pan to coat evenly.

2 Peel, core, and halve pears. Slice pears crosswise into ⅓-inch-thick slices. Evenly spread pears in pan, making sure bottom of pan is covered.

3 Mix together flour, ground ginger, baking powder, baking soda, and salt on a sheet of wax paper. With electric mixer, beat together oil, granulated sugar, lime zest, and coconut extract in large bowl. Beat in whole egg and egg white until thick.

4 With a spatula, alternately fold flour mixture and buttermilk into egg mixture, beginning and ending with flour mixture, until just blended.

5 Pour batter over pears, smoothing top to cover pears completely. Bake until a toothpick inserted in center comes out clean, about 35 minutes. Transfer to a wire rack. Let cake cool in pan on rack for 10 minutes, then invert onto a platter. Let cool slightly before slicing.

STEP 2 *Arrange sliced pears evenly over brown sugar in cake pan.*

STEP 3 *Beat whole egg and egg white into sugar mixture.*

STEP 5 *Spread batter evenly over pears in cake pan.*

Cook's Clue

Gently wash pears once peeled, and douse with lemon, lime, or orange juice to prevent browning. To cut the pear, use an apple corer, and remove the core from the base, then cut it into the necessary size and shape. When the recipe does not specify, leave the peel on all fruit for added nutritional benefits.

way back when… Ginger stems back 3,000 years. This root, so well known to the ancient Romans, disappeared after the fall of the Roman Empire. Marco Polo reintroduced ginger, and it soon became highly desirable and expensive. The invention of the gingerbread man was credited to Queen Elizabeth I of England.

(Source: http://homecooking.about.com)

HEALTH HINT

The soluble fiber in pears, including pectin, helps prevent cholesterol from being absorbed in the body. Pears also supply the mineral potassium, which helps ward off strokes.

 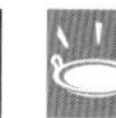  

Cocoa Crater Cake

Wow—there's no other word for this cake! It's reminiscent of those popular tunnel cakes of the 1960s, but this one's much healthier. It's a chocolate angel food, instead of the traditional fudgy butter cake—with only half the sugar, one-fourth the nuts, and egg whites instead of whole eggs. Its filling is chocolate pudding, not gooey chocolate frosting. Serve it proudly, as a special treat!

PER SERVING

187 calories / 14% from fat
1 g saturated fat, 3 g total fat
2 mg cholesterol
125 mg sodium
34 g total carbohydrate
1 g dietary fiber
6 g protein

PREP TIME 30 min. | COOK TIME 45 min. + chilling | SERVES 16

- 1 cup cake flour
- 1½ cups granulated sugar
- ⅓ cup unsweetened cocoa powder
- 14 egg whites (about 2 cups), at room temperature
- 1 teaspoon cream of tartar
- ¼ teaspoon salt
- 2 teaspoons vanilla
- 1 box (3⅛ ounces) chocolate pudding mix
- 1 tablespoon freeze-dried coffee granules
- 2 cups reduced-fat milk (2%)
- ½ cup finely chopped walnuts
- 2 tablespoons confectioners' sugar

1 Preheat oven to 325°F. Generously coat a 10-inch tube pan with removable bottom or 10-inch Bundt pan with nonstick cooking spray. Whisk cake flour, ¾ cup granulated sugar, and cocoa powder in medium bowl; set aside. Beat egg whites, cream of tartar, and salt in large bowl with electric mixer at medium speed until whites begin to hold their shape, about 4 minutes. Increase speed to high, and slowly add remaining sugar in steady stream until whites are glossy and hold soft peaks, about 4 minutes longer. Beat in vanilla.

2 Sift flour mixture, one-third at a time, over egg whites and gently fold in until flour disappears. Spoon batter into pan. Bake until cake is firm to touch, about 45 minutes. Cool cake completely in pan on rack, about 1 hour. Release cake with thin knife and turn out onto rack. Transfer cake to serving plate, top-side up.

3 Meanwhile, stir pudding mix and coffee granules in medium saucepan, then stir in milk until dissolved. Prepare according to package instructions. Remove from heat, stir in walnuts, and transfer to heatproof bowl. Lay piece of plastic wrap directly on top of pudding and refrigerate until cool but not completely set, about 30 minutes.

4 Cut 1-inch slice horizontally off top of cake. Tear out tunnel in cake, leaving 1-inch shell on bottom, center, and sides. Spoon pudding into tunnel and replace top of cake, pressing down lightly to adhere. Chill cake until serving time.

secret to success

Buy heavy, whole walnuts, with shells uncracked, unpierced, and unstained. Stains indicate mold, which is unsafe to eat. Shelled walnuts are usually available in prepackaged containers and in bulk. When purchasing, avoid any that appear rubbery or shriveled up. Whenever possible, smell walnuts to check for spoilage.

Cook's Clue

A little vinegar or cream of tartar stabilizes beaten egg whites (don't use a copper bowl, as it may cause a reaction). Use only a little salt because it can weaken the whites.

How to Fill a Cocoa Crater

Cut a 1-inch horizontal slice off top of cake.

Fill crater (tunnel) with chocolate pudding.

Replace top of cake, pressing down slightly.

HEALTH HINT

Like all angel food cakes, which are made with stiffly beaten egg whites, this one is heart-healthy because it's low in fat and cholesterol.

Daffodil Cake

Just as homemakers did in the 1930s, usher in spring by baking a daffodil cake—a fragrant, delicate sponge cake with swirls of yellow and white in every slice. This festive treat is lightly flavored with orange, and it boasts a mere 1 gram of fat per serving. A dessert as cheerful as spring itself.

PER SERVING

145 calories / 16% from fat
0.5 g saturated fat, 1 g total fat
53 mg cholesterol
110 mg sodium
29 g total carbohydrate
0 g dietary fiber
4 g protein

PREP TIME 20 min.	COOK TIME 35 min. + cooling	SERVES 16

- 10 large eggs, separated
- 1½ cups granulated sugar
- 2 teaspoons grated orange zest
- 1 tablespoon vanilla
- ½ teaspoon salt
- 1 teaspoon cream of tartar
- 1⅓ cups sifted cake flour
- ⅓ cup sifted confectioners' sugar

1 Preheat oven to 375°F. Beat 4 egg yolks (reserve remaining 6 yolks for another recipe), ¼ cup granulated sugar, and orange zest in large bowl with electric mixer at high speed until batter is thick and lemon-colored, about 10 minutes. Scrape down bowl occasionally with spatula. Beat in vanilla.

2 Beat all 10 egg whites and salt in separate large bowl with clean beaters at high speed until foamy. Add cream of tartar and beat until soft peaks form. Add remaining granulated sugar, 2 tablespoons at a time, beating at high speed until sugar has dissolved and stiff, glossy peaks form.

3 Sift flour over egg whites, ⅓ cup at a time, gently folding in each addition with a wire whisk just until flour is no longer visible. Fold one-third of egg white mixture into yolk mixture.

4 Alternately spoon heaping tablespoons of yellow and white batters into a 9- or 10-inch tube pan. Swirl thin spatula or knife through batter to marbleize. Lightly swirl top of cake. Bake until cake springs back when lightly touched, about 35 minutes.

5 Invert cake in pan onto bottle and cool completely. Run knife around pan to loosen cake. Remove cake from pan, place on serving plate, and sprinkle cake with confectioners' sugar.

STEP 4 *Swirl spatula through yellow and white batter in pan.*

STEP 5 *Cool cake upside down in pan.*

HEALTH HINT

Several compounds in citrus zest, polymethoxylated flavones, can potentially lower cholesterol more than prescription drugs. The most common fruits with these compounds are tangerines and oranges. Just a tablespoon of the peel may result in lowered cholesterol. In a study executed on hamsters, blood levels of total cholesterol were reduced significantly, and it appeared to have no effect on HDL ("good") cholesterol.

secret to success

Increasing the egg whites and cutting back on the yolks cuts the fat and yields a higher cake. Each slice weighs in at only 1 gram of fat.

When beating egg whites, always use a clean bowl and clean beaters. Even a trace of fat or egg yolk can cause the egg whites to collapse or prevent them from forming stiff peaks. Cream of tartar added to the egg whites gives the cake a fine grain and helps keep it from pulling away from the sides of the pan.

Lemon Angel Food Cake with Strawberries

Angel food cake is a dream dessert for those who are cholesterol-conscious. Whipped up from a dozen egg whites—but no yolks—this lofty delight is confected with no shortening at all. The vividly colorful fruit sauce makes the cake worthy of a festive occasion.

PER SERVING

159 calories / 0% from fat
0 g saturated fat, 0 g total fat
0 mg cholesterol
153 mg sodium
35 g total carbohydrate
1 g dietary fiber
5 g protein

PREP TIME 20 min. | COOK TIME 50 min. | SERVES 12

- 1 bag (20 ounces) frozen strawberries, thawed
- ½ cup orange juice
- 12 large egg whites, at room temperature
- 1¼ teaspoons cream of tartar
- ½ teaspoon salt
- 1¼ cups granulated sugar
- 3 tablespoons grated lemon zest
- 1 teaspoon vanilla
- 1 cup flour

1 Combine strawberries and orange juice in large bowl. Refrigerate.

2 Preheat oven to 325°F. Beat egg whites, cream of tartar, and salt in large bowl with electric mixer until foamy. Gradually beat in granulated sugar, 2 tablespoons at a time, until thick, soft peaks form. Beat in lemon zest and vanilla.

3 Gently fold flour into egg-white mixture, ¼ cup at a time, until incorporated. Spoon into ungreased 10-inch angel food or tube pan. Bake until top springs back when lightly pressed, about 50 minutes.

4 Invert cake pan to cool. If pan does not have legs, hang pan over the neck of a bottle. Cool cake completely. Run metal spatula around edges and center of pan, then invert onto cake platter. Serve with strawberries and their juice.

STEP 2 *Whip egg whites until soft peaks form.*

STEP 3 *With a rubber spatula, gently fold flour into beaten egg whites.*

STEP 4 *Angel food cake pans have "legs" to cool the cake upside down.*

HEALTH HINT

Strawberries contain high amounts of vitamin C, K, and dietary fiber, making them a heart-healthy fruit. They also contain a good amount of manganese, vitamin B_5, vitamin B_1, vitamin B_6, iodine, and folate. They contain a high source of phenols, which act as antioxidants that help protect cell structures and prevent oxygen damage in the body's organ systems. This phenol content helps strawberries protect the heart.

Cook's Clue

Egg whites won't whip up to maximum volume if there's the tiniest bit of fat in the bowl. Two tips: Use a glass or stainless-steel bowl (plastic holds grease), and separate the eggs carefully to avoid getting any of the fatty yolk into the whites. The best way to separate eggs is in two steps. Separate each egg white into a cup, then add the white to a large bowl that will hold all the whites. This way, if a yolk breaks, you'll only have to discard the one egg, not the whole batch.

Chocolate Snacking Cake

PER SERVING

77 calories / 12% from fat

0.5 g saturated fat, 1 g total fat

0 mg cholesterol

68 mg sodium

15 g total carbohydrate

1 g dietary fiber

1 g protein

Craving some chocolate? Each of these luscious little gems has only 77 calories and 1 gram of fat. Go ahead and indulge yourself! Because these are low-cholesterol chocolate treats, you can satisfy that craving while both your heart and conscience thank you.

PREP TIME 15 min.	COOK TIME 35 min. + cooling	SERVES 36

- 1⅓ cups sifted self-rising flour
- 1 cup plus 2 teaspoons unsweetened cocoa powder
- ¼ cup fat-free buttermilk
- 1 tablespoon instant espresso powder
- 1 cup granulated sugar
- ½ cup packed light brown sugar
- ½ cup unsweetened applesauce
- 2 teaspoons vanilla
- 2 large egg whites
- ½ cup mini chocolate chips
- 1 tablespoon confectioners' sugar

1 Preheat oven to 325°F. Line 8-inch square baking pan with foil, leaving 1-inch overhang. Sift flour and 1 cup cocoa together into small bowl. Heat buttermilk and espresso in small saucepan over low heat until espresso is dissolved.

2 Mix granulated and brown sugars, applesauce, buttermilk mixture, and vanilla in medium bowl. Stir in flour mixture just until blended. Beat egg whites in large bowl with electric mixer at high speed just until soft peaks form. Fold egg whites into batter. Stir in chocolate chips.

3 Scrape batter into pan. Bake 35 minutes or just until set (do not overbake). Cool in pan on wire rack 15 minutes. Lift out cake and set on rack to cool completely. Sift confectioners' sugar and remaining cocoa over cake. Cut into thirty-six 1½-inch squares.

STEP 1 *Sift flour and cocoa into small bowl. If you don't have a sifter, use a sieve.*

STEP 2 *Fold egg whites gently into cake batter with a rubber spatula.*

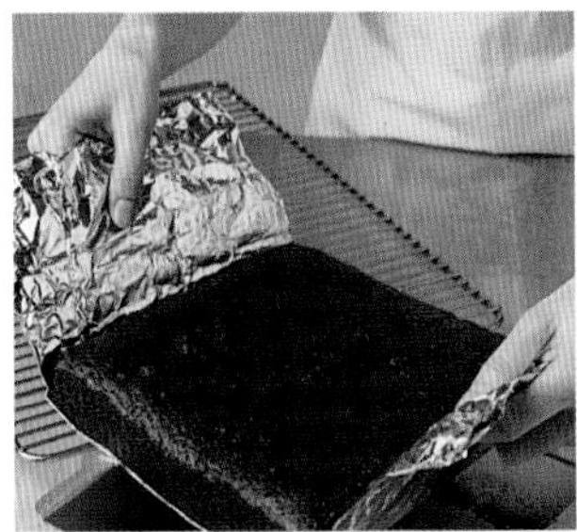

STEP 3 *Lift cake from pan by grasping the foil collar.*

secret to success

Smart substitutions trim the fat from this cake. Applesauce stands in for butter, and beaten egg whites, instead of whole eggs, provide leavening. Unsweetened cocoa powder is virtually fat-free, and instant espresso powder heightens the cake's rich chocolate flavor.

HEALTH HINT

Many recipes that require fats or oils can substitute unsweetened applesauce. For ultimate flavor and texture, replace half the amount with applesauce. Apples have enough fiber to lower cholesterol, reducing the risk of artery hardening and heart attack. Studies indicate that the soluble fiber pectin reduces LDL ("bad") cholesterol, and because apples are a high fiber food, they help prevent heart disease.

Cook's Clue

Lining the baking pan with foil eliminates the calories of greasing the pan and makes cleanup a breeze. Be sure to leave an overhang of foil to make it easy to remove the cake from the pan.

Pumpkin Pie with Pumpkin Seed Crust

The last thing you want after a heavy holiday meal is a fat-laden, guilt-inducing dessert. Instead, serve this silken, spicy pumpkin pie with a graham cracker–pumpkin seed crust. It's low in fat and boasts the heart-saving benefits of polyunsaturated oil in place of artery-clogging butter.

PER SERVING

261 calories / 24% from fat
1.5 g saturated fat, 7 g total fat
22 mg cholesterol
294 mg sodium
43 g total carbohydrate
2 g dietary fiber
7 g protein

PREP TIME 15 min.	COOK TIME 1 hour + chilling	SERVES 10

- 32 individual squares graham crackers (about 8 ounces), broken into small pieces
- ¼ cup hulled pumpkin seeds
- 2 tablespoons granulated sugar
- ½ teaspoon salt
- 1½ tablespoons pumpkin seed oil or walnut oil
- 3 tablespoons water
- 1 can (15 ounces) solid-pack pumpkin puree
- ¾ cup packed light brown sugar
- 1¼ cups low-fat (1%) milk
- 1 large egg plus 2 large egg whites
- 2 tablespoons bourbon or rum
- 2 teaspoons pumpkin pie spice

1 Preheat oven to 375°F. In food processor, process graham crackers, pumpkin seeds, granulated sugar, and ¼ teaspoon of salt until finely ground. Add oil and water and process until thoroughly moistened.

2 Spray 9-inch deep-dish glass or ceramic pie plate with nonstick cooking spray. Press crumb mixture into bottom and up sides of pie plate. Bake 10 minutes until crisp and set. Cool on wire rack.

3 Combine remaining ¼ teaspoon salt, pumpkin puree, brown sugar, milk, whole egg, egg whites, bourbon, and pumpkin pie spice in large bowl. Stir until well combined.

4 Pour pumpkin filling into pie shell and bake 45 to 50 minutes or until knife inserted between center and edge of pie comes out clean. Let the pie cool to room temperature, then refrigerate for at least 2 hours before serving.

STEP 2 *Carefully press graham cracker mixture into bottom and up sides of pie plate.*

STEP 3 *Combine pumpkin pie spice to pumpkin puree and egg mixture.*

STEP 4 *A knife inserted into pie somewhere between center and edge should come out clean when pie is done.*

HEALTH HINT

Popular in Austria, pumpkin seed oil is rich in nourishing compounds such as plant sterols, which may protect your heart by helping lower cholesterol levels. Look for it in gourmet food stores or any market that carries traditional Austrian foods.

secret to success

A few tips about using bourbon or rum in recipes: Bourbon offers a light flavor of caramel, vanilla, charcoal, and wood to a recipe, and instead of buying regular sized bottles, liquor stores sell single serving sizes. If you use rum and want a strong flavor, choose dark rum. Light rum has a less distinct flavor. Keep in mind that spiced rums should complement the main ingredients.

Cook's Clue

Make your own pumpkin seeds! Remove seeds from the pumpkin, and clean them with a moist paper towel. This removes any pulp on the seeds. Spread them on a paper bag to let them dry overnight. Once fully dried, put them on a cookie sheet, and sprinkle or spray them with olive oil and seasoning. Bake for 30 minutes at 300°F. Sporadically shake the pan to prevent burning.

Checkerboard Cherry Pie

PER SERVING
303 calories / 15% from fat
2 g saturated fat, 5 g total fat
6 mg cholesterol
200 mg sodium
61 g total carbohydrate
2 g dietary fiber
5 g protein

Life is a bowl of cherries when you dig into a wedge of this juicy pie. Enjoy—without feeling guilty! The crust bakes up delectably flaky, and the airy lattice top and sweet-tart filling make the pie light, but just as good as Grandma's.

PREP TIME 25 min.+chilling | **COOK TIME** 45 min. | **SERVES** 8

- 2 cups all-purpose flour
- 1 cup granulated sugar
- ½ teaspoon salt
- 2 tablespoons cold margarine, cut up
- ½ cup reduced-fat sour cream
- 3 to 4 tablespoons ice water
- 2 cans (14½ ounces each) sour cherries packed in water, drained
- 2 tablespoons cornstarch
- ¼ teaspoon almond extract
- 1 egg white beaten with 1 teaspoon water

1 Pulse flour, 2 tablespoons sugar, and ¼ teaspoon salt in food processor to mix. Add margarine and pulse until coarse crumbs form. With motor running, add sour cream, then water, 1 tablespoon at a time, and process until pastry holds together. Shape into two 8-inch disks, wrap in plastic, and refrigerate 30 minutes. Meanwhile, combine cherries, ¾ cup granulated sugar, cornstarch, almond extract, and remaining salt in large bowl. Set aside.

2 Coat 9-inch pie plate with nonstick cooking spray. Lightly flour work surface and roll out pastry disk into 15-inch round. Gently roll pastry onto rolling pin and ease into pie plate. Trim edge, leaving 1-inch overhang. Brush pastry with about 2 teaspoons egg-white mixture. Spoon in cherry filling.

3 Preheat oven to 425°F and arrange oven rack in center. Roll out remaining disk of pastry into 12-inch round. Cut pastry into ¾-inch-wide strips with fluted pastry or pizza wheel. Weave strips on top of pie filling to make lattice pattern *(see photos, right)*. Trim strips, leaving 1-inch overhang. Make 1-inch stand-up edge, folding in the ends of lattice strips as you go. Flute edge.

4 Brush top of pie with remaining egg-white mixture and sprinkle with remaining sugar. Place pie on foil-lined baking sheet to catch any overflow. Bake 10 minutes. Reduce temperature to 350°F and bake until crust is lightly browned and juices are bubbling in center, 35 to 40 minutes.

HEALTH HINT

The health benefits of cherries are unfolding. According to recent research, tart cherries contain lots of antioxidants that help fight cancer and heart disease. These cherries are naturally low in fat and contain potassium, vitamin C, iron, fiber, and natural carbohydrates, which give you energy. Tart cherries also contain a significant amount of melatonin, a powerful antioxidant. These antioxidants protect artery walls from damage that could lead to heart disease.

secret to success

Adding 1 teaspoon of vinegar or lemon juice for each cup of flour in a pastry and pie dough recipes does not affect the flavor, but it creates a more tender product.

How to Checker Your Pie

Fold back every other horizontal strip.

Repeat, adding vertical strips and folding back alternate horizontal strips.

Complete weaving lattice, leaving 1-inch overhang.

Cook's Clue

Can't find canned cherries? Use 4 cups pitted frozen cherries. Thaw before using.

Chocolate Mousse Tart

Celebrating a special occasion? Go ahead, indulge! This rich, creamy, very special treat is much lower in fat than a traditional chocolate tart, so you can enjoy a bit of guilt-free decadence. More good news: Even though the cocoa butter in chocolate is a saturated fat, it doesn't appear to raise the body's cholesterol level like other saturated fats.

PER SERVING

300 calories / 18% from fat
3 g saturated fat, 6 g total fat
14 mg cholesterol
118 mg sodium
58 g total carbohydrate
3 g dietary fiber
4 g protein

PREP TIME 20 min.	COOK TIME 12 min.+ chilling	SERVES 8

- 1¾ cups chocolate graham cracker crumbs (about 9 large crackers)
- 1 large egg white
- 2 tablespoons honey
- 1 packet unflavored gelatin
- 1 cup granulated sugar
- ¾ cup unsweetened cocoa powder, plus extra for dusting
- ⅓ cup reduced-fat milk (2%), warmed
- 1 teaspoon vanilla
- ½ cup heavy cream
- 1 container (12 ounces) fat-free frozen nondairy whipped topping, thawed
- 1 bar (3 ounces) semi-sweet chocolate, made into curls (optional)

1 Preheat oven to 350°F. Lightly coat 10-inch nonstick tart pan with removable bottom with nonstick cooking spray. Toss cracker crumbs, egg white, and honey with fork in medium bowl until evenly moistened. Pat crumb mixture into bottom and up side of tart pan. Bake 10 minutes. Cool.

2 Put 3 tablespoons water in small saucepan and sprinkle with gelatin. Let stand 1 minute. Stir over low heat until gelatin completely dissolves, about 2 minutes. Remove from heat.

3 Mix granulated sugar and cocoa in large bowl. Stir in milk and vanilla until cocoa dissolves. Blend in gelatin. Cool.

4 Whip cream in medium bowl until stiff. Fold whipped cream and half of whipped topping into cooled cocoa mixture until blended. Pour into crust. Swirl remaining whipped topping in center. Refrigerate until filling sets, at least 2 hours or overnight. Dust with cocoa powder. Decorate with chocolate curls (*see photos, right*), if you wish.

secret to success

Fat-free frozen whipped topping and unsweetened cocoa powder are heart-healthy stand-ins for heavy cream and the chocolate in the filling. That helps keep the fat low enough that you can indulge in a pure chocolate curl or two.

HEALTH HINT

Chocolate contains some nutrients such as iron, calcium, and vitamins A, B_1, C, D, and E, but most importantly, cocoa is the highest natural source of magnesium. A diet lacking in magnesium can increase the risk for hypertension and heart disease. Certain phytochemicals in cocoa help block free radicals from damaging arteries. Chocolate inhibits platelet aggregation, which could lead to heart attack or stroke.

How to Make Chocolate Curls

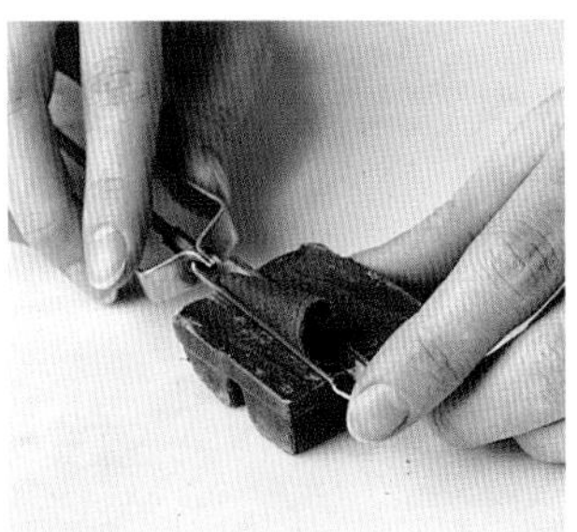

Be sure the chocolate is at room temperature. Draw the blade of a vegetable peeler across entire bar, pressing down firmly.

Lift curls with a toothpick or skewer. (Using your fingers might melt the curls.)

Cook's Clue

Gelatin is used in place of traditional eggs to thicken the mousse filling. It sets up the same, and the tart slices just as easily. Don't let the gelatin boil while dissolving, or it could lose its thickening power.

Fruit with Cannoli Cream

Italian cannoli pastries pack quite a wallop in the fat and cholesterol department: The dough is fried, and the filling is made with full-fat ricotta cheese. Save your heart and skip the fried dough. Instead, dip fresh fruit into chocolate-flecked cannoli "cream" made with sweetened low-fat cottage cheese and fat-free half-and-half.

PER SERVING

194 calories / 12% from fat

1 g saturated fat, 2.5 g total fat

2 mg cholesterol

233 mg sodium

38 g total carbohydrate

5 g dietary fiber

8 g protein

PREP TIME 15 min. | COOK TIME 0 min. | SERVES 4

1 cup low-fat (1%) cottage cheese

2 tablespoons fat-free half-and-half

2 tablespoons granulated sugar

½ teaspoon vanilla

¼ cup dried apricots, coarsely chopped

2 tablespoons mini chocolate chips

2 Bartlett pears, cut into ½-inch wedges

2 large apples, cut into ½-inch wedges

1 Combine cottage cheese, half-and-half, granulated sugar, and vanilla in a food processor and puree until smooth.

2 Transfer to bowl and stir in apricots and chocolate chips. (Recipe can be prepared to this point a day ahead. Cover and refrigerate until serving time.)

3 Arrange pears and apples on a platter, and serve the cannoli cream in the center.

Round Out the Meal

Children and grandchildren love this dessert. Make the meal completely hands on, and start out with make-your-own pizza with low-fat shredded mozzarella cheese. It is never too early to eat heart smart!

Cook's Clue

Any ingredient goes further when it's cut into small pieces, and that's true of chocolate chips, too. Mini-size chips make more of an impression in desserts because you get more of them per bite. If your market doesn't stock mini chips, you can finely chop up half an ounce of semisweet chocolate.

HEALTH HINT

To maintain good health, the United States Department of Agriculture (USDA) recommends 2 to 4 servings of fruit a day. If your family is reluctant to eat as much fruit as they should, try recipes such as this one that include bits of chocolate and a sweet creamy sauce.

secret to success

Rinse fruit under running water, and to retain nutritional benefits, avoid peeling unless the recipe requires it. Oxidation causes the fruit to brown, but applying lemon, lime, or orange juice to the sliced fruit can prevent it.

Coring and Cutting Pears

Halve the pears lengthwise, and use a melon baller to scoop out the seeds.

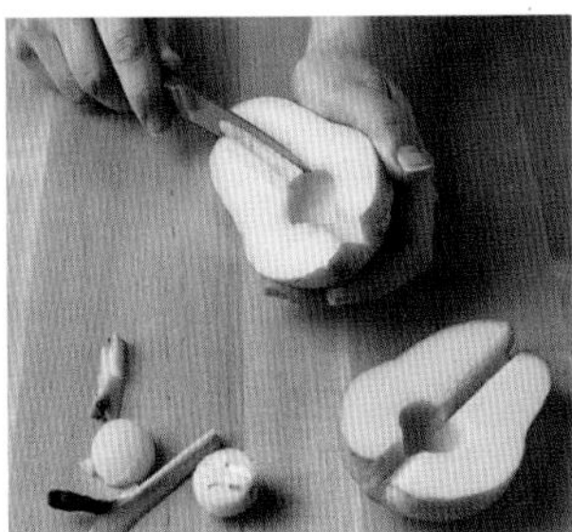

Remove the stringy core of the pear by cutting a lengthwise V-shaped channel.

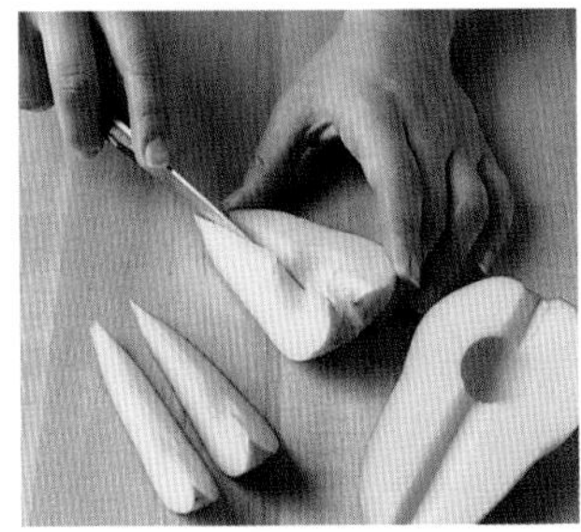

Then, cut each pear half lengthwise into wedges.

Key Lime Pudding Parfaits

In case you haven't heard, eating low-fat dairy products may help lower your blood pressure. Celebrate the good news with this lush, layered dessert made with pureed fat-free cottage cheese and low-fat evaporated milk—a miraculous ingredient for heart-smart cooks because it's improbably thick, rich, and velvety.

PER SERVING

210 calories / 13% from fat

1.5 g saturated fat, 3 g total fat

11 mg cholesterol

296 mg sodium

40 g total carbohydrate

1 g dietary fiber

8 g protein

PREP TIME 15 min.	COOK TIME 5 min. + chilling	SERVES 6

- 1½ cups low-fat evaporated milk
- ½ cup fat-free cottage cheese
- 2 tablespoons cornstarch
- 2 teaspoons grated lime zest
- ⅔ cup fresh lime juice
- ½ cup plus 2 teaspoons granulated sugar
- ¼ teaspoon salt
- 5 individual squares graham crackers
- ¼ cup toasted wheat germ

1 Combine ½ cup evaporated milk and cottage cheese in food processor or blender and puree until very smooth.

2 Place cornstarch in medium saucepan. Stir in remaining 1 cup evaporated milk, lime zest, lime juice, ½ cup granulated sugar, and salt. Stir in cottage cheese mixture. Cook pudding over medium heat, stirring constantly, until mixture comes to a boil. Cook, stirring, until thick, about 1 minute.

3 Transfer pudding to bowl, let cool to room temperature, then refrigerate until completely chilled, about 2 hours.

4 Meanwhile, place graham cracker squares in a food processor and pulse until coarse crumbs form. Combine graham cracker crumbs, remaining 2 teaspoons sugar, and wheat germ in small skillet. Cook over medium heat, stirring frequently, until graham cracker crumbs are lightly toasted, about 5 minutes. Cool to room temperature.

5 Dividing evenly, alternate layers of graham cracker mixture and pudding in 6 parfait glasses, beginning and ending with graham crackers. Refrigerate until serving time.

STEP 2 *Stir pureed cottage cheese into evaporated milk mixture in saucepan.*

STEP 4 *Toast graham cracker–wheat germ mixture in small skillet.*

STEP 5 *Alternate layers of pudding mixture and graham cracker mixture in parfait glasses or wine glasses.*

HEALTH HINT

Wheat germ adds crunchy texture and nutty flavor while providing fiber, vitamin E, and other essential vitamins and minerals. The antioxidant vitamin E plays an important role in protecting your cells from the damage caused by toxic free radicals.

Cook's Clue

Keep lime juice and zest leftovers for later use. Pour juice into ice cube trays until frozen, and store them in plastic bags in the freezer. Zest can be stored in a cool, dry place in an airtight glass container. Limes produce more juice when they're warmer, so squeeze juice when at room temperature. Extract more juice by rolling them on a flat surface.

secret to success

Another way to de-lump cottage cheese is to push the cottage cheese through a sieve. Fat-free cottage cheese has almost half the calories of regular cottage cheese, so try it in other desserts, such as cheesecake.

Toasted Almond Rice Pudding

PER SERVING

224 calories / 18% from fat

0.5 g saturated fat, 4.5 g total fat

0 mg cholesterol

230 mg sodium

41 g total carbohydrate

2 g dietary fiber

4 g protein

Nuts about rice pudding? You'll love our easy-to-prepare version, made with toasted almonds and almond milk. And the rice itself—delicate basmati or jasmine—contributes its own nutlike flavor and fragrance.

PREP TIME 5 min.  COOK TIME 25 min. + chilling | SERVES 4

- ¼ cup sliced almonds
- 2 cups almond milk (almond beverage)
- ½ cup jasmine or basmati rice
- 3 tablespoons granulated sugar
- ¼ teaspoon salt
- ¼ teaspoon almond extract
- ¼ cup dried cherries or cranberries
- ⅓ cup fat-free half-and-half

1 Preheat oven to 350°F. Place almonds on a baking sheet and toast until crisp and lightly golden, about 5 minutes; set aside.

2 Meanwhile, combine almond milk and rice in medium saucepan. Bring to a boil over medium heat. Reduce to a simmer, cover, and cook until rice is tender, about 20 minutes.

3 Remove from heat and stir in sugar, salt, and almond extract. Cool to room temperature. Stir in almonds, cherries, and half-and-half. Chill until serving time.

STEP 1 *Toast almonds on a baking sheet in oven.*

STEP 2 *Combine rice and almond milk in medium saucepan.*

STEP 3 *After rice has cooled to room temperature, stir in toasted almonds, cherries, and half-and-half.*

HEALTH HINT

One of the advantages of using almond milk instead of cow's milk is its rich nutritional makeup may help prevent heart disease. Almond milk contains lots of heart-protective monounsaturated fats and vitamin E, as well as potassium and magnesium. Look for almond milk fortified with the same bone-building compounds—calcium and vitamin D—as dairy milk.

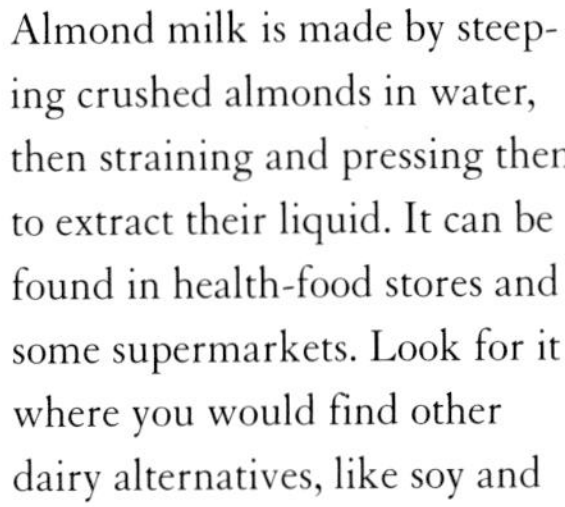

Cook's Clue

Almond milk is made by steeping crushed almonds in water, then straining and pressing them to extract their liquid. It can be found in health-food stores and some supermarkets. Look for it where you would find other dairy alternatives, like soy and rice beverages.

secret to success

Rinse the rice under water, and use your fingers to help clean it. The amount of water added varies depending on the rice. Reduce the amount of water required since jasmine and basmati rice usually require less water. Add texture by plumping with chopsticks before adding to the pudding.

way back when... Walnuts have been around for centuries, even millenniums. English walnuts came from India. In 4th century A.D., Romans brought the walnut to European countries, and it has been grown there since. Walnut trees have life spans several times that of humans. The tree provides food, shelter, lamp oil, and medicine. It is believed that walnuts grown in North America earned the nickname "English" walnuts because they were brought to America by English merchant ships.

(Source: www.whfoods.com)

Blueberry Bavarian

Spoon up a tangy-sweet mouthful of our custardy berry blend, and discover how sublime a low-fat dessert can be. Instead of heavy cream and whole eggs, this lush dessert is made with low-fat milk, fat-free dry milk, and fat-free sour cream, bolstered with unflavored gelatin. The berries offer a bonus in the form of pectin, a cholesterol-fighting soluble fiber.

PER SERVING

202 calories / 4% from fat
0.5 g saturated fat, 1 g total fat
2 mg cholesterol
178 mg sodium
43 g total carbohydrate
3 g dietary fiber
7 g protein

PREP TIME 10 min.	COOK TIME 15 min. + chilling	SERVES 6

- 1 cup low-fat (1%) milk
- ¼ cup fat-free dry milk
- 2 packages (12 ounces each) frozen blueberries, thawed
- ½ cup plus 1 tablespoon granulated sugar
- ¼ teaspoon salt
- 1 cup fat-free sour cream
- 1 packet unflavored gelatin
- ¼ cup cold water
- ½ cup fresh blueberries

1 Combine milk and dry milk in small bowl and whisk until well blended. Place in freezer for up to 30 minutes.

2 Combine frozen blueberries, ½ cup granulated sugar, and salt in medium saucepan over low heat. Bring to a simmer and cook until sugar has dissolved, berries have broken up, and mixture has reduced to 2¼ cups, about 10 minutes. Let cool to room temperature. Stir in ⅔ cup sour cream.

3 Sprinkle gelatin over cold water in heatproof measuring cup. Let stand 5 minutes to soften. Set measuring cup in small saucepan of simmering water, and heat until gelatin has melted, about 2 minutes. Let cool to room temperature.

4 With an electric mixer, beat chilled milk until thick, soft peaks form. Beat in remaining 1 tablespoon sugar until stiff peaks form. Beat in gelatin mixture.

5 Fold milk mixture into blueberry mixture. Spoon into 6 dessert bowls or glasses. Chill until set, about 2 hours. At serving time, top each with a dollop of remaining sour cream and fresh blueberries.

STEP 2 *Stir sour cream into cooled blueberry mixture.*

STEP 4 *With electric mixer, beat chilled milk mixture until soft peaks form before adding sugar.*

STEP 5 *With rubber spatula, gently fold whipped milk into blueberry mixture.*

HEALTH HINT

Blueberries are brimming with cardioprotective nutrients including potassium, folate, magnesium, soluble fiber, and vitamin C. With the exception of a small loss of vitamin C, frozen blueberries retain all the nutritive power of fresh berries.

Round Out the Meal

Serve blueberry or cranberry Bavarians at Thanksgiving or after a turkey dinner. This light dessert will perk you up after that holiday nap.

secret to success

Add fat-free dry milk to low-fat milk, and you'll get a thick "super-milk" that can be whipped like heavy cream when well chilled. The mixture is stabilized with gelatin to keep it firm. For best results, chill the bowl and beaters before whipping the milk.

Peach–Berry Cobbler

Want to put big smiles on their faces? Bring this luscious dessert straight from the oven to the table. Dripping with juicy fruit and topped with fluffy pecan dumplings, it's sure to please. And don't worry if they ask for seconds—it's a low-fat treat that can't be beat!

PER SERVING

292 calories / 28% from fat

1 g saturated fat, 9 g total fat

4 mg cholesterol

346 mg sodium

52 g total carbohydrate

6 g dietary fiber

4 g protein

PREP TIME 30 min.	COOK TIME 55 min.	SERVES 12

- 3 pounds peaches (about 8), peeled and sliced
- 2 pints blackberries
- ¾ cup packed light brown sugar
- 1 tablespoon cornstarch
- 2 tablespoons fresh lemon juice
- 2 cups self-rising flour
- ⅓ cup pecans, toasted and chopped
- ¼ teaspoon nutmeg
- 6 tablespoons cold margarine, cut into pieces
- ¾ cup plus 2 tablespoons reduced-fat milk (2%)
- 2 tablespoons granulated sugar

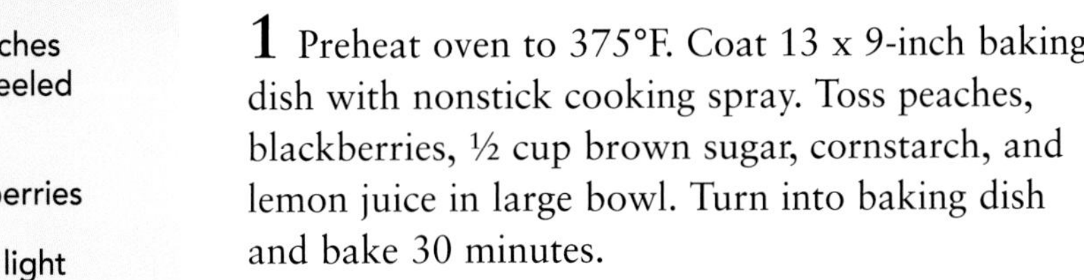

1 Preheat oven to 375°F. Coat 13 x 9-inch baking dish with nonstick cooking spray. Toss peaches, blackberries, ½ cup brown sugar, cornstarch, and lemon juice in large bowl. Turn into baking dish and bake 30 minutes.

2 Combine flour, pecans, remaining brown sugar, and nutmeg in large bowl. Cut in margarine with pastry blender or two knives until mixture resembles very coarse crumbs. Add ¾ cup milk, and stir with fork until thick batter forms, adding water if necessary.

3 Drop batter on top of fruit, spacing evenly, to make 12 dumplings.

4 Lightly brush dumplings with remaining milk. Sprinkle with granulated sugar, and bake until toothpick inserted in center of dumpling comes out with moist crumbs clinging, 25 to 30 minutes. Serve warm or at room temperature.

STEP 3 *Drop batter by heaping tablespoons, spacing evenly.*

STEP 4 *Sprinkle with granulated sugar for crispy dumplings.*

secret to success

Pecans bought unshelled should be heavy for their size, uncracked, and blemish-free. If the nuts rattle in the shell when shaken, this indicates they're old. Be wary of expiration dates. Since pecans absorb odors and flavors easily, store them in a closed container. Toasting enhances their aroma and creates a crunchy texture. Bake about 5 minutes at 375°F.

Cook's Clue

If you don't have self-rising flour, substitute 2 cups sifted all-purpose flour mixed with 1 tablespoon baking powder and ¼ teaspoon salt. When fresh berries are scarce, use a 20-ounce package of frozen blackberries.

HEALTH HINT

Choose ripe peaches: not only are they sweeter and more fragrant, but ripe peaches also contain more vitamin C. Peaches also have caroteins and flavonoids. Caroteins act like antioxidants, which protect the heart, and flavonoids block free radicals.

Pineapple Foster

Bananas Foster is a beloved New Orleans dessert, created in the 1950s at Brennan's Restaurant. This pineapple variation, in which the fruit is sautéed in butter, rum, and brown sugar and then flambéed, will bring raves. So cool a hot summer down or warm a rough winter up with this low-in-fat and high-in-vitamin-C showstopper!

PER SERVING

225 calories / 16% from fat

2 g saturated fat, 4 g total fat

9 mg cholesterol

40 mg sodium

37 g total carbohydrate

2 g dietary fiber

3 g protein

PREP TIME 15 min. | COOK TIME 10 min. | SERVES 4

- 1 large ripe pineapple
- 1 tablespoon unsalted butter
- 3 tablespoons packed light brown sugar
- ¼ teaspoon ground nutmeg
- 3 tablespoons dark rum
- 2 tablespoons Grand Marnier or other orange liqueur
- 1⅓ cups vanilla nonfat frozen yogurt

1 Cut off leaves and stem end from pineapple. Remove skin and "eyes." Slice pineapple, ¾ inch thick. Cut each slice into thirds and remove hard core.

2 In large skillet, melt butter over moderate heat. When butter begins to foam, add brown sugar and nutmeg and heat until sugar melts. Stir in rum and bring to a simmer. Add pineapple and cook, turning often, until the pineapple is warmed through, about 4 minutes.

3 Leaving skillet on heat, drizzle Grand Marnier over pineapple. Standing back, ignite liqueur with long match. Shake pan gently until alcohol burns off. Spoon pineapple slices and sauce over frozen yogurt.

secret to success

If there's no rum around, substitute rum extract, but only if the recipe requires less than ¼ cup. In this recipe, use about 1½ tablespoons rum extract for the dark rum. If you want a less intense flavor, add about a ¼ tablespoon of rum extract, as this will taste like a lighter rum.

HEALTH HINT

Pineapple is high in soluble dietary fiber, which helps control high blood cholesterol. It is also a good source of vitamin C, an important antioxidant that defends against free radicals that attack healthy cells. Free radicals can cause artery plaque, which can lead to atherosclerosis or diabetic heart disease.

Cook's Clue

Once picked, a pineapple won't get any sweeter. Fruit labeled "jet-shipped" is your best bet for peak ripeness. Choose a large, plump, heavy specimen with fresh green leaves. A ripe pineapple may have a sweet fragrance, but if it's chilled, it may not be detectable.

How to Prepare Fresh Pineapple

To start, twist off the leafy "crown."

Use a chef's knife to slice downward through the rind; don't cut too deeply or you'll lose fruit.

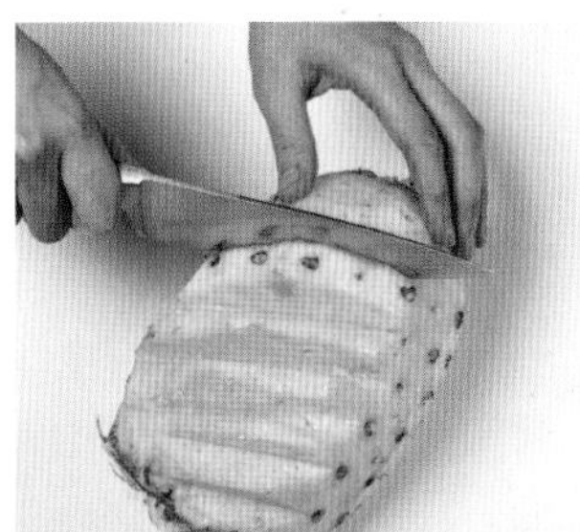

Pineapple "eyes" run in a diagonal pattern. Cut long diagonal notches about ¼" deep around the pineapple to remove them.

Chewy Granola Bars

Start with a double dose of cholesterol-lowering oats, and you're on your way to a heart-healthy snack. For a holiday gift, wrap the bars in wax paper or plastic wrap, then in colorful wrapping paper, and tuck them into a pretty basket. They'll keep about one week in the wrapping.

PER BAR

145 calories / 16% from fat
0.5 g saturated fat, 3 g total fat
0 mg cholesterol
52 mg sodium
29 g total carbohydrate
3 g dietary fiber
4 g protein

PREP TIME 15 min. | COOK TIME 35 min. | 12 BARS

- 1½ cups old-fashioned or quick-cooking oats
- ½ cup oat bran
- ⅓ cup flour
- ⅔ cup dried apricots, coarsely chopped
- ⅓ cup walnuts, coarsely chopped
- 2 tablespoons toasted wheat germ
- ¼ teaspoon salt
- ¼ cup frozen pineapple juice concentrate
- 2 tablespoons packed light brown sugar
- 2 tablespoons honey
- 1 teaspoon vanilla

1 Preheat oven to 350°F. Line 11 x 7-inch metal baking pan with foil, leaving 1 or 2 inches hanging over ends. Spray with nonstick cooking spray; set aside.

2 Place oats and oat bran in jelly roll pan and toast until oats are lightly browned and fragrant, about 10 minutes. Transfer to large mixing bowl and add flour, apricots, walnuts, wheat germ, and salt.

3 Combine pineapple juice concentrate, brown sugar, and honey in small skillet. Cook over medium heat until brown sugar has dissolved, about 4 minutes. Remove from heat and stir in vanilla. Pour honey mixture over oat mixture, stirring to coat.

4 Spoon oat mixture into baking pan. With moistened hands, press mixture into even layer in pan. Bake until firm, about 20 minutes. Using foil, carefully lift out bars and cool on wire rack. On work surface, cut into 12 bars.

STEP 2 *Add apricots and walnuts to toasted oats.*

STEP 3 *Before adding vanilla to the pineapple juice–honey mixture, remove pan from heat.*

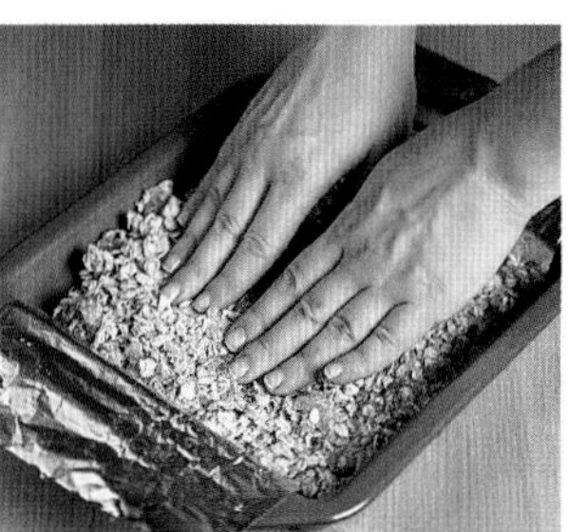

STEP 4 *Press oat mixture into an even layer in baking pan.*

Cook's Clue

If you're partial to the taste of honey, choose a strong-flavored variety, such as buckwheat; for a milder flavor, use clover honey.

HEALTH HINT

Oats are rich in a type of soluble fiber called beta-glucan, which helps usher cholesterol out of the body. Oat fiber may also help control blood sugar and improve insulin sensitivity, which is useful for people with diabetes or insulin resistance.

secret to success

Though sometimes hard to find, the raw honey sold at farmer's markets, which tends to not be pasteurized, clarified, or filtered, is the best honey to use in most recipes. Regular honey should be translucent; creamy is opaque. Remember, the darker the color of honey, the deeper flavor.

Pecan Icebox Cookies

Remember Grandma's cookie jar? It never seemed to be empty. With these cookies, it's easy to keep yours the same way. These are the traditional icebox cookies—where the dough is made ahead and kept in the refrigerator or freezer until it's time to bake them. Freshly baked cookies are always only 10 minutes away. The best part: These icebox cookies deliver only half the fat of Grandma's favorites!

PER COOKIE

34 calories / 27% from fat
0 g saturated fat, 1 g total fat
3 mg cholesterol
22 mg sodium
6 g total carbohydrate
0 g dietary fiber
0 g protein

PREP TIME 15 min. + chilling	COOK TIME 10 min.	MAKES 72

- 1¾ cups all-purpose flour
- ½ teaspoon cinnamon
- ¼ teaspoon salt
- ¼ teaspoon baking soda
- ¼ cup (½ stick) margarine, softened
- ⅔ cup granulated sugar
- ⅓ cup packed light brown sugar
- 1 large egg
- 1 tablespoon vanilla
- ⅓ cup fat-free sour cream
- ⅓ cup chopped pecans, toasted

1 Whisk flour, cinnamon, salt, and baking soda in medium bowl. Cream margarine, granulated sugar, and brown sugar in large bowl with electric mixer at high speed until light and fluffy, about 4 minutes. Add egg and vanilla and beat until well blended. Using a wooden spoon, stir in flour mixture, and then sour cream and pecans.

2 Tear off 20-inch sheet of plastic wrap and sprinkle lightly with flour. Transfer dough to plastic wrap and shape into 15-inch log. Tightly roll in plastic and refrigerate until firm, about 2 hours. (Or wrap dough in heavy-duty foil and freeze up to 1 month.)

3 Preheat oven to 375°F. Cut dough into rounds 3/16 inch thick, making approximately 6 dozen cookies. Working in batches, place ½ inch apart on ungreased baking sheets. Bake just until crisp and golden brown around edges, about 8 minutes (do not overbake). If using frozen dough, bake 10 minutes. Transfer cookies to wire racks to cool completely before storing in airtight container.

STEP 1 *Gently stir (don't beat) in pecans with wooden spoon.*

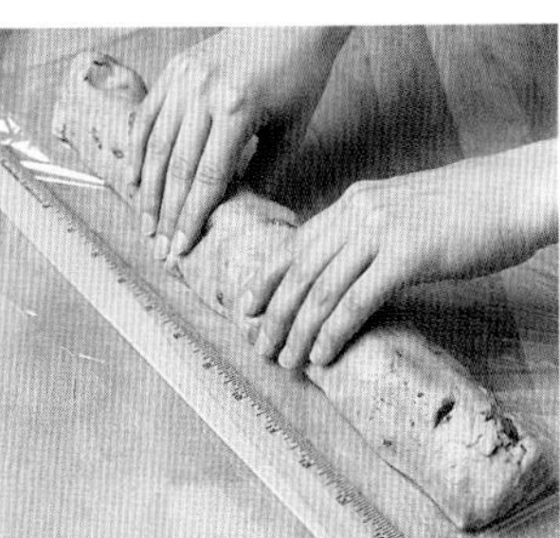

STEP 2 *Shape into a log about 15 inches long and 1½ inches in diameter.*

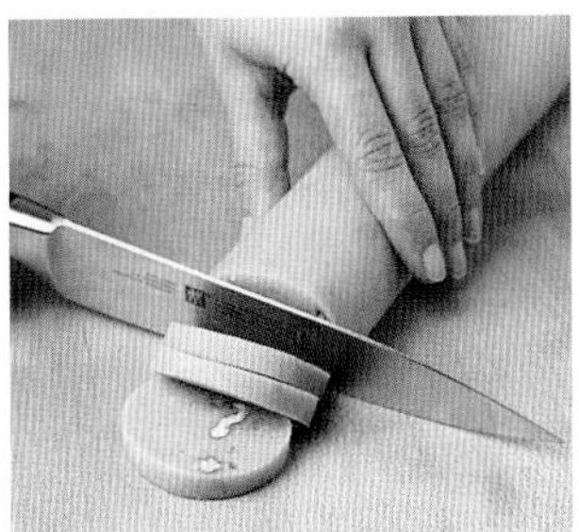

STEP 3 *Slice dough about 3/16 inch thick, making approximately 6 dozen cookies.*

HEALTH HINT

Pecans are packed with unsaturated fats, the heart-healthy kinds, and recent studies prove that eating pecans helps lower cholesterol. They are filled with vitamins and are naturally cholesterol-free. Studies show that diets high in pecans lowered total and LDL cholesterol twice as much as the American Heart Association Step 1 diet. Diets with pecans help maintain HDL ("good") cholesterol because they contain heart-healthy fats.

secret to success

Even though the fat in pecans is predominantly monounsaturated (the "good" kind of fat), nuts are still a high-calorie, high-fat food. Since toasted nuts add so much flavor, you can use a lot fewer in recipes like this.

Cook's Clue

Love chocolate? This recipe makes great Chocolate Icebox Cookies. At beginning of Step 1, whisk ⅓ cup unsweetened cocoa into the flour mixture. Increase the margarine to ⅓ cup and sour cream to ½ cup.

Chocolate Chip–Oatmeal Cookies

Look what has happened to the traditional chocolate chip cookie! This one has only half the fat of the original, plus old-fashioned oats that give a fiber boost. Yet all of this trimming has not slimmed down the flavor. These cookies will still vanish just as fast!

PER COOKIE

85 calories / 27% from fat

1 g saturated fat, 2.5 g total fat

7 mg cholesterol

70 mg sodium

14 g total carbohydrate

0.5 g dietary fiber

1 g protein

PREP TIME 15 min. | COOK TIME 10 min. + cooling | MAKES 36

- 1 cup all-purpose flour
- ½ teaspoon baking soda
- ½ teaspoon salt
- 1 cup old-fashioned oats
- 4 tablespoons margarine
- ⅔ cup packed light brown sugar
- ½ cup granulated sugar
- 1 large egg
- 1½ teaspoons vanilla
- ⅓ cup reduced-fat sour cream
- ¾ cup semisweet chocolate chips

1 Preheat oven to 375°F. Line two large baking sheets with parchment paper. Whisk flour, baking soda, and salt in medium bowl. Stir in oats.

2 Cream margarine, brown sugar, and granulated sugar in large bowl with electric mixer at high speed until well blended. Add egg and vanilla, and beat until light yellow and creamy, about 3 minutes.

3 Blend in sour cream with wooden spoon, then flour mixture all at once, just until combined (don't overmix or the cookies may become tough). Stir in chocolate chips.

4 Drop dough by heaping teaspoonfuls 2 inches apart onto baking sheets. Bake cookies until golden, about 10 minutes. Cool on baking sheets 2 minutes, then transfer to wire racks and cool completely. Store in airtight container for up to 2 weeks or freeze for up to 3 months.

STEP 2 *Cream margarine, sugars, egg, and vanilla with electric mixer at high speed.*

STEP 3 *Stir in flour and oatmeal mixture with spoon.*

STEP 4 *Drop dough onto baking sheets, making a total of 36 cookies.*

HEALTH HINT

Eating soluble oat fiber every day may lower total cholesterol, which decreases the risk of heart disease. Research suggests that fiber helps remove cholesterol from the digestive system, preventing it from entering the bloodstream. The antioxidant compounds in oats also protect against heart disease by preventing free radicals from damaging cholesterol levels.

way back when... That first chocolate chip cookie was baked in a 1709 tollhouse, known to the neighbors as the Toll House Inn. In the 1930s, as the story goes, owner Mrs. Ruth Wakefield was experimenting with an old American cookie recipe of butter drop-do's. She decided to chop up a chocolate bar and throw it into the dough. Much to her amazement, the chocolate didn't melt in the oven, but remained as small bites of chocolate when baked. Little did she know that she had just created one of America's most loved cookies!

(Source: The Encyclopedia of American Food and Drink, *by John F. Mariani, Lebhar-Friedman Books, NY, 1999)*

secret to success

By using only half the fat and margarine instead of butter, you've significantly cut the saturated fat. The reduced-fat sour cream also helps to keep the melt-in-your-mouth taste high and the fat low. Old-fashioned oats add an extra helping of heart-healthy goodness.

Double-Decker Strawberry Shortcakes

Here's a tempting, good-for-you fruit dessert that's a breeze to make. Layers of fresh strawberries, a velvety cream topping, and melt-in-your-mouth shortcakes stack up to an impressive—and impressively healthful—way to end a meal.

PER SERVING

300 calories / 21% from fat

1 g saturated fat, 7 g total fat

2 mg cholesterol

470 mg sodium

54 g total carbohydrate

4 g dietary fiber

6 g protein

PREP TIME 30 min.	COOK TIME 12 min.	SERVES 8

- 2 large limes
- 2 quarts strawberries, hulled and halved
- 6 tablespoons granulated sugar
- 2½ cups reduced-fat buttermilk baking mix
- 3 tablespoons cold margarine, cut into pieces
- ¾ cup low-fat milk (1%)
- 1 cup fat-free sour cream
- 2 cups fat-free frozen nondairy whipped topping, thawed
- Fresh mint sprigs

1 Preheat oven to 425°F. Lightly coat baking sheet with nonstick cooking spray. Zest and juice limes. Toss strawberries, 2 tablespoons lime juice, and 3 tablespoons granulated sugar in large bowl and set aside.

2 Whisk baking mix, 2 tablespoons sugar, and 1 teaspoon lime zest in medium bowl. Cut in margarine.

3 Stir in milk with fork until soft dough begins to form. Dust work surface lightly with flour. Turn out dough and gently knead just until dough holds together.

4 Pat dough into large circle, about ½ inch thick. Cut out 8 rounds with 3-inch floured biscuit cutter (preferably fluted), rerolling scraps as you go. Set shortcakes 1 inch apart on baking sheet. Sprinkle with remaining sugar. Bake until puffed and golden, about 12 minutes. Cool biscuits on wire rack.

5 Meanwhile, fold sour cream into nondairy whipped topping. Split biscuits with serrated knife. Generously layer with berries and sour cream mixture on dessert plates. Sprinkle with remaining lime zest, and garnish with mint sprigs.

STEP 2 *Cut in margarine with pastry blender.*

STEP 3 *Stir in milk with fork until soft dough begins to form.*

STEP 4 *Cut straight down into dough with fluted cutter.*

Cook's Clue

If you wish to omit the limes in this recipe, but still keep a sweet flavor, add 2 tablespoons of granulated sugar to the strawberries after washing them. Strawberries are juicier when crushed, so crush a few before sugaring. Let them sit for about an hour before adding to the recipe.

HEALTH HINT

Strawberries are a good source of pectin and other soluble fibers that may help lower cholesterol. They also provide folate—a heart-healthy B vitamin—and major amounts of vitamin C and potassium.

secret to success

Using a pastry blender to cut in fats, as in this recipe, creates a flakier biscuit. By mixing in the milk with a fork, the biscuit will be tender. Don't overmix the dough, and when you are kneading, pat lightly (with just your fingertips).

Carrot Cake with Cream Cheese Frosting

Go ahead, take another bite. This cake is melt-in-your-mouth delicious, plus it's really good for you! Each bite provides beta-carotene, which helps protect your heart. And you don't need to be a pastry chef in a four-star restaurant to make it.

PER SERVING

364 calories / 25% from fat

3 g saturated fat, 10 g total fat

52 mg cholesterol

605 mg sodium

62 g total carbohydrate

2 g dietary fiber

7 g protein

PREP TIME 20 min. | **COOK TIME 50 min. + cooling** | **SERVES 16**

- 8 medium carrots, peeled
- 3¾ cups self-rising flour
- 1½ tablespoons pumpkin pie spice
- 1½ teaspoons baking soda
- 2 cups plus 1 tablespoon low-fat buttermilk
- 6 tablespoons vegetable oil
- 1½ cups granulated sugar
- 3 large eggs
- 1 tablespoon vanilla
- 8 ounces Neufchâtel cheese, room temperature
- 2 cups sifted confectioners' sugar

Cook's Clue

The cake is done when it shrinks slightly from the sides of the pan or if it springs back when you touch it. If the top of the cake browns too quickly, place a pan of warm water on the oven rack above the cake while baking.

1 Preheat oven to 350°F. Generously coat 10-inch Bundt or angel food cake pan with nonstick cooking spray. Dust pan with a little flour, tapping out excess. Finely shred carrots using a hand grater or food processor fitted with shredding disk (3 cups).

2 Whisk flour, pumpkin pie spice, and baking soda in large bowl and make a well. Whisk 2 cups buttermilk, oil, granulated sugar, eggs, and 2 teaspoons vanilla in medium bowl until blended and frothy. Pour into well, and whisk just until combined.

3 Fold in carrots. Pour batter into pan, spreading top evenly. Tap pan lightly on flat surface a few times to break up large air bubbles. Bake until toothpick inserted in center comes out clean, about 50 minutes. Cool cake in pan on wire rack 10 minutes, then turn out onto rack. Flip cake top-side up on rack and cool completely.

4 Beat cheese with remaining vanilla and buttermilk in medium bowl until softened. Gradually blend in confectioners' sugar just until frosting is smooth. Place cake on serving plate and frost, letting frosting drip down sides. Refrigerate cake until ready to serve.

HEALTH HINT

Cooking carrots, as in this recipe, breaks down cellular walls holding the heart-healthy beta-carotene, thus increasing the availability of this vital nutrient to the body.

STEP 2 *Pour buttermilk mixture into flour well.*

STEP 3 *Fold in carrots.*

STEP 4 *Frost top of cooled cake, letting some frosting drip down the sides.*

secret to success

This heart-smart cake recipe uses about ⅓ the oil of the traditional recipe, only 3 eggs instead of 5, and low-fat buttermilk for extra moistness.

Index

D

E

F

G

T

U

V

W

Y

Z